Parallel and Concurrent Programming in Haskell

Simon Marlow

Beijing · Cambridge · Farnham · Köln · Sebastopol · Tokyo

Parallel and Concurrent Programming in Haskell

by Simon Marlow

Published by O'Reilly Media, Inc., 1005 Gravenstein Highway North, Sebastopol, CA 95472.

O'Reilly books may be purchased for educational, business, or sales promotional use. Online editions are also available for most titles (*http://my.safaribooksonline.com*). For more information, contact our corporate/institutional sales department: 800-998-9938 or *corporate@oreilly.com*.

Editors: Andy Oram and Maria Gulick	**Indexer:** WordCo Indexing Services
Production Editor: Melanie Yarbrough	**Cover Designer:** Randy Comer
Copyeditor: Gillian McGarvey	**Interior Designer:** David Futato
Proofreader: Julie Van Keuren	**Illustrator:** Rebecca Demarest

July 2013:   First Edition

Revision History for the First Edition:

2013-07-10:   First release

See *http://oreilly.com/catalog/errata.csp?isbn=9781449335946* for release details.

ISBN: 978-1-449-33594-6

[LSI]

Table of Contents

Part II.   Concurrent Haskell

Preface

As one of the developers of the Glasgow Haskell Compiler (GHC) for almost 15 years, I have seen Haskell grow from a niche research language into a rich and thriving ecosystem. I spent a lot of that time working on GHC's support for parallelism and concurrency. One of the first things I did to GHC in 1997 was to rewrite its runtime system, and a key decision we made at that time was to build concurrency right into the core of the system rather than making it an optional extra or an add-on library. I like to think this decision was founded upon shrewd foresight, but in reality it had as much to do with the fact that we found a way to reduce the overhead of concurrency to near zero (previously it had been on the order of 2%; we've always been performance-obsessed). Nevertheless, having concurrency be non-optional meant that it was always a first-class part of the implementation, and I'm sure that this decision was instrumental in bringing about GHC's solid and lightning-fast concurrency support.

Haskell has a long tradition of being associated with parallelism. To name just a few of the projects, there was the pH variant of Haskell derived from the Id language, which was designed for parallelism, the GUM system for running parallel Haskell programs on multiple machines in a cluster, and the GRiP system: a complete computer architecture designed for running parallel functional programs. All of these happened well before the current multicore revolution, and the problem was that this was the time when Moore's law was still giving us ever-faster computers. Parallelism was difficult to achieve, and didn't seem worth the effort when ordinary computers were getting exponentially faster.

Around 2004, we decided to build a parallel implementation of the GHC runtime system for running on shared memory multiprocessors, something that had not been done before. This was just before the multicore revolution. Multiprocessor machines were fairly common, but multicores were still around the corner. Again, I'd like to think the decision to tackle parallelism at this point was enlightened foresight, but it had more to do with the fact that building a shared-memory parallel implementation was an interesting research problem and sounded like fun. Haskell's purity was essential—it meant that we could avoid some of the overheads of locking in the runtime system and garbage collector, which in turn meant that we could reduce the overhead of using parallelism to a low-single-digit percentage. Nevertheless, it took more research, a rewrite of the scheduler, and a new parallel garbage collector before the implementation was really usable and able to speed up a wide range of programs. The paper I presented at the International Conference on Functional Programming (ICFP) in 2009 marked the turning point from an interesting prototype into a usable tool.

All of this research and implementation was great fun, but good-quality resources for teaching programmers how to use parallelism and concurrency in Haskell were conspicuously absent. Over the last couple of years, I was fortunate to have had the opportunity to teach two summer school courses on parallel and concurrent programming in Haskell: one at the Central European Functional Programming (CEFP) 2011 summer school in Budapest, and the other the CEA/EDF/INRIA 2012 Summer School at Cadarache in the south of France. In preparing the materials for these courses, I had an excuse to write some in-depth tutorial matter for the first time, and to start collecting good illustrative examples. After the 2012 summer school I had about 100 pages of tutorial, and thanks to prodding from one or two people (see the Acknowledgments), I decided to turn it into a book. At the time, I thought I was about 50% done, but in fact it was probably closer to 25%. There's a lot to say! I hope you enjoy the results.

Audience

You will need a working knowledge of Haskell, which is not covered in this book. For that, a good place to start is an introductory book such as *Real World Haskell* (O'Reilly), *Programming in Haskell* (Cambridge University Press), *Learn You a Haskell for Great Good!* (No Starch Press), or *Haskell: The Craft of Functional Programming* (Addison-Wesley).

How to Read This Book

The main goal of the book is to get you programming competently with Parallel and Concurrent Haskell. However, as you probably know by now, learning about programming is not something you can do by reading a book alone. This is why the book is deliberately practical: There are lots of examples that you can run, play with, and extend. Some of the chapters have suggestions for exercises you can try out to get familiar with the topics covered in that chapter, and I strongly recommend that you either try a few of these, or code up some of your own ideas.

As we explore the topics in the book, I won't shy away from pointing out pitfalls and parts of the system that aren't perfect. Haskell has been evolving for over 20 years but is moving faster today than at any point in the past. So we'll encounter inconsistencies and parts that are less polished than others. Some of the topics covered by the book are very recent developments: Chapters 4, 5, 6, and pass:[14 cover frameworks that were developed in the last few years.

The book consists of two mostly independent parts: Part I and Part II. You should feel free to start with either part, or to flip between them (i.e., read them concurrently!). There is only one dependency between the two parts: Chapter 13 will make more sense if you have read Part I first, and in particular before reading "The ParIO monad" on page 237, you should have read Chapter 4.

While the two parts are mostly independent from each other, the chapters should be read sequentially within each part. This isn't a reference book; it contains running examples and themes that are developed across multiple chapters.

Conventions Used in This Book

The following typographical conventions are used in this book:

Italic
: Used for emphasis, new terms, URLs, Unix commands and utilities, and file and directory names.

`Constant width`
: Indicates variables, functions, types, parameters, objects, and other programming constructs.

> This icon signifies a tip, suggestion, or a general note.

> This icon indicates a trap or pitfall to watch out for, typically something that isn't immediately obvious.

Code samples look like this:

timetable1.hs

```
search :: ( partial -> Maybe solution )    -- ❶
       -> ( partial -> [ partial ] )
       -> partial
       -> [solution]
```

The heading gives the filename of the source file containing the code snippet, which may be found in the sample code; see "Sample Code" on page 4 for how to obtain the sample code. When there are multiple snippets quoted from the same file, usually only the first will have the filename heading.

❶ There will often be commentary referring to individual lines in the code snippet, which look like this.

Commands that you type into the shell look like this:

```
$ ./logger
hello
bye
logger: stop
```

The $ character is the prompt, the command follows it, and the rest of the lines are the output generated by the command.

GHCi sessions look like this:

```
> extent arr
(Z :. 3) :. 5
> rank (extent arr)
2
> size (extent arr)
15
```

I often set GHCi's prompt to the character > followed by a space, because GHCi's default prompt gets overly long when several modules are imported. You can do the same using this command in GHCi:

```
Prelude> :set prompt "> "
>
```

Using Sample Code

The sample code that accompanies the book is available online; see "Sample Code" on page 4 for details on how to get it and build it. For information on your rights to use, modify, and redistribute the sample code, see the file *LICENSE* in the sample code distribution.

Safari® Books Online

Safari Books Online is an on-demand digital library that delivers expert content in both book and video form from the world's leading authors in technology and business.

Technology professionals, software developers, web designers, and business and creative professionals use Safari Books Online as their primary resource for research, problem solving, learning, and certification training.

Safari Books Online offers a range of product mixes and pricing programs for organizations, government agencies, and individuals. Subscribers have access to thousands of books, training videos, and prepublication manuscripts in one fully searchable database from publishers like O'Reilly Media, Prentice Hall Professional, Addison-Wesley Professional, Microsoft Press, Sams, Que, Peachpit Press, Focal Press, Cisco Press, John Wiley & Sons, Syngress, Morgan Kaufmann, IBM Redbooks, Packt, Adobe Press, FT Press, Apress, Manning, New Riders, McGraw-Hill, Jones & Bartlett, Course Technology, and dozens more. For more information about Safari Books Online, please visit us online.

How to Contact Us

Please address comments and questions concerning this book to the publisher:

> O'Reilly Media, Inc.
> 1005 Gravenstein Highway North
> Sebastopol, CA 95472
> 800-998-9938 (in the United States or Canada)
> 707-829-0515 (international or local)
> 707-829-0104 (fax)

We have a web page for this book, where we list errata, examples, and any additional information. You can access this page at *http://oreil.ly/parallel-concurrent-prog-haskell*.

To comment or ask technical questions about this book, send email to *bookques tions@oreilly.com*.

For more information about our books, courses, conferences, and news, see our website at *http://www.oreilly.com*.

Find us on Facebook: *http://facebook.com/oreilly*

Follow us on Twitter: *http://twitter.com/oreillymedia*

Watch us on YouTube: *http://www.youtube.com/oreillymedia*

Acknowledgments

For several months I have had a head full of Parallel and Concurrent Haskell without much room for anything else, so firstly and most importantly I would like to thank my wife for her encouragement, patience, and above all, cake, during this project.

Secondly, all of this work owes a lot to Simon Peyton Jones, who has led the GHC project since its inception and has always been my richest source of inspiration. Simon's relentless enthusiasm and technical insight have been a constant driving force behind GHC.

Thanks to Mary Sheeran and Andres Löh (among others), who persuaded me to turn my tutorial notes into this book, and thanks to the organizers of the CEFP and CEA/EDF/INRIA summer schools for inviting me to give the courses that provided the impetus to get started, and to the students who attended those courses for being my guinea pigs.

Many thanks to my editor, Andy Oram, and the other folks at O'Reilly who helped this book become a reality.

The following people have helped with the book in some way, either by reviewing early drafts, sending me suggestions, commenting on the online chapters, writing some code that I borrowed (with attribution, I hope), writing a paper or blog post from which I took ideas, or something else (if I've forgotten you, I'm sorry): Joey Adams, Lennart Augustsson, Tuncer Ayaz, Jost Berthold, Manuel Chakravarty, Duncan Coutts, Andrew Cowie, Iavor Diatchki, Chris Dornan, Sigbjorn Finne, Kevin Hammonad, Tim Harris, John Hughes, Mikolaj Konarski, Erik Kow, Chris Kuklewicz, John Launchbury, Roman Leshchinskiy, Ben Lippmeier, Andres Löh, Hans-Wolfgang Loidl, Ian Lynagh, Trevor L. McDonell, Takayuki Muranushi, Ryan Newton, Mary Sheeran, Wren ng Thornton, Bryan O'Sullivan, Ross Paterson, Thomas Schilling, Michael Snoyman, Simon Thomson, Johan Tibell, Phil Trinder, Bas Van Dijk, Phil Wadler, Daniel Winograd-Cort, Nicolas Wu, and Edward Yang.

Finally, thanks to the Haskell community for being one of the most friendly, inclusive, helpful, and stimulating online open source communities I've come across. We have a lot to be proud of, folks; keep it up.

CHAPTER 1

Introduction

For a long time, the programming community has known that programming with threads and locks is hard. It often requires an inordinate degree of expertise even for simple problems and leads to programs that have faults that are hard to diagnose. Still, threads and locks are general enough to express everything we might need to write, from parallel image processors to concurrent web servers, and there is an undeniable benefit in having a single general API. However, if we want to make programming concurrent and parallel software easier, we need to embrace the idea that different problems require different tools; a single tool just doesn't cut it. Image processing is naturally expressed in terms of parallel array operations, whereas threads are a good fit in the case of a concurrent web server.

So in Haskell, we aim to provide the right tool for the job, for as many jobs as possible. If a job is found for which Haskell doesn't have the right tool, then we try to find a way to build it. The inevitable downside of this diversity is that there is a lot to learn, and that is what this book is all about. In this book, I'll discuss how to write parallel and concurrent programs in Haskell, ranging from the simple uses of parallelism to speed up computation-heavy programs to the use of lightweight threads for writing high-speed concurrent network servers. Along the way, we'll see how to use Haskell to write programs that run on the powerful processor in a modern graphics card (GPU), and to write programs that can run on multiple machines in a network (distributed programming).

That is not to say that I plan to cover every experimental programming model that has sprung up; if you peruse the packages on Hackage, you'll encounter a wide variety of libraries for parallel and concurrent programming, many of which were built to scratch a particular itch, not to mention all the research projects that aren't ready for real-world use yet. In this book I'm going to focus on the APIs that can be used right now to get work done and are stable enough to rely upon in production. Furthermore, my aim is to leave you with a firm grasp of how the lowest layers work, so that you can build your own abstractions on top of them if you should need to.

Terminology: Parallelism and Concurrency

In many fields, the words *parallel* and *concurrent* are synonyms; not so in programming, where they are used to describe fundamentally different concepts.

A *parallel* program is one that uses a multiplicity of computational hardware (e.g., several processor cores) to perform a computation more quickly. The aim is to arrive at the answer earlier, by delegating different parts of the computation to different processors that execute at the same time.

By contrast, *concurrency* is a program-structuring technique in which there are multiple *threads of control*. Conceptually, the threads of control execute "at the same time"; that is, the user sees their effects interleaved. Whether they actually execute at the same time or not is an implementation detail; a concurrent program can execute on a single processor through interleaved execution or on multiple physical processors.

While parallel programming is concerned only with efficiency, concurrent programming is concerned with structuring a program that needs to interact with multiple independent external agents (for example, the user, a database server, and some external clients). Concurrency allows such programs to be *modular*; the thread that interacts with the user is distinct from the thread that talks to the database. In the absence of concurrency, such programs have to be written with event loops and callbacks, which are typically more cumbersome and lack the modularity that threads offer.

The notion of "threads of control" does not make sense in a purely functional program, because there are no effects to observe, and the evaluation order is irrelevant. So concurrency is a structuring technique for effectful code; in Haskell, that means code in the IO monad.

A related distinction is between *deterministic* and *nondeterministic* programming models. A deterministic programming model is one in which each program can give only one result, whereas a nondeterministic programming model admits programs that may have different results, depending on some aspect of the execution. Concurrent programming models are necessarily nondeterministic because they must interact with external agents that cause events at unpredictable times. Nondeterminism has some notable drawbacks, however: Programs become significantly harder to test and reason about.

For parallel programming, we would like to use deterministic programming models if at all possible. Since the goal is just to arrive at the answer more quickly, we would rather not make our program harder to debug in the process. Deterministic parallel programming is the best of both worlds: Testing, debugging, and reasoning can be performed on the sequential program, but the program runs faster with the addition of more processors. Indeed, most computer processors themselves implement deterministic parallelism in the form of pipelining and multiple execution units.

While it is possible to do parallel programming using concurrency, that is often a poor choice because concurrency sacrifices determinism. In Haskell, most parallel programming models are deterministic. However, it is important to note that deterministic programming models are not sufficient to express all kinds of parallel algorithms; there are algorithms that depend on internal nondeterminism, particularly problems that involve searching a solution space. Moreover, we sometimes want to parallelize programs that really do have side effects, and then there is no alternative but to use nondeterministic parallel or concurrent programming.

Finally, it is entirely reasonable to want to mix parallelism and concurrency in the same program. Most interactive programs need to use concurrency to maintain a responsive user interface while compute-intensive tasks are being performed in the background.

Tools and Resources

To try out the sample programs and exercises from this book, you will need to install the Haskell Platform (*http://hackage.haskell.org/platform*). The Haskell Platform includes the GHC compiler and all the important libraries, including the parallel and concurrent libraries we shall be using. The code in this book was tested with the Haskell Platform version 2012.4.0.0, but the sample code will be updated as new versions of the platform are released.

Some chapters require the installation of additional packages. Instructions for installing the extra dependencies can be found in "Sample Code" on page 4.

Additionally, I recommend installing ThreadScope. ThreadScope is a tool for visualizing the execution of Haskell programs and is particularly useful for gaining insight into the behavior of Parallel and Concurrent Haskell code. On a Linux system, ThreadScope is probably available direct from your distribution, and this is by far the easiest way to get it. For example, on Ubuntu, you can install it through a simple:

```
$ sudo apt-get install threadscope
```

For instructions on how to install ThreadScope on other systems, see the Haskell website (*http://bit.ly/1aC5uHW*).

While reading this book, I recommend that you have the following Documentation in hand:

- The GHC User's Guide (*http://bit.ly/15fGRwZ*).

- The Haskell Platform library documentation, which can be found on the main Haskell Platform site (*http://bit.ly/19To77y*). Any types or functions that are used in this book that are not explicitly described can be found documented there.

- Documentation for packages not in the Haskell Platform, which can be found on Hackage (*http://hackage.haskell.org*). To search for documentation for a particular function or type, use Hoogle (*http://www.haskell.org/hoogle*).

It should be noted that the majority of the APIs used in this book are *not* part of the Haskell 2010 standard. They are provided by add-on packages, some of which are part of the Haskell Platform, while the rest are available on Hackage.

Sample Code

The sample code is collected together in the package `parconc-examples` on Hackage. To download and unpack it, run:

```
$ cabal unpack parconc-examples
```

Then, install the dependent packages:

```
$ cd parconc-examples
$ cabal install --only-dependencies
```

Next, build all the sample programs:

```
$ cabal build
```

The `parconc-examples` package will be updated as necessary to follow future changes in the Haskell Platform or other APIs.

PART I

Parallel Haskell

Now that processor manufacturers have largely given up trying to squeeze more performance out of individual processors and have refocused their attention on providing us with more processors instead, the biggest gains in performance are to be had by using parallel techniques in our programs so as to make use of these extra cores. Parallel Haskell is aimed at providing access to multiple processors in a natural and robust way.

You might wonder whether the compiler could automatically parallelize programs for us. After all, it should be easier to do this in a purely functional language, where the only dependencies between computations are data dependencies, which are mostly perspicuous and thus readily analyzed. However, even in a purely functional language, automatic parallelization is thwarted by an age-old problem: To make the program faster, we have to gain more from parallelism than we lose due to the overhead of adding it, and compile-time analysis cannot make good judgments in this area. An alternative approach is to use runtime profiling to find good candidates for parallelization and to feed this information back into the compiler. Even this, however, has not been terribly successful in practice.

Fully automatic parallelization is still a pipe dream. However, the parallel programming models provided by Haskell do succeed in eliminating some mundane or error-prone aspects traditionally associated with parallel programming:

- Parallel programming in Haskell is *deterministic*: The parallel program always produces the same answer, regardless of how many processors are used to run it. So parallel programs can be debugged without actually running them in parallel. Furthermore, the programmer can be confident that adding parallelism will not introduce lurking race conditions or deadlocks that would be hard to eliminate with testing.

- Parallel Haskell programs are high-level and declarative and do not explicitly deal with concepts like *synchronization* or *communication*. The programmer indicates where the parallelism is, and the details of actually running the program in parallel are left to the runtime system. This is both a blessing and a curse:

  — By embodying fewer operational details, parallel Haskell programs are abstract and are therefore likely to work on a wide range of parallel hardware.

  — Parallel Haskell programs can take advantage of existing highly tuned technology in the runtime system, such as parallel garbage collection. Furthermore, the program gets to benefit from future improvements made to the runtime with no additional effort.

  — Because a lot of the details of execution are hidden, performance problems can be hard to understand. Moreover, the programmer has less control than he would in a lower-level programming language, so fixing performance problems can be tricky. Indeed, this problem is not limited to Parallel Haskell: It will be familiar to anyone who has tried to optimize Haskell programs at all. In this book, I hope to demonstrate how to identify and work around the most common issues that can occur in practice.

The main thing that the parallel Haskell programmer has to think about is *partitioning*: dividing up the problem into pieces that can be computed in parallel. Ideally, you want to have enough tasks to keep all the processors busy continuously. However, your efforts may be frustrated in two ways:

Granularity

If you make your tasks too small, the overhead of managing the tasks outweighs any benefit you might get from running them in parallel. So granularity should be large enough to dwarf overhead, but not too large, because then you risk not having enough work to keep all the processors busy, especially toward the end of the execution when there are fewer tasks left.

Data dependencies

When one task depends on another, they must be performed sequentially. The first two programming models we will be encountering in this book take different approaches to data dependencies: In Chapter 3, data dependencies are entirely implicit, whereas in Chapter 4 they are explicit. Programming with explicit data dependencies is less concise, but it can be easier to understand and fix problems when the data dependencies are not hidden.

In the following chapters, we will describe the various parallel programming models that Haskell provides:

- Chapters 2 and 3 introduce the Eval monad and Evaluation Strategies, which are suitable for expressing parallelism in Haskell programs that are not heavily numerical or array-based. These programming models are well established, and there are many good examples of using them to achieve parallelism.

- Chapter 4 introduces the Par monad, a more recent parallel programming model that also aims at parallelizing ordinary Haskell code but with a different trade-off: It affords the programmer more control in exchange for some of the conciseness and modularity of Strategies.

- Chapter 5 looks at the Repa library, which provides a rich set of combinators for building parallel array computations. You can express a complex array algorithm as the composition of several simpler operations, and the library automatically optimizes the composition into a single-pass algorithm using a technique called *fusion*. Furthermore, the implementation of the library automatically parallelizes the operation using the available processors.

- Chapter 6 discusses programming with a graphics processing unit (GPU) using the Accelerate library, which offers a similar programming model to Repa but runs the computation directly on the GPU.

Parallelizing Haskell code can be a joyful experience: Adding a small annotation to your program can suddenly make it run several times faster on a multicore machine. It can also be a frustrating experience. As we'll see over the course of the next few chapters, there are a number of pitfalls waiting to trap you. Some of these are Haskell-specific, and some are part and parcel of parallel programming in any language. Hopefully by the end you'll have built up enough of an intuition for parallel programming that you'll be able to achieve decent parallel speedups in your own code using the techniques covered.

Keep in mind while reading this part of the book that obtaining reliable results with parallelism is inherently difficult because in today's complex computing devices, performance depends on a vast number of interacting components. For this reason, the results I get from running the examples on my computers might differ somewhat from the results you get on your hardware. Hopefully the difference isn't huge—if it is, that might indicate a problem in GHC that you should report. The important thing is to be aware that performance is fragile, especially where parallelism is concerned.

CHAPTER 2

Basic Parallelism: The Eval Monad

This chapter will teach you the basics of adding parallelism to your Haskell code. We'll start with some essential background about lazy evaluation in the next section before moving on to look at how to use parallelism in "The Eval Monad, rpar, and rseq" on page 15.

Lazy Evaluation and Weak Head Normal Form

Haskell is a *lazy* language which means that expressions are not evaluated until they are required.[1] Normally, we don't have to worry about how this happens; as long as expressions are evaluated when they are needed and not evaluated if they aren't, everything is fine. However, when adding parallelism to our code, we're telling the compiler something about how the program should be run: Certain things should happen in parallel. To be able to use parallelism effectively, it helps to have an intuition for how lazy evaluation works, so this section will explore the basic concepts using GHCi as a playground.

Let's start with something very simple:

```
Prelude> let x = 1 + 2 :: Int
```

This binds the variable x to the expression 1 + 2 (at type Int, to avoid any complications due to overloading). Now, as far as Haskell is concerned, 1 + 2 is equal to 3: We could have written let x = 3 :: Int here, and there is no way to tell the difference by writing ordinary Haskell code. But for the purposes of parallelism, we really do care about the difference between 1 + 2 and 3, because 1 + 2 is a computation that has not taken place yet, and we might be able to compute it in parallel with something else. Of course in

---

1. Technically, this is not correct. Haskell is actually a *non-strict* language, and lazy evaluation is just one of several valid implementation strategies. But GHC uses lazy evaluation, so we ignore this technicality for now.

practice, you wouldn't want to do this with something as trivial as 1 + 2, but the principle of an unevaluated computation is nevertheless important.

We say at this point that x is *unevaluated*. Normally in Haskell, you wouldn't be able to tell that x was unevaluated, but fortunately GHCi's debugger provides some commands that inspect the structure of Haskell expressions in a noninvasive way, so we can use those to demonstrate what's going on. The `:sprint` command prints the value of an expression without causing it to be evaluated:

```
Prelude> :sprint x
x = _
```

The special symbol _ indicates "unevaluated." Another term you may hear in this context is "thunk," which is the object in memory representing the unevaluated computation 1 + 2. The thunk in this case looks something like Figure 2-1.

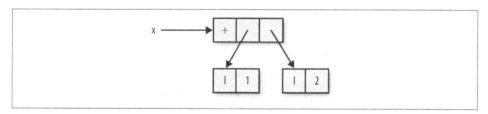

Figure 2-1. The thunk representing 1 + 2

Here, x is a pointer to an object in memory representing the function + applied to the integers 1 and 2.

The thunk representing x will be evaluated whenever its value is required. The easiest way to cause something to be evaluated in GHCi is to print it; that is, we can just type x at the prompt:

```
Prelude> x
3
```

Now if we inspect the value of x using `:sprint`, we'll find that it has been evaluated:

```
Prelude> :sprint x
x = 3
```

In terms of the objects in memory, the thunk representing 1 + 2 is actually overwritten by the (boxed) integer 3.[2] So any future demand for the value of x gets the answer immediately; this is how lazy evaluation works.

---

2. Strictly speaking, it is overwritten by an indirect reference to the value, but the details aren't important here. Interested readers can head over to the GHC wiki (*http://trac.haskell.org/ghc*) to read the documentation about the implementation and the many papers written about its design.

That was a trivial example. Let's try making something slightly more complex.

```
Prelude> let x = 1 + 2 :: Int
Prelude> let y = x + 1
Prelude> :sprint x
x = _
Prelude> :sprint y
y = _
```

Again, we have x bound to 1 + 2, but now we have also bound y to x + 1, and :sprint shows that both are unevaluated as expected. In memory, we have a structure like Figure 2-2.

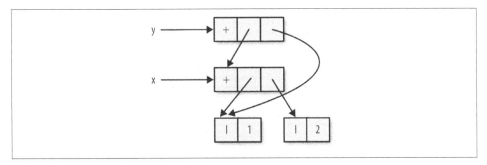

Figure 2-2. One thunk referring to another

Unfortunately there's no way to directly inspect this structure, so you'll just have to trust me.

Now, in order to compute the value of y, the value of x is needed: y depends on x. So evaluating y will also cause x to be evaluated. This time we'll use a different way to force evaluation: Haskell's built-in seq function.

```
Prelude> seq y ()
()
```

The seq function evaluates its first argument, here y, and then returns its second argument—in this case, just (). Now let's inspect the values of x and y:

```
Prelude> :sprint x
x = 3
Prelude> :sprint y
y = 4
```

Both are now evaluated, as expected. So the general principles so far are:

- Defining an expression causes a thunk to be built representing that expression.
- A thunk remains unevaluated until its value is required. Once evaluated, the thunk is replaced by its value.

Let's see what happens when a data structure is added:

```
Prelude> let x = 1 + 2 :: Int
Prelude> let z = (x,x)
```

This binds z to the pair (x,x). The :sprint command shows something interesting:

```
Prelude> :sprint z
z = (_,_)
```

The underlying structure is shown in Figure 2-3.

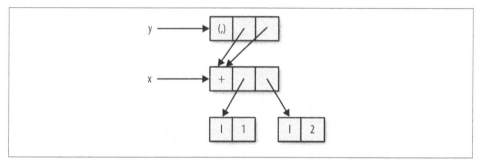

Figure 2-3. A pair with both components referring to the same thunk

The variable z itself refers to the pair (x,x), but the components of the pair both point to the unevaluated thunk for x. This shows that we can build data structures with unevaluated components.

Let's make z into a thunk again:

```
Prelude> import Data.Tuple
Prelude Data.Tuple> let z = swap (x,x+1)
```

The swap function is defined as: swap (a,b) = (b,a). This z is unevaluated as before:

```
Prelude Data.Tuple> :sprint z
z = _
```

The point of this is so that we can see what happens when z is evaluated with seq:

```
Prelude Data.Tuple> seq z ()
()
Prelude Data.Tuple> :sprint z
z = (_,_)
```

Applying seq to z caused it to be evaluated to a pair, *but the components of the pair are still unevaluated*. The seq function evaluates its argument only as far as the first constructor, and doesn't evaluate any more of the structure. There is a technical term for this: We say that seq evaluates its first argument to *weak head normal form*. The reason for this terminology is somewhat historical, so don't worry about it too much. We often use the acronym WHNF instead. The term *normal form* on its own means "fully evaluated," and we'll see how to evaluate something to normal form in "Deepseq" on page 29.

The concept of weak head normal form will crop up several times over the next two chapters, so it's worth taking the time to understand it and get a feel for how evaluation happens in Haskell. Playing around with expressions and :sprint in GHCi is a great way to do that.

Just to finish the example, we'll evaluate x:

```
Prelude Data.Tuple> seq x ()
()
```

What will we see if we print the value of z?

```
Prelude Data.Tuple> :sprint z
z = (_,3)
```

Remember that z was defined to be swap (x,x+1), which is (x+1,x), and we just evaluated x, so the second component of z is now evaluated and has the value 3.

Finally, we'll take a look at an example with lists and a few of the common list functions. You probably know the definition of map, but here it is for reference:

```
map :: (a -> b) -> [a] -> [b]
map f []     = []
map f (x:xs) = f x : map f xs
```

The map function builds a lazy data structure. This might be clearer if we rewrite the definition of map to make the thunks explicit:

```
map :: (a -> b) -> [a] -> [b]
map f []     = []
map f (x:xs) = let
                    x'  = f x
                    xs' = map f xs
                in
                    x' : xs'
```

This behaves identically to the previous definition of map, but now we can see that both the head and the tail of the list that map returns are thunks: f x and map f xs, respectively. That is, map builds a structure like Figure 2-4.

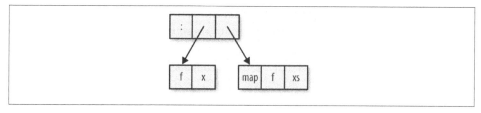

Figure 2-4. Thunks created by a map

Let's define a simple list structure using `map`:

```
Prelude> let xs = map (+1) [1..10] :: [Int]
```

Nothing is evaluated yet:

```
Prelude> :sprint xs
xs = _
```

Now we evaluate this list to weak head normal form:

```
Prelude> seq xs ()
()
Prelude> :sprint xs
xs = _ : _
```

We have a list with at least one element, but that is all we know about it so far. Next, we'll apply the `length` function to the list:

```
Prelude> length xs
10
```

The `length` function is defined like this:

```
length :: [a] -> Int
length []     = 0
length (_:xs) = 1 + length xs
```

Note that `length` ignores the head of the list, recursing on the tail, `xs`. So when `length` is applied to a list, it will descend the structure of the list, evaluating the list cells but not the elements. We can see the effect clearly with `:sprint`:

```
Prelude> :sprint xs
xs = [_,_,_,_,_,_,_,_,_,_]
```

GHCi noticed that the list cells were all evaluated, so it switched to using the bracketed notation rather than infix `:` to display the list.

Even though we have now evaluated the entire spine of the list, it is still not in normal form (but it is still in weak head normal form). We can cause it to be fully evaluated by applying a function that demands the values of the elements, such as `sum`:

```
Prelude> sum xs
65
```

```
Prelude> :sprint xs
xs = [2,3,4,5,6,7,8,9,10,11]
```

We have scratched the surface of what is quite a subtle and complex topic. Fortunately, most of the time, when writing Haskell code, you don't need to worry about understanding when things get evaluated. Indeed, the Haskell language definition is very careful not to specify exactly how evaluation happens; the implementation is free to choose its own strategy as long as the program gives the right answer. And as programmers, most of the time that's all we care about, too. However, when writing parallel code, it becomes important to understand when things are evaluated so that we can arrange to parallelize computations.

An alternative to using lazy evaluation for parallelism is to be more explicit about the data flow, and this is the approach taken by the Par monad in Chapter 4. This avoids some of the subtle issues concerning lazy evaluation in exchange for some verbosity. Nevertheless, it's worthwhile to learn about both approaches because there are situations where one is more natural or more efficient than the other.

The Eval Monad, rpar, and rseq

Next, we introduce some basic functionality for creating parallelism, which is provided by the module Control.Parallel.Strategies:

```
data Eval a
instance Monad Eval

runEval :: Eval a -> a

rpar :: a -> Eval a
rseq :: a -> Eval a
```

Parallelism is expressed using the Eval monad, which comes with two operations, rpar and rseq. The rpar combinator creates parallelism: It says, "My argument could be evaluated in parallel"; while rseq is used for forcing sequential evaluation: It says, "Evaluate my argument and wait for the result." In both cases, evaluation is to weak head normal form. It's also worth noting that the argument to rpar should be an unevaluated computation—a thunk. If the argument is already evaluated, nothing useful happens, because there is no work to perform in parallel.

The Eval monad provides a runEval operation that performs the Eval computation and returns its result. Note that runEval is completely pure; there's no need to be in the IO monad here.

To see the effects of rpar and rseq, suppose we have a function f, along with two arguments to apply it to, x and y, and we would like to calculate the results of f x and f y in parallel. Let's say that f x takes longer to evaluate than f y. We'll look at a few different ways to code this and investigate the differences between them. First, suppose we used rpar with both f x and f y, and then returned a pair of the results, as shown in Example 2-1.

Example 2-1. rpar/rpar

```
runEval $ do
    a <- rpar (f x)
    b <- rpar (f y)
    return (a,b)
```

Execution of this program fragment proceeds as shown in Figure 2-5.

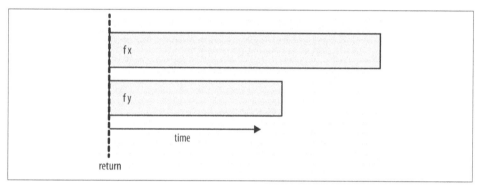

Figure 2-5. rpar/rpar timeline

We see that f x and f y begin to evaluate in parallel, while the return happens immediately: It doesn't wait for either f x or f y to complete. The rest of the program will continue to execute while f x and f y are being evaluated in parallel.

Let's try a different variant, replacing the second rpar with rseq:

Example 2-2. rpar/rseq

```
runEval $ do
    a <- rpar (f x)
    b <- rseq (f y)
    return (a,b)
```

Now the execution will look like Figure 2-6.

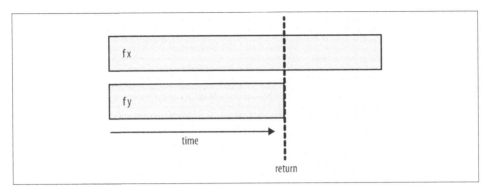

Figure 2-6. rpar/rseq timeline

Here f x and f y are still evaluated in parallel, but now the final return doesn't happen until f y has completed. This is because we used rseq, which waits for the evaluation of its argument before returning.

If we add an additional rseq to wait for f x, we'll wait for both f x and f y to complete:

Example 2-3. rpar/rseq/rseq

```
runEval $ do
  a <- rpar (f x)
  b <- rseq (f y)
  rseq a
  return (a,b)
```

Note that the new rseq is applied to a, namely the result of the first rpar. This results in the ordering shown in Figure 2-7.

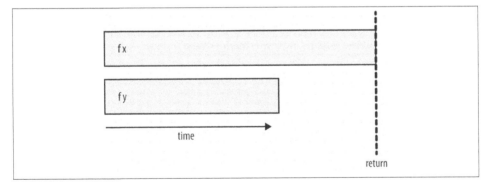

Figure 2-7. rpar/rseq/rseq timeline

The code waits until both f x and f y have completed evaluation before returning.

Which of these patterns should we use?

- *rpar/rseq* is unlikely to be useful because the programmer rarely knows in advance which of the two computations takes the longest, so it makes little sense to wait for an arbitrary one of the two.

- The choice between *rpar/rpar* or *rpar/rseq/rseq* styles depends on the circumstances. If we expect to be generating more parallelism soon and don't depend on the results of either operation, it makes sense to use *rpar/rpar*, which returns immediately. On the other hand, if we have generated all the parallelism we can, or we need the results of one of the operations in order to continue, then *rpar/rseq/rseq* is an explicit way to do that.

There is one final variant:

Example 2-4. rpar/rpar/rseq/rseq

```
runEval $ do
    a <- rpar (f x)
    b <- rpar (f y)
    rseq a
    rseq b
    return (a,b)
```

This has the same behavior as *rpar/rseq/rseq*, waiting for both evaluations before returning. Although it is the longest, this variant has more symmetry than the others, so it might be preferable for that reason.

To experiment with these variants yourself, try the sample program *rpar.hs*, which uses the Fibonacci function to simulate the expensive computations to run in parallel. In order to use parallelism with GHC, we have to use the -threaded option. Compile the program like this:

```
$ ghc -O2 rpar.hs -threaded
```

To try the *rpar/rpar* variant, run it as follows. The +RTS -N2 flag tells GHC to use two cores to run the program (ensure that you have at least a dual-core machine):

```
$ ./rpar 1 +RTS -N2
time: 0.00s
(24157817,14930352)
time: 0.83s
```

The first timestamp is printed when the rpar/rseq fragment returns, and the second timestamp is printed when the last calculation finishes. As you can see, the return here happened immediately. In *rpar/rseq*, it happens after the second (shorter) computation has completed:

```
$ ./rpar 2 +RTS -N2
time: 0.50s
(24157817,14930352)
time: 0.82s
```

In *rpar/rseq/rseq*, the return happens at the end:

```
$ ./rpar 3 +RTS -N2
time: 0.82s
(24157817,14930352)
time: 0.82s
```

Example: Parallelizing a Sudoku Solver

In this section, we'll walk through a case study, exploring how to add parallelism to a program that performs the same computation on multiple input data. The computation is an implementation of a Sudoku solver. This solver is fairly fast as Sudoku solvers go, and can solve all 49,000 of the known 17-clue puzzles in about 2 minutes.

The goal is to parallelize the solving of multiple puzzles. We aren't interested in the details of how the solver works; for the purposes of this discussion, the solver will be treated as a black box. It's just an example of an expensive computation that we want to perform on multiple data sets, namely the Sudoku puzzles.

We will use a module Sudoku that provides a function solve with type:

```
solve :: String -> Maybe Grid
```

The String represents a single Sudoku problem. It is a flattened representation of the 9×9 board, where each square is either empty, represented by the character ., or contains a digit 1–9.

The function solve returns a value of type Maybe Grid, which is either Nothing if a problem has no solution, or Just g if a solution was found, where g has type Grid. For the purposes of this example, we are not interested in the solution itself, the Grid, but only in whether the puzzle has a solution at all.

We start with some ordinary sequential code to solve a set of Sudoku problems read from a file:

sudoku1.hs

```
import Sudoku
import Control.Exception
import System.Environment
import Data.Maybe

main :: IO ()
main = do
  [f] <- getArgs                           -- ❶
  file <- readFile f                       -- ❷

  let puzzles   = lines file               -- ❸
      solutions = map solve puzzles        -- ❹

  print (length (filter isJust solutions)) -- ❺
```

This short program works as follows:

❶ Grab the command-line arguments, expecting a single argument, the name of the file containing the input data.

❷ Read the contents of the given file.

❸ Split the file into lines; each line is a single puzzle.

❹ Solve all the puzzles by mapping the solve function over the list of lines.

❺ Calculate the number of puzzles that had solutions, by first filtering out any results that are Nothing and then taking the length of the resulting list. This length is then printed. Even though we're not interested in the solutions themselves, the filter isJust is necessary here: Without it, the program would never evaluate the elements of the list, and the work of the solver would never be performed (recall the length example at the end of "Lazy Evaluation and Weak Head Normal Form" on page 9).

Let's check that the program works by running over a set of sample problems. First, compile the program:

```
$ ghc -O2 sudoku1.hs -rtsopts
[1 of 2] Compiling Sudoku          ( Sudoku.hs, Sudoku.o )
[2 of 2] Compiling Main            ( sudoku1.hs, sudoku1.o )
Linking sudoku1 ...
```

Remember that when working on performance, it is important to compile with full optimization (-O2). The goal is to make the program run faster, after all.

Now we can run the program on 1,000 sample problems:

```
$ ./sudoku1 sudoku17.1000.txt
1000
```

All 1,000 problems have solutions, so the answer is 1,000. But what we're really interested in is how long the program took to run, because we want to make it go faster. So let's run it again with some extra command-line arguments:

```
$ ./sudoku1 sudoku17.1000.txt +RTS -s
1000
   2,352,273,672 bytes allocated in the heap
      38,930,720 bytes copied during GC
         237,872 bytes maximum residency (14 sample(s))
          84,336 bytes maximum slop
               2 MB total memory in use (0 MB lost due to fragmentation)

                                Tot time (elapsed)  Avg pause  Max pause
  Gen  0      4551 colls,     0 par    0.05s    0.05s     0.0000s    0.0003s
  Gen  1        14 colls,     0 par    0.00s    0.00s     0.0001s    0.0003s
```

```
INIT    time    0.00s  (   0.00s elapsed)
MUT     time    1.25s  (   1.25s elapsed)
GC      time    0.05s  (   0.05s elapsed)
EXIT    time    0.00s  (   0.00s elapsed)
Total   time    1.30s  (   1.31s elapsed)

%GC     time            4.1%  (4.1% elapsed)

Alloc rate    1,883,309,531 bytes per MUT second

Productivity  95.9% of total user, 95.7% of total elapsed
```

The argument +RTS -s instructs the GHC runtime system to emit the statistics shown. These are particularly helpful as a first step in analyzing performance. The output is explained in detail in the GHC User's Guide, but for our purposes we are interested in one particular metric: Total time. This figure is given in two forms: the total CPU time used by the program and the *elapsed* or wall-clock time. Since we are running on a single processor core, these times are almost identical (sometimes the elapsed time might be slightly longer due to other activity on the system).

We shall now add some parallelism to make use of two processor cores. We have a list of problems to solve, so as a first attempt we'll divide the list in two and solve the problems in both halves of the list in parallel. Here is some code to do just that:

sudoku2.hs

```
main :: IO ()
main = do
  [f] <- getArgs
  file <- readFile f

  let puzzles = lines file

      (as,bs) = splitAt (length puzzles `div` 2) puzzles  -- ❶

      solutions = runEval $ do
                    as' <- rpar (force (map solve as))     -- ❷
                    bs' <- rpar (force (map solve bs))     -- ❸
                    rseq as'                               -- ❹
                    rseq bs'                               -- ❺
                    return (as' ++ bs')                    -- ❻

  print (length (filter isJust solutions))
```

❶ Divide the list of puzzles into two equal sublists (or almost equal, if the list had an odd number of elements).

❷ ❸ We're using the *rpar/rpar/rseq/rseq* pattern from the previous section to solve both halves of the list in parallel. However, things are not completely straightforward, because `rpar` only evaluates to weak head normal form. If we were to use `rpar (map solve as)`, the evaluation would stop at the first (`:`) constructor and go no further, so the `rpar` would not cause any of the work to take place in parallel. Instead, we need to cause the whole list and the elements to be evaluated, and this is the purpose of `force`:

```
force :: NFData a => a -> a
```

The `force` function evaluates the entire structure of its argument, reducing it to *normal form*, before returning the argument itself. It is provided by the `Control.DeepSeq` module. We'll return to the `NFData` class in "Deepseq" on page 29, but for now it will suffice to think of it as the class of types that can be evaluated to normal form.

Not evaluating deeply enough is a common mistake when using `rpar`, so it is a good idea to get into the habit of thinking, for each `rpar`, "How much of this structure do I want to evaluate in the parallel task?" (Indeed, it is such a common problem that in the `Par` monad to be introduced later, the designers went so far as to make `force` the default behavior).

❹ ❺ Using `rseq`, we wait for the evaluation of both lists to complete.

❻ Append the two lists to form the complete list of solutions.

Let's run the program and measure how much performance improvement we get from the parallelism:

```
$ ghc -O2 sudoku2.hs -rtsopts -threaded
[2 of 2] Compiling Main            ( sudoku2.hs, sudoku2.o )
Linking sudoku2 ...
```

Now we can run the program using two cores:

```
$ ./sudoku2 sudoku17.1000.txt +RTS -N2 -s
1000
  2,360,292,584 bytes allocated in the heap
     48,635,888 bytes copied during GC
      2,604,024 bytes maximum residency (7 sample(s))
        320,760 bytes maximum slop
              9 MB total memory in use (0 MB lost due to fragmentation)

                                 Tot time (elapsed)  Avg pause  Max pause
  Gen  0      2979 colls,  2978 par    0.11s    0.06s     0.0000s    0.0003s
  Gen  1         7 colls,     7 par    0.01s    0.01s     0.0009s    0.0014s

  Parallel GC work balance: 1.49 (6062998 / 4065140, ideal 2)
```

```
                    MUT time (elapsed)        GC time  (elapsed)
Task  0 (worker) :   0.81s  (  0.81s)        0.06s   (  0.06s)
Task  1 (worker) :   0.00s  (  0.88s)        0.00s   (  0.00s)
Task  2 (bound)  :   0.52s  (  0.83s)        0.04s   (  0.04s)
Task  3 (worker) :   0.00s  (  0.86s)        0.02s   (  0.02s)

SPARKS: 2 (1 converted, 0 overflowed, 0 dud, 0 GC'd, 1 fizzled)

INIT    time    0.00s  (  0.00s elapsed)
MUT     time    1.34s  (  0.81s elapsed)
GC      time    0.12s  (  0.06s elapsed)
EXIT    time    0.00s  (  0.00s elapsed)
Total   time    1.46s  (  0.88s elapsed)

Alloc rate     1,763,903,211 bytes per MUT second

Productivity  91.6% of total user, 152.6% of total elapsed
```

Note that the `Total time` now shows a marked difference between the CPU time (1.46s) and the elapsed time (0.88s). Previously, the elapsed time was 1.31s, so we can calculate the *speedup* on 2 cores as 1.31/0.88 = 1.48. Speedups are always calculated as a ratio of wall-clock times. The CPU time is a helpful metric for telling us how busy our cores are, but as you can see here, the CPU time when running on multiple cores is often greater than the wall-clock time for a single core, so it would be misleading to calculate the speedup as the ratio of CPU time to wall-clock time (1.66 here).

Why is the speedup only 1.48, and not 2? In general, there could be a host of reasons for this, not all of which are under the control of the Haskell programmer. However, in this case the problem is partly of our doing, and we can diagnose it using the *Thread-Scope* tool. To profile the program using *ThreadScope*, we need to first recompile it with the `-eventlog` flag and then run it with `+RTS -l`. This causes the program to emit a log file called `sudoku2.eventlog`, which we can pass to `threadscope`:

```
$ rm sudoku2; ghc -O2 sudoku2.hs -threaded -rtsopts -eventlog
[2 of 2] Compiling Main             ( sudoku2.hs, sudoku2.o )
Linking sudoku2 ...
$ ./sudoku2 sudoku17.1000.txt +RTS -N2 -l
1000
$ threadscope sudoku2.eventlog
```

The *ThreadScope* profile is shown in Figure 2-8. This graph was generated by selecting "Export image" from *ThreadScope*, so it includes the timeline graph only, and not the rest of the *ThreadScope* GUI.

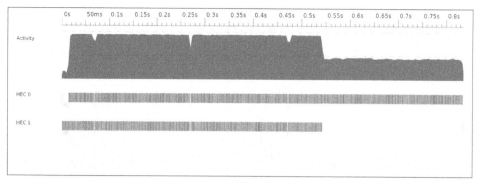

Figure 2-8. sudoku2 ThreadScope profile

The x-axis of the graph is time, and there are three horizontal bars showing how the program executed over time. The topmost bar is known as the "activity" profile, and it shows how many cores were executing Haskell code (as opposed to being idle or garbage collecting) at a given point in time. Underneath the activity profile is one bar per core, showing what that core was doing at each point in the execution. Each bar has two parts: The upper, thicker bar is green when that core is executing Haskell code, and the lower, narrower bar is orange or green when that core is performing garbage collection.

As we can see from the graph, there is a period at the end of the run where just one processor is executing and the other one is idle (except for participating in regular garbage collections, which is necessary for GHC's parallel garbage collector). This indicates that our two parallel tasks are uneven: One takes much longer to execute than the other. We are not making full use of our two cores, and this results in less-than-perfect speedup.

Why should the workloads be uneven? After all, we divided the list in two, and we know the sample input has an even number of problems. The reason for the unevenness is that each problem does not take the same amount of time to solve: It all depends on the searching strategy used by the Sudoku solver.[3]

This illustrates an important principle when parallelizing code: Try to avoid partitioning the work into a small, fixed number of chunks. There are two reasons for this:

- In practice, chunks rarely contain an equal amount of work, so there will be some imbalance leading to a loss of speedup, as in the example we just saw.
- The parallelism we can achieve is limited to the number of chunks. In our example, even if the workloads were even, we could never achieve a speedup of more than two, regardless of how many cores we use.

---

3. In fact, I sorted the problems in the sample input so as to clearly demonstrate the problem.

Even if we tried to solve the second problem by dividing the work into as many segments as we have cores, we would still have the first problem, namely that the work involved in processing each segment may differ.

GHC doesn't force us to use a fixed number of rpar calls; we can call it as many times as we like, and the system will automatically distribute the parallel work among the available cores. If the work is divided into smaller chunks, then the system will be able to keep all the cores busy for longer.

A fixed division of work is often called *static partitioning*, whereas distributing smaller units of work among processors at runtime is called *dynamic partitioning*. GHC already provides the mechanism for dynamic partitioning; we just have to supply it with enough tasks by calling rpar often enough so that it can do its job and balance the work evenly.

The argument to rpar is called a *spark*. The runtime collects sparks in a pool and uses this as a source of work when there are spare processors available, using a technique called *work stealing*. Sparks may be evaluated at some point in the future, or they might not—it all depends on whether there is a spare core available. Sparks are very cheap to create: rpar essentially just writes a pointer to the expression into an array.

So let's try to use dynamic partitioning with the Sudoku problem. First, we define an abstraction that will let us apply a function to a list in parallel, parMap:

```
parMap :: (a -> b) -> [a] -> Eval [b]
parMap f [] = return []
parMap f (a:as) = do
   b <- rpar (f a)
   bs <- parMap f as
   return (b:bs)
```

This is rather like a monadic version of map, except that we have used rpar to lift the application of the function f to the element a into the Eval monad. Hence, parMap runs down the whole list, eagerly creating sparks for the application of f to each element, and finally returns the new list. When parMap returns, it will have created one spark for each element of the list. Now, the evaluation of all the results can happen in parallel:

sudoku3.hs

```
main :: IO ()
main = do
  [f] <- getArgs
  file <- readFile f

  let puzzles   = lines file
      solutions = runEval (parMap solve puzzles)

  print (length (filter isJust solutions))
```

Note how this version is nearly identical to the first version, *sudoku1.hs*. The only difference is that we've replaced `map solve puzzles` by `runEval (parMap solve puzzles)`.

Running this new version yields more speedup:

```
Total   time    1.42s (  0.72s elapsed)
```

which corresponds to a speedup of 1.31/0.72 = 1.82, approaching the ideal speedup of 2. Furthermore, the GHC runtime system tells us how many sparks were created:

```
SPARKS: 1000 (1000 converted, 0 overflowed, 0 dud, 0 GC'd, 0 fizzled)
```

We created exactly 1,000 sparks, and they were all *converted* (that is, turned into real parallelism at runtime). Here are some other things that can happen to a spark:

overflowed

The spark pool has a fixed size, and if we try to create sparks when the pool is full, they are dropped and counted as overflowed.

dud

When `rpar` is applied to an expression that is already evaluated, this is counted as a *dud* and the `rpar` is ignored.

GC'd

The sparked expression was found to be unused by the program, so the runtime removed the spark. We'll discuss this in more detail in "GC'd Sparks and Speculative Parallelism" on page 48.

fizzled

The expression was unevaluated at the time it was sparked but was later evaluated independently by the program. Fizzled sparks are removed from the spark pool.

The *ThreadScope* profile for this version looks much better (Figure 2-9). Furthermore, now that the runtime is managing the work distribution for us, the program will automatically scale to more processors. On an 8-core machine, for example, I measured a speedup of 5.83 for the same program.[4]

---

4. This machine was an Amazon EC2 High-CPU extra-large instance.

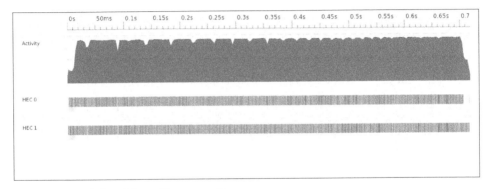

Figure 2-9. sudoku3 ThreadScope profile

If we look closely at the two-processor profile, there appears to be a short section near the beginning where not much work is happening. In fact, zooming in on this section in *ThreadScope* (Figure 2-10) reveals that both processors are working, but most of the activity is garbage collection, and only one processor is performing most of the garbage collection work. In fact, what we are seeing here is the program reading the input file (lazily) and dividing it into lines, driven by the demand of parMap, which traverses the whole list of lines. Splitting the file into lines creates a lot of data, and this seems to be happening on the second core here. However, note that even though splitting the file into lines is sequential, the program doesn't wait for it to complete before the parallel work starts. The parMap function creates the first spark when it has the first element of the list, so two processors can be working before we've finished splitting the file into lines. Lazy evaluation helps the program be more parallel, in a sense.

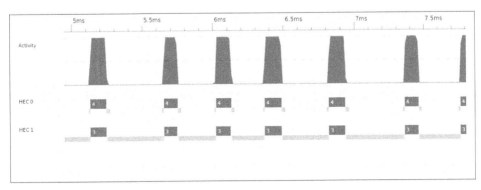

Figure 2-10. sudoku3: zoomed ThreadScope profile

We can experiment with forcing the splitting into lines to happen all at once before we start the main computation, by adding the following (see *sudoku3.hs*):

```
evaluate (length puzzles)
```

The `evaluate` function is like a `seq` in the `IO` monad: it evaluates its argument to weak head normal form and then returns it:

```
evaluate :: a -> IO a
```

Forcing the lines to be evaluated early reduces the parallelism slightly, because we no longer get the benefit of overlapping the line splitting with the solving. Our two-core runtime is now 0.76s. However, we can now clearly see the boundary between the sequential and parallel parts in *ThreadScope* (Figure 2-11).

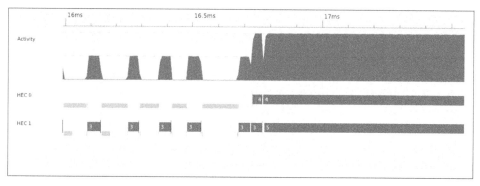

Figure 2-11. sudoku4 ThreadScope profile

Looking at the profile, we can see that the program is sequential until about 16.7ms, when it starts executing in parallel. A program that has a sequential portion like this can never achieve perfect speedup, and in fact we can calculate the maximum achievable speedup for a given number of cores using Amdahl's law. Amdahl's law gives the maximum speedup as the ratio:

$$1 / ((1 - P) + P/N)$$

where P is the portion of the runtime that can be parallelized, and N is the number of processors available. In our case, P is $(0.76 - 0.0167)/0.76 = 0.978$, and the maximum speedup is 1.96. The sequential fraction here is too small to make a significant impact on the theoretical maximum speedup with two processors, but when we have more processors, say 64, it becomes much more important: $1 / ((1-0.978) + 0.978/64) = 26.8$. So no matter what we do, this tiny sequential part of our program will limit the maximum speedup we can obtain with 64 processors to 26.8. In fact, even with 1,024 cores, we could achieve only around 44 speedup, and it is impossible to achieve a speedup of 46 no matter how many cores we have. Amdahl's law tells us that not only does parallel speedup become harder to achieve the more processors we add, but in practice most programs have a theoretical maximum amount of parallelism.

Deepseq

We encountered `force` earlier, with this type:

```
force :: NFData a => a -> a
```

The `force` function fully evaluates its argument and then returns it. This function isn't built-in, though: Its behavior is defined for each data type through the `NFData` class. The name stands for normal-form data, where normal-form is a value with no unevaluated subexpressions, and "data" because it isn't possible to put a function in normal form; there's no way to "look inside" a function and evaluate the things it mentions.[5]

The `NFData` class has only one method:

```
class NFData a where
  rnf :: a -> ()
  rnf a = a `seq` ()
```

The `rnf` name stands for "reduce to normal-form." It fully evaluates its argument and then returns `()`. The default definition uses `seq`, which is convenient for types that have no substructure; we can just use the default. For example, the instance for `Bool` is defined as simply:

```
instance NFData Bool
```

And the `Control.Deepseq` module provides instances for all the other common types found in the libraries.

You may need to create instances of `NFData` for your own types. For example, if we had a binary tree data type:

```
data Tree a = Empty | Branch (Tree a) a (Tree a)
```

then the `NFData` instance should look like this:

```
instance NFData a => NFData (Tree a) where
  rnf Empty = ()
  rnf (Branch l a r) = rnf l `seq` rnf a `seq` rnf r
```

The idea is to just recursively apply `rnf` to the components of the data type, composing the calls to `rnf` together with `seq`.

There are some other operations provided by `Control.DeepSeq`:

```
deepseq :: NFData a => a -> b -> b
deepseq a b = rnf a `seq` b
```

---

5. However, there is an instance of `NFData` for functions, which evaluates the function to WHNF. This is purely for convenience, because we often have data structures that contain functions and nevertheless want to evaluate them as much as possible.

The function deepseq is so named for its similarity with seq; it is like seq, but if we think of weak head normal form as being *shallow* evaluation, then normal form is *deep* evaluation, hence deepseq.

The force function is defined in terms of deepseq:

```
force :: NFData a => a -> a
force x = x `deepseq` x
```

You should think of force as turning WHNF into NF: If the program evaluates force x to WHNF, then x will be evaluated to NF.

 Evaluating something to normal form involves traversing the whole of its structure, so you should bear in mind that it is $O(n)$ for a structure of size n, whereas seq is $O(1)$. It is therefore a good idea to avoid repeated uses of force or deepseq on the same data.

WHNF and NF are two ends of a scale; there may be lots of intermediate "degrees of evaluation," depending on the data type. For example, we saw earlier that the length function evaluates only the *spine* of a list; that is, the list cells but not the elements. The module Control.Seq (from the parallel package) provides a set of combinators that can be composed together to evaluate data structures to varying degrees. We won't need it for the examples in this book, but you may find it useful.

CHAPTER 3

Evaluation Strategies

Evaluation Strategies, or simply Strategies, are a means for modularizing parallel code by separating the algorithm from the parallelism. Sometimes they require you to rewrite your algorithm, but once you do so, you will be able to parallelize it in different ways just by substituting a new Strategy.

Concretely, a `Strategy` is a function in the `Eval` monad that takes a value of type `a` and returns the same value:

```
type Strategy a = a -> Eval a
```

The idea is that a Strategy takes a data structure as input, traverses the structure creating parallelism with `rpar` and `rseq`, and then returns the original value.

Here's a simple example: Let's create a Strategy for pairs that evaluates the two components of the pair in parallel. We want a function `parPair` with the following type:

```
parPair :: Strategy (a,b)
```

From the definition of the `Strategy` type previously shown, we know that this type is the same as `(a,b) -> Eval (a,b)`. So `parPair` is a function that takes a pair, does some computation in the `Eval` monad, and returns the pair again. Here is its definition:

strat.hs

```
parPair :: Strategy (a,b)
parPair (a,b) = do
  a' <- rpar a
  b' <- rpar b
  return (a',b')
```

This is similar to the *rpar/rpar* pattern that we saw in "The Eval Monad, rpar, and rseq" on page 15. The difference is that we've packaged it up as a Strategy: It takes a data structure (in this case a pair), creates some parallelism using `rpar`, and then returns the same data structure.

We'll see this in action in a moment, but first we need to know how to use a Strategy. Using a Strategy consists of applying it to its input and running the `Eval` computation to get the output. We could write that directly with `runEval`; for example, to evaluate the pair (`fib 35, fib 36`) in parallel, we could write:

```
runEval (parPair (fib 35, fib 36))
```

This works just fine, but it turns out to be much nicer to package up the application of a Strategy into a function named `using`:

```
using :: a -> Strategy a -> a
x `using` s = runEval (s x)
```

The `using` function takes a value of type `a` and a Strategy for `a`, and applies the Strategy to the value. We normally write `using` infix, as its definition suggests. Here is the `parPair` example above rewritten with `using`:

```
(fib 35, fib 36) `using` parPair
```

Why write it this way? Well, a Strategy returns the same value that it was passed, so we know that aside from its performance, the above code is equivalent to just:

```
(fib 35, fib 36)
```

So we've clearly separated the code that describes what the program *does* (the pair) from the code that adds the parallelism (`` `using` parPair``). Indeed, everywhere we see `x ` `using` s` in our program, we can delete the `` `using` `` s part and the program should produce the same result.[1] Conversely, someone who is interested in parallelizing the program can focus on modifying the Strategy without worrying about breaking the program.

The example program *strat.hs* contains the `parPair` example just shown; try running it yourself with one and two processors to see it compute the two calls to `fib` in parallel.

Parameterized Strategies

The `parPair` Strategy embodies a fixed policy: It always evaluates the components of the pair in parallel, and always to weak head normal form. If we wanted to do something different with a pair—fully evaluate the components to normal form, for example—we would have to write a completely new Strategy. A better way to factor things is to write a *parameterized* Strategy, which takes as arguments the Strategies to apply to the components of the data structure. Here is a parameterized Strategy for pairs:

---

1. This comes with a couple of minor caveats that we'll describe in "The Identity Property" on page 55.

strat.hs

```
evalPair :: Strategy a -> Strategy b -> Strategy (a,b)
evalPair sa sb (a,b) = do
  a' <- sa a
  b' <- sb b
  return (a',b')
```

This Strategy no longer has parallelism built in, so I've called it `evalPair` instead of `parPair`.[2] It takes two `Strategy` arguments, `sa` and `sb`, applies them to the respective components of the pair, and then returns the pair.

Compared with `parPair`, we are passing in the functions to apply to a and b instead of making fixed calls to `rpar`. So to define `parPair` in terms of `evalPair`, we can just pass `rpar` as the arguments:

```
parPair :: Strategy (a,b)
parPair = evalPair rpar rpar
```

This means we're using `rpar` itself as a `Strategy`:

```
rpar :: Strategy a
```

The type of `rpar` is `a -> Eval a`, which is equivalent to `Strategy a`; `rpar` is therefore a Strategy for any type, with the effect of starting the evaluation of its argument while the enclosing `Eval` computation proceeds in parallel. (The `rseq` operation is also a `Strategy`.)

But `parPair` is still restrictive, in that the components of the pair are always evaluated to weak head normal form. What if we wanted to fully evaluate the components using `force`, for example? We can make a `Strategy` that fully evaluates its argument:

```
rdeepseq :: NFData a => Strategy a
rdeepseq x = rseq (force x)
```

But how do we combine `rpar` with `rdeepseq` to give us a single Strategy that fully evaluates its argument in parallel? We need one further combinator, which is provided by `Control.Parallel.Strategies`:

```
rparWith :: Strategy a -> Strategy a
```

Think of `rparWith` s as wrapping the Strategy s in an `rpar`.

Now we can provide a parameterized version of `parPair` that takes the Strategies to apply to the components:

```
parPair :: Strategy a -> Strategy b -> Strategy (a,b)
parPair sa sb = evalPair (rparWith sa) (rparWith sb)
```

---

2. The `evalPair` function is provided by `Control.Parallel.Strategies` as `evalTuple2`.

And we can use parPair to write a Strategy that fully evaluates both components of a pair in parallel:

```
parPair rdeepseq rdeepseq :: (NFData a, NFData b) => Strategy (a,b)
```

To break down what happens when this Strategy is applied to a pair: parPair calls evalPair, and evalPair calls rparWith rdeepseq on each component of the pair. So the effect is that each component will be fully evaluated to normal form in parallel.

When using these parameterized Strategies, we sometimes need a way to say, "Don't evaluate this component at all." The Strategy that does no evaluation is called r0:

```
r0 :: Strategy a
r0 x = return x
```

For example, we can write a Strategy over a pair of pairs that evaluates the first component (only) of both pairs in parallel.

```
evalPair (evalPair rpar r0) (evalPair rpar r0) :: Strategy ((a,b),(c,d))
```

The first rpar applies to a and the first r0 to b, while the second rpar applies to c and the second r0 to d.

A Strategy for Evaluating a List in Parallel

In Chapter 2, we defined a function parMap that would map a function over a list in parallel. We can think of parMap as a composition of two parts:

- The algorithm: map
- The parallelism: evaluating the elements of a list in parallel

And indeed, with Strategies, we can express it exactly this way:

```
parMap :: (a -> b) -> [a] -> [b]
parMap f xs = map f xs `using` parList rseq
```

The parList function is a Strategy on lists that evaluates the list elements in parallel. To define parList, we can take the same approach that we took with pairs earlier and first define a parameterized Strategy on lists, called evalList:

parlist.hs

```
evalList :: Strategy a -> Strategy [a]
evalList strat []     = return []
evalList strat (x:xs) = do
  x'  <- strat x
  xs' <- evalList strat xs
  return (x':xs')
```

Note that evalList walks the list recursively, applying the Strategy parameter strat to each of the elements and building the result list. Now we can define parList in terms of evalList, using rparWith:

```
parList :: Strategy a -> Strategy [a]
parList strat = evalList (rparWith strat)
```

In fact, both evalList and parList are already provided by Control.Parallel.Strategies so you don't have to define them yourself, but it's useful to see that their implementations are not mysterious.

As with parPair, the parList function is a parameterized Strategy. That is, it takes as an argument a Strategy on values of type a and returns a Strategy for lists of a. So parList describes a family of Strategies on lists that evaluate the list elements in parallel.

The parList Strategy covers a wide range of uses for parallelism in typical Haskell programs; in many cases, a single parList is all that is needed to expose plenty of parallelism.

Returning to our Sudoku solver from Chapter 2 for a moment: instead of our own hand-written parMap, we could have used parList:

sudoku5.hs

```
let solutions = map solve puzzles `using` parList rseq
```

Using rseq as the Strategy for the list elements is enough here: The result of solve is a Maybe, so evaluating it to weak head normal form forces the solver to determine whether the puzzle has a solution.

This version has essentially the same performance as the version that used parMap in Chapter 2.

Example: The K-Means Problem

Let's look at a slightly more involved example. In the *K-Means* problem, the goal is to partition a set of data points into clusters. Figure 3-1 shows an example data set, and the circles indicate the locations of the clusters that the algorithm should derive. From the locations of the clusters, partitioning the points is achieved by simply finding the closest cluster to each point.

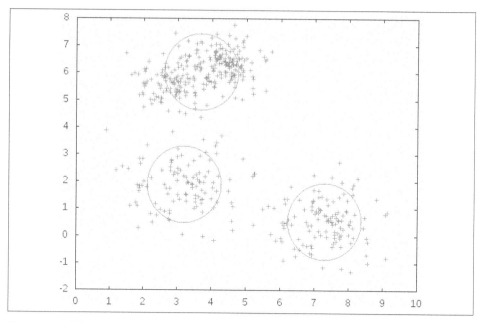

Figure 3-1. The K-Means problem

Finding an optimal solution to the problem is too expensive to be practical. However, there are several heuristic techniques that are fast, and even though they don't guarantee an optimal solution, in practice, they give good results. The most well-known heuristic technique for K-Means is Lloyd's algorithm, which finds a solution by iteratively improving an initial guess. The algorithm takes as a parameter the number of clusters to find and makes an initial guess at the center of each cluster. Then it proceeds as follows:

1. Assign each point to the cluster to which it is closest. This yields a new set of clusters.
2. Find the *centroid* of each cluster (the average of all the points in the cluster).
3. Repeat steps 1 and 2 until the cluster locations stabilize. We cut off processing after an arbitrarily chosen number of iterations, because sometimes the algorithm does not converge.

The initial guess can be constructed by randomly assigning each point in the data set to a cluster and then finding the centroids of those clusters.

The algorithm works in any number of dimensions, but we will use two for ease of visualization.

A complete Haskell implementation can be found in the directory *kmeans* in the sample code.

A data point is represented by the type `Point`, which is just a pair of `Double`s representing the x and y coordinates respectively:[3]

```
data Point = Point !Double !Double
```

There are a couple of basic operations on `Point`:

kmeans/KMeansCore.hs

```
zeroPoint :: Point
zeroPoint = Point 0 0

sqDistance :: Point -> Point -> Double
sqDistance (Point x1 y1) (Point x2 y2) = ((x1-x2)^2) + ((y1-y2)^2)
```

We can make a zero point with `zeroPoint`, and find the square of the distance between two points with `sqDistance`. The actual distance between the points would be given by the square root of this value, but since we will only be comparing distances, we can save time by comparing squared distances instead.

Clusters are represented by the type `Cluster`:

```
data Cluster
  = Cluster { clId   :: Int
            , clCent :: Point
            }
```

A `Cluster` contains its number (`clId`) and its centroid (`clCent`).

We will also need an intermediate type called `PointSum`:

```
data PointSum = PointSum !Int !Double !Double
```

A `PointSum` represents the sum of a set of points; it contains the number of points in the set and the sum of their x and y coordinates respectively. A `PointSum` is constructed incrementally, by repeatedly adding points using `addToPointSum`:

kmeans/kmeans.hs

```
addToPointSum :: PointSum -> Point -> PointSum
addToPointSum (PointSum count xs ys) (Point x y)
  = PointSum (count+1) (xs + x) (ys + y)
```

A `PointSum` can be turned into a `Cluster` by computing the centroid. The x coordinate of the centroid is the sum of the x coordinates of the points in the cluster divided by the total number of points, and similarly for the y coordinate.

```
pointSumToCluster :: Int -> PointSum -> Cluster
pointSumToCluster i (PointSum count xs ys) =
  Cluster { clId   = i
```

---

3. The actual implementation adds UNPACK pragmas for efficiency, which I have omitted here for clarity.

```
                , clCent  = Point (xs / fromIntegral count) (ys / fromIntegral count)
                }
```

The roles of the types Point, PointSum, and Cluster in the algorithm are as follows. The input is a set of points represented as [Point], and an initial guess represented as [Cluster]. The algorithm will iteratively refine the clusters until convergence is reached.

- Step 1 divides the points into new sets by finding the Cluster to which each Point is closest. However, instead of collecting sets of Points, we build up a PointSum for each cluster. This is an optimization that avoids constructing the intermediate data structure and allows the algorithm to run in constant space. We'll represent the output of this step as Vector PointSum.

- The Vector PointSum is fed into step 2, which makes a Cluster from each PointSum, giving [Cluster].

- The result of step 2 is fed back into step 1 until convergence is reached.

The function assign implements step 1 of the algorithm, assigning points to clusters and building a vector of PointSums:

```
assign :: Int -> [Cluster] -> [Point] -> Vector PointSum
assign nclusters clusters points = Vector.create $ do
    vec <- MVector.replicate nclusters (PointSum 0 0 0)
    let
        addpoint p = do
          let c = nearest p; cid = clId c
          ps <- MVector.read vec cid
          MVector.write vec cid $! addToPointSum ps p

    mapM_ addpoint points
    return vec
  where
    nearest p = fst $ minimumBy (compare `on` snd)
                        [ (c, sqDistance (clCent c) p) | c <- clusters ]
```

Given a set of clusters and a set of points, the job of assign is to decide, for each point, which cluster is closest. For each cluster, we build up a PointSum of the points that were found to be closest to it. The code has been carefully optimized, using mutable vectors from the vector package; the details aren't important here.

The function makeNewClusters implements step 2 of the algorithm:

```
makeNewClusters :: Vector PointSum -> [Cluster]
makeNewClusters vec =
  [ pointSumToCluster i ps
  | (i,ps@(PointSum count _ _)) <- zip [0..] (Vector.toList vec)
  , count > 0
  ]
```

Here we make a new `Cluster`, using `pointSumToCluster`, from each `PointSum` produced by `assign`. There is a slight complication in that we have to avoid creating a cluster with no points, because it cannot have a centroid.

Finally `step` combines `assign` and `makeNewClusters` to implement one complete iteration:

```
step :: Int -> [Cluster] -> [Point] -> [Cluster]
step nclusters clusters points
  = makeNewClusters (assign nclusters clusters points)
```

To complete the algorithm, we need a loop to repeatedly apply the `step` function until convergence. The function `kmeans_seq` implements this:

```
kmeans_seq :: Int -> [Point] -> [Cluster] -> IO [Cluster]
kmeans_seq nclusters points clusters =
  let
      loop :: Int -> [Cluster] -> IO [Cluster]
      loop n clusters | n > tooMany = do          -- ❶
        putStrLn "giving up."
        return clusters
      loop n clusters = do
        printf "iteration %d\n" n
        putStr (unlines (map show clusters))
        let clusters' = step nclusters clusters points    -- ❷
        if clusters' == clusters                          -- ❸
            then return clusters
            else loop (n+1) clusters'
  in
  loop 0 clusters

tooMany = 80
```

❶ The first argument to `loop` is the number of iterations completed so far. If this figure reaches the limit `tooMany`, then we bail out (sometimes the algorithm does not converge).

❷ After printing the iteration number and the current clusters for diagnostic purposes, we calculate the next iteration by calling the function `step`. The arguments to `step` are the number of clusters, the current set of clusters, and the set of points.

❸ If this iteration did not change the clusters, then the algorithm has converged, and we return the result. Otherwise, we do another iteration.

We compile this program in the same way as before:

```
$ cd kmeans
$ ghc -O2 -threaded -rtsopts -eventlog kmeans.hs
```

The sample code comes with a program to generate some input data, *GenSamples.hs*, which uses the normaldistribution package to generate a realistically clustered set of values. The data set is large, so it isn't included with the sample code, but you can generate it using GenSamples:

```
$ ghc -O2 GenSamples.hs
$ ./GenSamples 5 50000 100000 1010
```

This should generate a data set of about 340,000 points with 5 clusters in the file points.bin.

Run the kmeans program using the sequential algorithm:

```
$ ./kmeans seq
```

The program will display the clusters at each iteration and should converge after 65 iterations.

Note that the program displays its own running time at the end; this is because there is a significant amount of time spent reading in the sample data at the beginning, and we want to be able to calculate the parallel speedup for the portion of the runtime spent computing the K-Means algorithm only.

Parallelizing K-Means

How can this algorithm be parallelized? One place that looks profitable to parallelize is the assign function because it is essentially just a map over the points, and indeed that is where we will concentrate our efforts. The operations are too fine-grained here to use a simple parMap or parList as we did before; the overhead of the parMap will swamp the parallelism, so we need to increase the size of the operations. One way to do that is to divide the list of points into chunks, and process the chunks in parallel. First we need some code to split a list into chunks:

```
split :: Int -> [a] -> [[a]]
split numChunks xs = chunk (length xs `quot` numChunks) xs

chunk :: Int -> [a] -> [[a]]
chunk n [] = []
chunk n xs = as : chunk n bs
  where (as,bs) = splitAt n xs
```

So we can split the list of points into chunks and map assign over the list of chunks. But what do we do with the results? We have a list of Vector PointSums that we need to combine into a single Vector PointSum. Fortunately, PointSums can be added together:

```
addPointSums :: PointSum -> PointSum -> PointSum
addPointSums (PointSum c1 x1 y1) (PointSum c2 x2 y2)
  = PointSum (c1+c2) (x1+x2) (y1+y2)
```

And using this, we can combine vectors of PointSums:

```
combine :: Vector PointSum -> Vector PointSum -> Vector PointSum
combine = Vector.zipWith addPointSums
```

We now have all the pieces to define a parallel version of step:

```
parSteps_strat :: Int -> [Cluster] -> [[Point]] -> [Cluster]
parSteps_strat nclusters clusters pointss
  = makeNewClusters $
      foldr1 combine $
        (map (assign nclusters clusters) pointss
          `using` parList rseq)
```

The arguments to parSteps_strat are the same as for step, except that the list of points is now a list of lists of points, that is, the list of points divided into chunks by split. We want to pass in the chunked data rather than call split inside parSteps_strat so that we can do the chunking of the input data just once instead of repeating it for each iteration.

The kmeans_strat function below is our parallel version of kmeans_seq, the only differences being that we call split to divide the list of points into chunks (❶) and we call parSteps_strat instead of steps (❷):

```
kmeans_strat :: Int -> Int -> [Point] -> [Cluster] -> IO [Cluster]
kmeans_strat numChunks nclusters points clusters =
  let
      chunks = split numChunks points                        -- ❶

      loop :: Int -> [Cluster] -> IO [Cluster]
      loop n clusters | n > tooMany = do
        printf "giving up."
        return clusters
      loop n clusters = do
        printf "iteration %d\n" n
        putStr (unlines (map show clusters))
        let clusters' = parSteps_strat nclusters clusters chunks -- ❷
        if clusters' == clusters
           then return clusters
           else loop (n+1) clusters'
  in
  loop 0 clusters
```

Note that the number of chunks doesn't have to be related to the number of processors; as we saw earlier, it is better to produce plenty of sparks and let the runtime schedule them automatically, because this should enable the program to scale over a wide range of processors.

Performance and Analysis

Next we're going on an exploration of the performance of this parallel program. Along the way, we'll learn several lessons about the kinds of things that can go wrong when parallelizing Haskell code, how to look out for them using ThreadScope, and how to fix them.

We'll start by taking some measurements of the speedup for various numbers of cores. When running the program in parallel, we get to choose the number of chunks to divide the input into, and for these measurements I'll use 64 (but we'll revisit this in "Granularity" on page 47). The program is run in parallel like this:

```
$ ./kmeans strat 64 +RTS -N2
```

strat indicates that we want to use the Strategies version of the algorithm, and 64 is the number of chunks to divide the input data into. Here, I'm telling the GHC runtime to use two cores.

Here are the speedup results I get on my computer for the kmeans program I showed earlier.[4] For each measurement, I ran the program a few times and took the average runtime.[5]

Cores	Time (s)	Speedup
1	2.56	1
2	1.42	1.8
3	1.06	2.4
4	0.97	2.6

We can see that speedup is quite good for two to three cores but starts to drop off at four cores. Still, a 2.6 speedup on 4 cores is reasonably respectable.

The ThreadScope profile gives us some clues about why the speedup might be less than we hope. The overall view of the four-core run can be seen in Figure 3-2.

---

4. A quad-core Intel i7-3770

5. To do this scientifically, you would need to be much more rigorous, but the goal here is just to optimize our program, so rough measurements are fine.

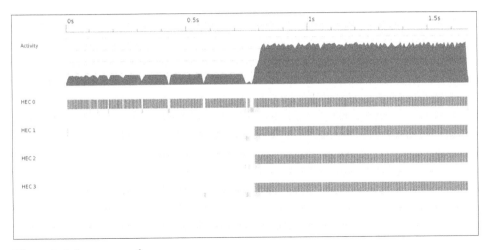

Figure 3-2. kmeans on four cores

We can clearly see the sequential section at the start, where the program reads in the input data. But that isn't a problem; remember that the program emits its own timing results, which begin at the parallel part of the run. The parallel section itself looks quite good; all cores seem to be running for the duration. Let's zoom in on the beginning of the parallel section, as shown in Figure 3-3.

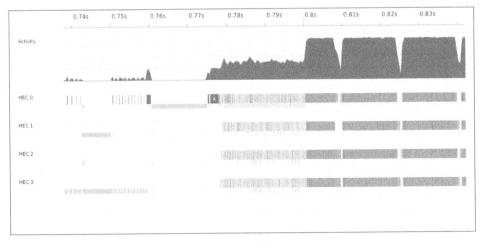

Figure 3-3. kmeans on four cores, start of parallel execution

There's a segment between 0.78s and 0.8s where, although parallel execution has started, there is heavy GC activity. This is similar to what we saw in "Example: Parallelizing a Sudoku Solver" on page 19, where the work of splitting the input data into lines was overlapped with the parallel execution. In the case of kmeans, the act of splitting the data set into chunks is causing the extra work.

The sequential version of the algorithm doesn't need to split the data into chunks, so chunking is a source of extra overhead in the parallel version. This is one reason that we aren't achieving full speedup. If you're feeling adventurous, you might want to see whether you can avoid this chunking overhead by using Vector instead of a list to represent the data set, because Vectors can be sliced in $O(1)$ time.

Let's look at the rest of the parallel section in more detail (see Figure 3-4).

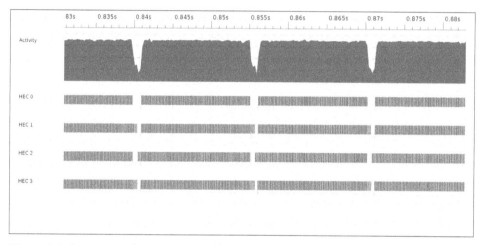

Figure 3-4. kmeans on four cores, parallel execution

The parallel execution, which at first looked quite uniform, actually consists of a series of humps when we zoom in. Remember that the algorithm performs a series of iterations over the data set—these humps in the profile correspond to the iterations. Each iteration is a separate parallel segment, and between the iterations lies some sequential execution. We expect a small amount of sequential execution corresponding to makeNewClusters, combine, and the comparison between the new and old clusters in the outer loop.

Let's see whether the reality matches our expectations by zooming in on one of the gaps to see more clearly what happens between iterations (Figure 3-5).

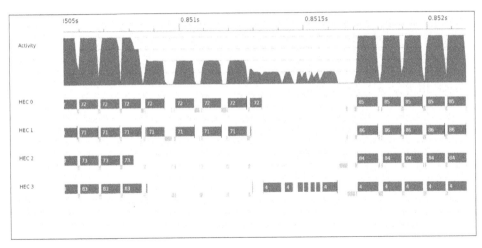

Figure 3-5. kmeans on four cores, gap between iterations

There's quite a lot going on here. We can see the parallel execution of the previous iteration tailing off, as a couple of cores run longer than the others. Following this, there is some sequential execution on HEC 3 before the next iteration starts up in parallel.

Looking more closely at the sequential bit on HEC 3, we can see some gaps where nothing appears to be happening at all. In the ThreadScope GUI, we can show the detailed events emitted by the RTS (look for the "Raw Events" tab in the lower pane), and if we look at the events for this section, we see:

```
0.851404792s HEC 3: stopping thread 4 (making a foreign call)
0.851405771s HEC 3: running thread 4
0.851406373s HEC 3: stopping thread 4 (making a foreign call)
0.851419669s HEC 3: running thread 4
0.851451713s HEC 3: stopping thread 4 (making a foreign call)
0.851452171s HEC 3: running thread 4
...
```

The program is popping out to make several foreign calls during this period. Thread-Scope doesn't tell us any more than this, but it's enough of a clue: A foreign call usually indicates some kind of I/O, which should remind us to look back at what happens between iterations in the kmeans_seq function:

```
loop n clusters = do
  printf "iteration %d\n" n
  putStr (unlines (map show clusters))
  ...
```

We're printing some output. Furthermore, we're doing this in the sequential part of the program, and Amdahl's law is making us pay for it in parallel speedup.

Commenting out these two lines (in both kmeans_seq and kmeans_strat, to be fair) improves the parallel speedup from 2.6 to **3.4** on my quad-core machine. It's amazing how easy it is to make a small mistake like this in parallel programming, but fortunately ThreadScope helps us identify the problem, or at least gives us clues about where we should look.

Visualizing Spark Activity

We can also use ThreadScope to visualize the creation and use of sparks during the run of the program. Figure 3-6 shows the profile for kmeans running on four cores, showing the spark pool size over time for each HEC (these graphs are enabled in the ThreadScope GUI from the "Traces" tab in the left pane).

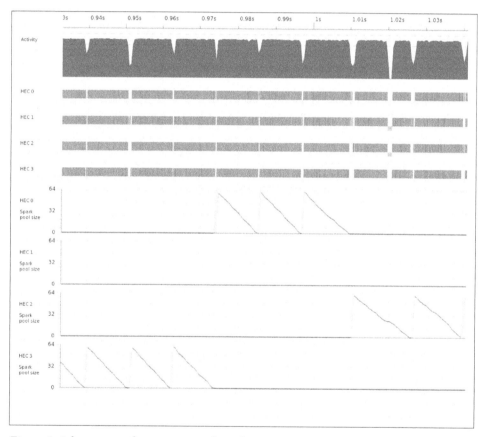

Figure 3-6. kmeans on four cores, spark pool sizes

The figure clearly shows that as each iteration starts, 64 sparks are created on one HEC and then are gradually consumed. What is perhaps surprising is that the sparks aren't always generated on the same HEC; this is the GHC runtime moving work behind the scenes as it tries to keep the load balanced across the cores.

There are more spark-related graphs available in ThreadScope, showing the rates of spark creation and conversion (running sparks). All of these can be valuable in understanding the performance characteristics of your parallel program.

Granularity

Looking back at Figure 3-5, I remarked earlier that the parallel section didn't finish evenly, with two cores running a bit longer than the others. Ideally, we would have all the cores running until the end to maximize our speedup.

As we saw in "Example: Parallelizing a Sudoku Solver" on page 19, having too few work items in our parallel program can impact the speedup, because the work items can vary in cost. To get a more even run, we want to create fine-grained work items and more of them.

To see the effect of this, I ran kmeans with various numbers of chunks from 4 up to 512, and measured the runtime on 4 cores. The results are shown in Figure 3-7.

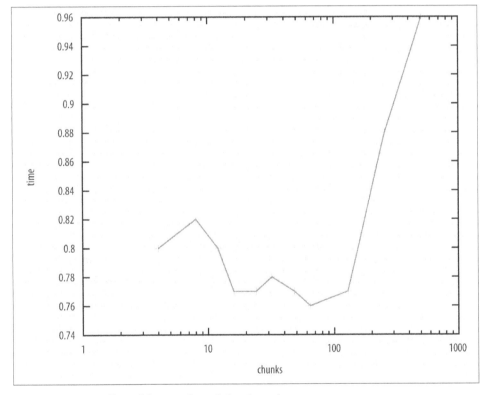

Figure 3-7. The effect of the number of chunks in kmeans

We can see not only that having too few chunks is not good for the reasons given above, but also having too many can have a severe impact. In this case, the sweet spot is somewhere around 50-100.

Why does having too many chunks increase the runtime? There are two reasons:

- There is some overhead per chunk in creating the spark and arranging to run it on another processor. As the chunks get smaller, this overhead becomes more significant.

- The amount of sequential work that the program has to do is greater. Combining the results from 512 chunks takes longer than 64, and because this is in the sequential part, it significantly impacts the parallel performance.

GC'd Sparks and Speculative Parallelism

Recall the definition of parList:

```
parList :: Strategy a -> Strategy [a]
parList strat = evalList (rparWith strat)
```

And the underlying parameterized Strategy on lists, evalList:

```
evalList :: Strategy a -> Strategy [a]
evalList strat []     = return []
evalList strat (x:xs) = do
  x'  <- strat x
  xs' <- evalList strat xs
  return (x':xs')
```

As evalList traverses the list applying the strategy strat to the list elements, it remembers each value returned by strat (bound to x'), and constructs a new list from these values. Why? Well, one answer is that a Strategy must return a data structure equal to the one it was passed.

But do we really need to build a new list? After all, this means that evalList is not *tail-recursive*; the recursive call to evalList is not the last operation in the do on its right-hand side, so evalList requires stack space linear in the length of the input list.

Couldn't we just write a tail-recursive version of parList instead? Perhaps like this:

```
parList :: Strategy a -> Strategy [a]
parList strat xs = do
  go xs
  return xs
 where
  go []     = return ()
  go (x:xs) = do rparWith strat x
                 go xs
```

After all, this is type-correct and seems to call rparWith on each list element as required.

Unfortunately, this version of parList has a serious problem: All the parallelism it creates will be discarded by the garbage collector. The omission of the result list turns out to be crucial. Let's take a look at the data structures that our original, correct implementations of parList and evalList created (Figure 3-8).

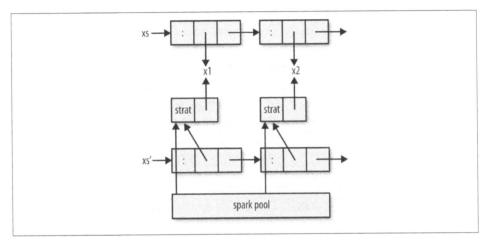

Figure 3-8. parList heap structures

At the top of the diagram is the input list xs: a linked list of cells, each of which points to a list element (x1, x2, and so forth). At the bottom of the diagram is the *spark pool*, the runtime system data structure that stores references to sparks in the heap. The other structures in the diagram are built by parList (the correct version, not the one I most recently showed). Each strat box represents the strategy strat applied to an element of the original list, and xs' is the linked list of cells in the output list. The spark pool contains pointers to each of the strat boxes; these are the pointers created by each call to rparWith.

The GHC runtime regularly checks the spark pool for any entries that are not required by the program and removes them. It would be bad to retain entries that aren't needed, because that could cause the program to hold on to memory unnecessarily, leading to a space leak. We don't want parallelism to have a negative impact on performance.

How does the runtime know whether an entry is needed? The same way it knows whether any item in memory is needed: There must be a pointer to it from something else that is needed. This is the reason that parList creates a new list xs'. Suppose we did not build the new list xs', as in the tail-recursive version of parList above. Then the only reference to each strat box in the heap would be from the spark pool, and hence the runtime would automatically sweep all those references from the spark pool, discarding the parallelism. So we build a new list xs' to hold references to the strat calls that we need to retain.

The automatic discarding of unreferenced sparks has another benefit besides avoiding space leaks; suppose that under some circumstances the program does not need the entire list. If the program simply forgets the unused remainder of the list, the runtime system will clean up the unreferenced sparks from the spark pool and will not waste any further parallel processing resources on evaluating those sparks. The extra parallelism in this case is termed *speculative*, because it is not necessarily required, and the runtime will automatically discard speculative tasks that it can prove will never be required—a useful property!

Although the runtime system's discarding of unreferenced sparks is certainly useful in some cases, it can be tricky to work with because there is no language-level support for catching mistakes. Fortunately, the runtime system will tell us if it garbage-collects unreferenced sparks. For example, if you use the tail-recursive parList with the Sudoku solver from Chapter 2, the +RTS -s stats will show something like this:

```
SPARKS: 1000 (2 converted, 0 overflowed, 0 dud, 998 GC'd, 0 fizzled)
```

Garbage-collected sparks are reported as "GC'd." ThreadScope will also indicate GC'd sparks in its spark graphs.

If you see that a large number of sparks are GC'd, it's a good indication that sparks are being removed from the spark pool before they can be used for parallelism. Unless you are using speculation, a non-zero figure for GC'd sparks is probably a bad sign.

All the combinators in the Control.Parallel.Strategies libraries retain references to sparks correctly. These are the rules of thumb for not shooting yourself in the foot:

- Use using to apply Strategies instead of runEval; it encourages the right pattern, in which the program uses the results of applying the Strategy.

- When writing your own Eval monad code, this is wrong:

```
do
  ...
  rpar (f x)
  ...
```

Equivalently, using rparWith without binding the result is wrong. However, this is OK:

```
do
  ...
  y <- rpar (f x)
  ... y ...
```

And this might be OK, as long as y is required by the program somewhere:

```
do
  ...
  rpar y
  ...
```

Parallelizing Lazy Streams with parBuffer

A common pattern in Haskell programming is to use a lazy list as a stream so that the program can consume input while simultaneously producing output and consequently run in constant space. Such programs present something of a challenge for parallelism; if we aren't careful, parallelizing the computation will destroy the lazy streaming property and the program will require space linear in the size of the input.

To demonstrate this, we will use the sample program *rsa.hs*, an implementation of RSA encryption and decryption. The program takes two command line arguments: the first specifies which action to take, encrypt or decrypt, and the second is either the filename of the file to read, or the character - to read from stdin. The output is always produced on stdout.

The following example uses the program to encrypt the message "Hello World!":

```
$ echo 'Hello World!' | ./rsa encrypt -
11656463941851871045300458781178110195032310900426966299882646602337646308966290
04616367852931838847898165226788260038683620100405280790394258940505884384435202
7497503612575260076123051034258985243174
```

And we can test that the program successfully decrypts the output, producing the original text, by piping the output back into rsa decrypt:

```
$ echo "Hello World!" | ./rsa encrypt - | ./rsa decrypt -
Hello World!
```

The rsa program is a stream transformer, consuming input and producing output lazily. We can see this by looking at the RTS stats:

```
$ ./rsa encrypt /usr/share/dict/words >/dev/null +RTS -s
   8,040,128,392 bytes allocated in the heap
      66,756,936 bytes copied during GC
         186,992 bytes maximum residency (71 sample(s))
          36,584 bytes maximum slop
               2 MB total memory in use (0 MB lost due to fragmentation)
```

The */usr/share/dict/words* file is about 1 MB in size, but the program has a maximum residency (live memory) of 186,992 bytes.

Let's try to parallelize the program. The program uses the lazy ByteString type from Data.ByteString.Lazy to achieve streaming, and the top-level encrypt function has this type:

```
encrypt :: Integer -> Integer -> ByteString -> ByteString
```

The two `Integer`s are the key with which to encrypt the data. The implementation of `encrypt` is a beautiful pipeline composition:

rsa.hs

```
encrypt n e = B.unlines                            -- ❶
            . map (B.pack . show . power e n . code)   -- ❷
            . chunk (size n)                           -- ❸
```

❸   Divide the input into chunks. Each chunk is encrypted separately; this has nothing to do with parallelism.

❷   Encrypt each chunk.

❶   Concatenate the result as a sequence of lines.

We won't delve into the details of the RSA implementation here, but if you're interested, go and look at the code in *rsa.hs* (it's fairly short). For the purposes of parallelism, all we need to know is that there's a `map` on the second line, so that's our target for parallelization.

First, let's try to use the `parList` Strategy that we have seen before:

rsa1.hs

```
encrypt n e = B.unlines
            . withStrategy (parList rdeepseq)        -- ❶
            . map (B.pack . show . power e n . code)
            . chunk (size n)
```

❶   I'm using `withStrategy` here, which is just a version of `using` with the arguments flipped; it is slightly nicer in situations like this. The Strategy is `parList`, with `rdeepseq` as the Strategy to apply to the list elements (the list elements are lazy `ByteStrings`, so we want to ensure that they are fully evaluated).

If we run this program on four cores, the stats show something interesting:

```
6,251,537,576 bytes allocated in the heap
   44,392,808 bytes copied during GC
    2,415,240 bytes maximum residency (33 sample(s))
      550,264 bytes maximum slop
           10 MB total memory in use (0 MB lost due to fragmentation)
```

The maximum residency has increased to 2.3 MB, because the `parList` Strategy forces the whole spine of the list, preventing the program from streaming in constant space. The speedup in this case was 2.2; not terrible, but not great either. We can do better.

The Control.Parallel.Strategies library provides a Strategy to solve exactly this problem, called parBuffer:

```
parBuffer :: Int -> Strategy a -> Strategy [a]
```

The parBuffer function has a similar type to parList but takes an Int argument as a buffer size. In contrast to parList which eagerly creates a spark for every list element, parBuffer N creates sparks for only the first N elements of the list, and then creates more sparks as the result list is consumed. The effect is that there will always be N sparks available until the end of the list is reached.

The disadvantage of parBuffer is that we have to choose a particular value for the buffer size, and as with the chunk factor we saw earlier, there will be a "best value" somewhere in the range. Fortunately, performance is usually not too sensitive to this value, and something in the range of 50-500 is often good. So let's see how well this works:

rsa2.hs

```
encrypt n e = B.unlines
            . withStrategy (parBuffer 100 rdeepseq)        -- ❶
            . map (B.pack . show . power e n . code)
            . chunk (size n)
```

❶   Here I replaced parList with parBuffer 100.

This programs achieves a speedup of 3.5 on 4 cores. Furthermore, it runs in much less memory than the parList version:

```
6,275,891,072 bytes allocated in the heap
   27,749,720 bytes copied during GC
      294,872 bytes maximum residency (58 sample(s))
       62,456 bytes maximum slop
            4 MB total memory in use (0 MB lost due to fragmentation)
```

We can expect it to need more memory than the sequential version, which required only 2 MB, because we're performing many computations in parallel. Indeed, a higher residency is common in parallel programs for the simple reason that they are doing more work, although it's not always the case; sometimes parallel evaluation can reduce memory overhead by evaluating thunks that were causing space leaks.

ThreadScope's spark pool graph shows that parBuffer really does keep a constant supply of sparks, as shown in Figure 3-9.

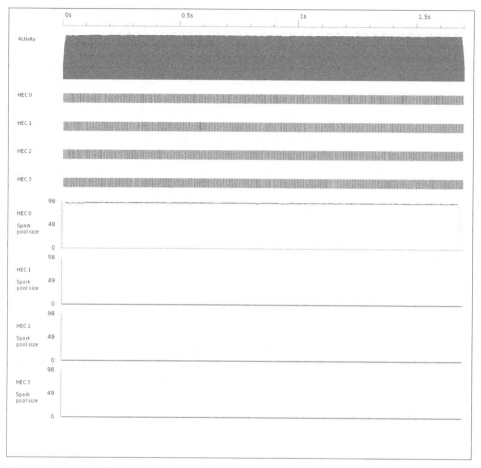

Figure 3-9. rsa on four cores, using parBuffer

The spark pool on HEC 0 constantly hovers around 90-100 sparks.

In programs with a multistage pipeline, interposing more calls to `withStrategy` in the pipeline can expose more parallelism.

Chunking Strategies

When parallelizing K-Means in "Parallelizing K-Means" on page 40, we divided the input data into chunks to avoid creating parallelism with excessively fine granularity. Chunking is a common technique, so the `Control.Parallel.Strategies` library provides a version of `parList` that has chunking built in:

```
parListChunk :: Int -> Strategy a -> Strategy [a]
```

The first argument is the number of elements in each chunk; the list is split in the same way as the chunk function that we saw earlier in the kmeans example. You might find parListChunk useful if you have a list with too many elements to spark every one, or when the list elements are too cheap to warrant a spark each.

The spark pool has a fixed size, and when the pool is full, subsequent sparks are dropped and reported as overflowed in the +RTS -s stats output. If you see some overflowed sparks, it is probably a good idea to create fewer sparks; replacing parList with parListChunk is a good way to do that.

Note that chunking the list incurs some overhead, as we noticed in the earlier kmeans example when we used chunking directly. For that reason, in kmeans we created the chunked list once and shared it amongst all the iterations of the algorithm, rather than using parListChunk, which would chunk the list every time.

The Identity Property

I mentioned at the beginning of this chapter that if we see an expression of this form:

```
x `using` s
```

We can delete `using` s, leaving an equivalent program. For this to be true, the Strategy s must obey the *identity property*; that is, the value it returns must be equal to the value it was passed. The operations provided by the Control.Parallel.Strategies library all satisfy this property, but unfortunately it isn't possible to enforce it for arbitrary user-defined Strategies. Hence we cannot *guarantee* that x `using` s == x, just as we cannot guarantee that all instances of Monad satisfy the monad laws, or that all instances of Eq are reflexive. These properties are satisfied by convention only; this is just something to be aware of.

There is one more caveat to this property. The expression x `using` s might be *less defined* than x, because it evaluates more structure of x than the context does. What does *less defined* mean? It means that the program containing x `using` s might fail with an error when simply x would not. A trivial example of this is:

```
print $ snd (1 `div` 0, "Hello!")
```

This program works and prints "Hello!", but:

```
print $ snd ((1 `div` 0, "Hello!") `using` rdeepseq)
```

This program fails with `divide by zero`. The original program didn't fail because the erroneous expression was never evaluated, but adding the Strategy has caused the program to fully evaluate the pair, including the division by zero.

This is rarely a problem in practice; if the Strategy evaluates more than the program would have done anyway, the Strategy is probably wasting effort and needs to be modified.

CHAPTER 4

Dataflow Parallelism: The Par Monad

In the previous two chapters, we looked at the Eval monad and Strategies, which work in conjunction with lazy evaluation to express parallelism. A Strategy consumes a lazy data structure and evaluates parts of it in parallel. This model has some advantages: it allows the decoupling of the algorithm from the parallelism, and it allows parallel evaluation strategies to be built compositionally. But Strategies and Eval are not always the most convenient or effective way to express parallelism. We might not want to build a lazy data structure, for example. Lazy evaluation brings the nice modularity properties that we get with Strategies, but on the flip side, lazy evaluation can make it tricky to understand and diagnose performance.

In this chapter, we'll explore another parallel programming model, the Par monad, with a different set of tradeoffs. The goal of the Par monad is to be more explicit about granularity and data dependencies, and to avoid the reliance on lazy evaluation, but without sacrificing the determinism that we value for parallel programming. In this programming model, the programmer has to give more detail but in return gains more control. The Par monad has some other interesting benefits; for example, it is implemented entirely as a Haskell library and the implementation can be readily modified to accommodate alternative scheduling strategies.

The interface is based around a monad called, unsurprisingly, Par:

```
newtype Par a
instance Applicative Par
instance Monad Par

runPar :: Par a -> a
```

A computation in the Par monad can be run using runPar to produce a pure result. The purpose of Par is to introduce parallelism, so we need a way to create parallel tasks:

```
fork :: Par () -> Par ()
```

The Par computation passed as the argument to fork (the "child") is executed in parallel with the caller of fork (the "parent"). But fork doesn't return anything to the parent, so you might be wondering how we get the result back if we start a parallel computation with fork. Values can be passed between Par computations using the IVar type[1] and its operations:

```
data IVar a  -- instance Eq

new :: Par (IVar a)
put :: NFData a => IVar a -> a -> Par ()
get :: IVar a -> Par a
```

Think of an IVar as a box that starts empty. The put operation stores a value in the box, and get reads the value. If the get operation finds the box empty, then it waits until the box is filled by a put. So an IVar lets you communicate values between parallel Par computations, because you can put a value in the box in one place and get it in another.

Once filled, the box stays full; the get operation doesn't remove the value from the box. It is an error to call put more than once on the same IVar.

The IVar type is a relative of the MVar type that we shall see later in the context of Concurrent Haskell ("Communication: MVars" on page 128), the main difference being that an IVar can be written only once. An IVar is also like a *future* or *promise*, concepts that may be familiar to you from other parallel or concurrent languages.

There is nothing in the types to stop you from returning an IVar from runPar and passing it to another call of runPar. This is a Very Bad Idea; don't do it. The implementation of the Par monad assumes that IVars are created and used within the same runPar, and breaking this assumption could lead to a runtime error, deadlock, or worse.

The library could prevent you from doing this using qualified types in the same way that the ST monad prevents you from returning an STRef from runST. This is planned for a future version.

Together, fork and IVars allow the construction of *dataflow* networks. Let's see how that works with a few simple examples.

We'll start in the same way we did in Chapter 2: write some code to perform two independent computations in parallel. As before, I'm going to use the fib function to simulate some work we want to do:

---

1. IVar has this name because it is an implementation of I-Structures, a concept from an early Parallel Haskell variant called *pH*.

parmonad.hs

```
runPar $ do
    i <- new                    -- ❶
    j <- new                    -- ❷
    fork (put i (fib n))        -- ❸
    fork (put j (fib m))        -- ❹
    a <- get i                  -- ❺
    b <- get j                  -- ❻
    return (a+b)                -- ❼
```

❶❷ Creates two new IVars to hold the results, i and j.

❸❹ fork two independent Par computations. The first puts the value of fib n into the IVar i, and the second puts the value of fib m into the IVar j.

❺❻ The parent of the two forks calls get to wait for the results from i and j.

❼   Finally, add the results and return.

When run, this program evaluates fib n and fib m in parallel. To try it yourself, compile *parmonad.hs* and run it passing two values for n and m, for example:

```
$ ./parmonad 34 35 +RTS -N2
```

The pattern in this program is represented graphically in Figure 4-1.

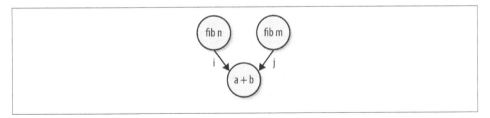

Figure 4-1. Simple Par example

The diagram makes it clear that what we are creating is a *dataflow graph*: that is, a graph in which the nodes (fib n, etc.) contain the computation and data flows down the edges (i and j). To be concrete, each fork in the program creates a node, each new creates an edge, and get and put connect the edges to the nodes.

From the diagram, we can see that the two nodes containing fib n and fib m are independent of each other, and that is why they can be computed in parallel, which is exactly what the monad-par library will do. However, the dataflow graph doesn't exist in any explicit form at runtime; the library works by keeping track of all the computations that can currently be performed (a *work pool*), and dividing those amongst the available processors using an appropriate scheduling strategy. The dataflow graph is just a way to visualize and understand the structure of the parallelism. Unfortunately, right now there's no way to generate a visual representation of the dataflow graph from some Par monad code, but hopefully in the future someone will write a tool to do that.

Using dataflow to express parallelism is quite an old idea; there were people experimenting with custom hardware architectures designed around dataflow back in the 1970s and 1980s. In contrast to those designs that were focused on exploiting very fine-grained parallelism automatically, here we are using dataflow as an explicit parallel programming model. But we are using dataflow here for the same reasons that it was attractive back then: instead of saying what is to be done in parallel, we only describe the data dependencies, thereby exposing all the implicit parallelism to be exploited.

While the Par monad is particularly suited to expressing dataflow networks, it can also express other common patterns. For example, we can build an equivalent of the parMap combinator that we saw earlier in Chapter 2. To make it easier to define parMap, let's first build a simple abstraction for a parallel computation that returns a result:

```
spawn :: NFData a => Par a -> Par (IVar a)
spawn p = do
  i <- new
  fork (do x <- p; put i x)
  return i
```

The spawn function forks a computation in parallel and returns an IVar that can be used to wait for the result. For convenience, spawn is already provided by Control.Monad.Par.

Parallel map consists of calling spawn to apply the function to each element of the list and then waiting for all the results:

```
parMapM :: NFData b => (a -> Par b) -> [a] -> Par [b]
parMapM f as = do
  ibs <- mapM (spawn . f) as
  mapM get ibs
```

(parMapM is also provided by Control.Monad.Par, albeit in a more generalized form than the version shown here.)

Note that the function argument, f, returns its result in the Par monad; this means that f itself can create further parallelism using fork and the other Par operations. When the function argument of a map is monadic, convention is to add the M suffix to the function name, hence parMapM.

It is straightforward to define a variant of parMapM that takes a non-monadic function instead, by inserting a return:

```
parMap :: NFData b => (a -> b) -> [a] -> Par [b]
parMap f as = do
  ibs <- mapM (spawn . return . f) as
  mapM get ibs
```

One other thing to note here is that, unlike the parMap we saw in Chapter 2, parMapM and parMap wait for all the results before returning. Depending on the context, this may or may not be the most useful behavior. If you don't want to wait for the results, then you could always just use mapM (spawn . f), which returns a list of IVars.

Strictness of put

The put function calls deepseq on the value it puts in the IVar, which is why its type has an NFData constraint. This is a deliberate design choice; in the Par monad, we want the work to happen where we expect it to, so we rule out the possibility that an unevaluated expression is transferred via an IVar.

This means that put causes a traversal of the value stored in the IVar, which can be expensive if the value is a large data structure. For this reason, there's a backdoor to use if you know what you're doing:

```
put_ :: IVar a -> a -> Par ()
```

The put_ operation evaluates the value to WHNF only. Replacing put with put_ can save some time if you know that the argument is already fully evaluated.

Example: Shortest Paths in a Graph

The Floyd-Warshall algorithm finds the lengths of the shortest paths between all pairs of nodes in a weighted directed graph. The algorithm is quite simple and can be expressed as a function over three vertices. Assuming vertices are numbered from one, and we have a function weight g i j that gives the weight of the edge from i to j in graph g, the algorithm is described by this pseudocode:

```
shortestPath :: Graph -> Vertex -> Vertex -> Vertex -> Weight
shortestPath g i j 0 = weight g i j
shortestPath g i j k = min (shortestPath g i j (k-1))
                           (shortestPath g i k (k-1) + shortestPath g k j (k-1))
```

You can think of the algorithm intuitively this way: shortestPath g i j k gives the length of the shortest path from i to j, passing through vertices up to k only. At k == 0, the paths between each pair of vertices consists of the direct edges only. For a nonzero k, there are two cases: either the shortest path from i to j passes through k, or it does not. The shortest path passing through k is given by the sum of the shortest path from i to k and from k to j. Then the shortest path from i to j is the minimum of the two choices, either passing through k or not.

We wouldn't want to implement the algorithm like this directly, because it requires an exponential number of recursive calls. This is a classic example of a dynamic programming problem: rather than recursing top-down, we can build the solution bottom-up, so that earlier results can be used when computing later ones. In this case, we want to start by computing the shortest paths between all pairs of nodes for k == 0, then for k == 1, and so on until k reaches the maximum vertex. Each step is $O(n^2)$ in the vertices, so the whole algorithm is $O(n^3)$.

The algorithm is often run over an adjacency matrix, which is a very efficient representation of a dense graph. But here we're going to assume a sparse graph (most pairs of vertices do not have an edge between them), and use a representation more suitable for this case:

fwsparse/SparseGraph.hs

```
type Vertex = Int
type Weight = Int

type Graph = IntMap (IntMap Weight)

weight :: Graph -> Vertex -> Vertex -> Maybe Weight
weight g i j = do
  jmap <- Map.lookup i g
  Map.lookup j jmap
```

The graph is essentially a mapping from pairs of nodes to weights, but it is represented more efficiently as a two-layer map. For example, to find the edge between i and j, we look up i in the outer map, yielding another map in which we look up j to find the weight. The function `weight` embodies this pair of lookups using the `Maybe` monad. If there is no edge between the two vertices, then `weight` returns `Nothing`.

Here is the sequential implementation of the shortest path algorithm:

fwsparse/fwsparse.hs

```
shortestPaths :: [Vertex] -> Graph -> Graph
shortestPaths vs g = foldl' update g vs           -- ❶
  where
    update g k = Map.mapWithKey shortmap g        -- ❷
      where
        shortmap :: Vertex -> IntMap Weight -> IntMap Weight
        shortmap i jmap = foldr shortest Map.empty vs -- ❸
          where shortest j m =
                  case (old,new) of               -- ❹
                    (Nothing, Nothing) -> m
                    (Nothing, Just w ) -> Map.insert j w m
                    (Just w,  Nothing) -> Map.insert j w m
                    (Just w1, Just w2) -> Map.insert j (min w1 w2) m
                  where
                    old = Map.lookup j jmap        -- ❺
                    new = do w1 <- weight g i k     -- ❻
                             w2 <- weight g k j
                             return (w1+w2)
```

`shortestPaths` takes a list of vertices in addition to the graph; we could have derived this from the graph, but it's slightly more convenient to pass it in. The result is also a `Graph`, but instead of containing the weights of the edges between vertices, it contains the lengths of the shortest paths between vertices. For simplicity, we're not returning the shortest paths themselves, although this can be added without affecting the asymptotic time or space complexity.

❶ The algorithm as a whole is a left-fold over the list of vertices; this corresponds to iterating over values of `k` in the pseudocode description shown earlier. At each stage we add a new vertex to the set of vertices that can be used to construct paths, until at the end we have paths that can use all the vertices. Note that we use the strict left-fold, `foldl'`, to ensure that we're evaluating the graph at every step and not building up a chain of thunks (we're also using a strict `IntMap` to avoid thunks building up inside the `Graph`; this turns out to be vital for avoiding a space leak).

❷ The `update` function computes each step by mapping the function `shortmap` over the outer `IntMap` in the graph. There's no need to map over the whole list of vertices because we know that any vertex that does not have an entry in the outer map cannot have a path to any other vertex (although it might have *incoming* paths).

❸ `shortmap` takes `i`, the current vertex, and `jmap`, the mapping of shortest paths from `i`. This function *does* need to consider every vertex in the graph as a possible destination because there may be vertices that we can reach from `i` via `k`, but which do not currently have an entry in `jmap`. So here we're building up a new `jmap` by folding over the list of vertices, `vs`.

❺ For a given `j`, look up the current shortest path from `i` to `j`, and call it `old`.

❻ Look up the shortest path from `i` to `j` via `k` (if one exists), and call it `new`.

❹ Find the minimum of `old` and `new`, and insert it into the new mapping. Naturally, one path is the winner if the other path does not exist.

The algorithm is a nest of three loops. The outer loop is a left-fold with a data dependency between iterations, so it cannot be parallelized (as a side note, folds can be parallelized only when the operation being folded is associative, and then the linear fold can be turned into a tree). The next loop, however, is a map:

```
update g k = Map.mapWithKey shortmap g
```

As we know, maps parallelize nicely. Will this give the right granularity? The map is over the outer `IntMap` of the `Graph`, so there will be as many tasks as there are vertices without edges. There will typically be at least hundreds of edges in the graph, so there are clearly enough separate work items to keep even tens of cores busy. Furthermore, each task is an $O(n)$ loop over the list of vertices, so we are unlikely to have problems with the granularity being too fine.

Let's consider how to add parallelism here. It's not an ordinary map—we're using the mapWithKey function provided by Data.IntMap to map directly over the IntMap. We could turn the IntMap into a list, run a standard parMap over that, and then turn it back into an IntMap, but the conversion to and from a list would add some overhead. Fortunately, the IntMap library provides a way to traverse an IntMap in a monad:

```
traverseWithKey :: Applicative t
                => (Key -> a -> t b)
                -> IntMap a
                -> t (IntMap b)
```

Don't worry if you're not familiar with the Applicative type class; most of the time, you can read Applicative as Monad and you'll be fine. All the standard Monad types are also Applicative, and in general any Monad can be made into an Applicative easily.[2]

So traverseWithKey essentially maps a monadic function over the IntMap, for any monad t. The monadic function is passed not only the element a, but also the Key, which is just what we need here: shortmap needs both the key (the source vertex) and the element (the map from destination vertices to weights).

So we want to behave like parMap, except that we'll use traverseWithKey to map over the IntMap. Here is the parallel code for update:

```
update g k = runPar $ do
  m <- Map.traverseWithKey (\i jmap -> spawn (return (shortmap i jmap))) g
  traverse get m
```

We've put runPar inside update; the rest of the shortestPaths function will remain as before, and all the parallelism is confined to update. We're calling traverseWithKey to spawn a call to shortmap for each of the elements of the IntMap. The result of this call will be an IntMap (IVar (IntMap Weight)); that is, there's an IVar in place of each element. To get the new Graph, we need to call get on each of these IVars and produce a new Graph with all the elements, which is what the final call to traverse does. The traverse function is from the Traversable class; for our purposes here, it is like traverseWithKey but doesn't pass the Key to the function.

Let's take a look at the speedup we get from this code. Running the original program on a random graph with 800 edges over 1,000 vertices:

```
$ ./fwsparse 1000 800 +RTS -s
...
  Total   time    4.16s  ( 4.17s elapsed)
```

2. For more details, see the documentation for Control.Monad.Applicative.

And our parallel version, first on one core:

```
$ ./fwsparse1 1000 800 +RTS -s
...
  Total   time     4.54s  (  4.57s elapsed)
```

Adding the parallel traversal has cost us about 10% overhead; this is quite a lot, and if we were optimizing this program for real, we would want to look into whether that overhead can be reduced. Perhaps it is caused by doing one `runPar` per iteration (a `runPar` is quite expensive) or perhaps `traverseWithKey` is expensive.

The speedup on four cores is fairly respectable:

```
$ ./fwsparse1 1000 800 +RTS -s -N4
...
  Total   time     5.27s  (  1.38s elapsed)
```

This gives us a speedup of 3.02 over the sequential version. To improve this speedup further, the first target would be to reduce the overhead of the parallel version.

Pipeline Parallelism

Next, we're going to look at a different way to expose parallelism: *pipeline* parallelism. Back in "Parallelizing Lazy Streams with parBuffer" on page 51, we saw how to use parallelism in a program that consumed and produced input lazily, although in that case we used *data parallelism*, which is parallelism between the stream elements. Here, we're going to show how to make use of parallelism between the stages of a pipeline. For example, we might have a pipeline that looks like this:

Each stage of the pipeline is doing some computation on the stream elements and maintaining state as it does so. When a pipeline stage maintains some state, we can't exploit parallelism between the stream elements as we did in "Parallelizing Lazy Streams with parBuffer" on page 51. Instead, we would like each of the pipeline stages to run on a separate core, with the data streaming between them. The `Par` monad, together with the techniques in this section, allows us to do that.

The basic idea is as follows: instead of representing the stream as a lazy list, use an explicit representation of a stream:

```
data IList a
  = Nil
  | Cons a (IVar (IList a))

type Stream a = IVar (IList a)
```

An ILList is a list with an IVar as the tail. This allows the producer to generate the list incrementally, while a consumer runs in parallel, grabbing elements as they are produced. A Stream is an IVar containing an IList.

We'll need a few functions for working with Streams. First, we need a generic producer that turns a lazy list into a Stream:

```
streamFromList :: NFData a => [a] -> Par (Stream a)
streamFromList xs = do
  var <- new                      -- ❶
  fork $ loop xs var              -- ❷
  return var                      -- ❸
 where
  loop [] var = put var Nil       -- ❹
  loop (x:xs) var = do            -- ❺
    tail <- new                   -- ❻
    put var (Cons x tail)         -- ❼
    loop xs tail                  -- ❽
```

❶ Creates the IVar that will be the Stream itself.

❷ forks the loop that will create the Stream contents.

❸ Returns the Stream to the caller. The Stream is now being created in parallel.

❹ This loop traverses the input list, producing the IList as it goes. The first argument is the list, and the second argument is the IVar into which to store the IList. In the case of an empty list, we simply store an empty IList into the IVar.

❺ In the case of a non-empty list,

❻ we create a new IVar for the tail,

❼ and store a Cons cell representing this element into the current IVar. Note that this fully evaluates the list element x, because put is strict.

❽ Recurse to create the rest of the stream.

Next, we'll write a consumer of Streams, streamFold:

```
streamFold :: (a -> b -> a) -> a -> Stream b -> Par a
streamFold fn !acc instrm = do
  ilst <- get instrm
  case ilst of
    Nil      -> return acc
    Cons h t -> streamFold fn (fn acc h) t
```

This is a left-fold over the Stream and is defined exactly as you would expect: recursing through the IList and accumulating the result until the end of the Stream is reached. If the streamFold consumes all the available stream elements and catches up with the producer, it will block in the get call waiting for the next element.

The final operation we'll need is a map over `Streams`. This is both a producer and a consumer:

```
streamMap :: NFData b => (a -> b) -> Stream a -> Par (Stream b)
streamMap fn instrm = do
  outstrm <- new
  fork $ loop instrm outstrm
  return outstrm
 where
  loop instrm outstrm = do
    ilst <- get instrm
    case ilst of
      Nil -> put outstrm Nil
      Cons h t -> do
        newtl <- new
        put outstrm (Cons (fn h) newtl)
        loop t newtl
```

There's nothing particularly surprising here—the pattern is a combination of the producer we saw in `streamFromList` and the consumer in `streamFold`.

To demonstrate that this works, I'll construct an example using the RSA encryption code that we saw earlier in "Parallelizing Lazy Streams with parBuffer" on page 51. However, this time, in order to construct a nontrivial pipeline, I'll compose together encryption and decryption; encryption will produce a stream that decryption consumes (admittedly this isn't a realistic use case, but it does demonstrate pipeline parallelism).

Previously, `encrypt` and `decrypt` consumed and produced lazy `ByteStrings`. Now they work over `Stream ByteString` in the `Par` monad, and are expressed as a `streamMap`:

rsa-pipeline.hs

```
encrypt :: Integer -> Integer -> Stream ByteString -> Par (Stream ByteString)
encrypt n e s = streamMap (B.pack . show . power e n . code) s

decrypt :: Integer -> Integer -> Stream ByteString -> Par (Stream ByteString)
decrypt n d s = streamMap (B.pack . decode . power d n . integer) s
```

The following function composes these together and also adds a `streamFromList` to create the input `Stream` and a `streamFold` to consume the result:

```
pipeline :: Integer -> Integer -> Integer -> ByteString -> ByteString
pipeline n e d b = runPar $ do
  s0 <- streamFromList (chunk (size n) b)
  s1 <- encrypt n e s0
  s2 <- decrypt n d s1
  xs <- streamFold (\x y -> (y : x)) [] s2
  return (B.unlines (reverse xs))
```

Note that the `streamFold` produces a list of `ByteStrings` at the end, to which we apply `unlines`, and then the caller prints out the result.

This works rather nicely: I see a speedup of 1.45 running the program over a large text file. What's the maximum speedup we can achieve here? Well, there are four independent pipeline stages: `streamFromList`, two `streamMaps`, and a `streamFold`, although only the two maps really involve any significant computation.[3] So the best we can hope for is to reduce the running time to the longer of the two maps. We can verify, by timing the *rsa.hs* program, that encryption takes approximately twice as long as decryption, which means that we can expect a speedup of about 1.5, which is close to the sample run here.

The ThreadScope profile of this program is quite revealing. Figure 4-2 is a typical section from it.

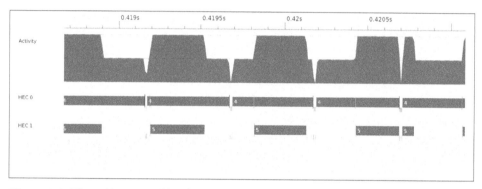

Figure 4-2. ThreadScope profile of rsa-pipeline

HEC 0 appears to be doing the encryption, and HEC 1 the decryption. Decryption is faster than encryption, so HEC 1 repeatedly gets stuck waiting for the next element of the encrypted stream; this accounts for the gaps in execution we see on HEC 1.

One interesting thing to note about this profile is that the pipeline stages tend to stay on the same core. This is because each pipeline stage is a single `fork` (a single node in the dataflow graph) and the `Par` scheduler will run a task to completion on the current core before starting on the next task. Keeping each pipeline stage running on a single core is good for locality.

Rate-Limiting the Producer

In our previous example, the consumer was faster than the producer. If, instead, the producer had been faster than the consumer, then there would be nothing to stop the producer from getting a long way ahead of the consumer and building up a long `IList` chain in memory. This is undesirable, because large heap data structures incur overhead due to garbage collection, so we might want to rate-limit the producer to avoid it getting

---

3. You can verify this for yourself by profiling the *rsa.hs* program. Most of the execution time is spent in `power`.

too far ahead. There's a trick that adds some automatic rate-limiting to the stream API. It entails adding another constructor to the `IList` type:

```
data IList a
  = Nil
  | Cons a (IVar (IList a))
  | Fork (Par ()) (IList a)  -- ❶
```

❶   The idea is that the creator of the `IList` produces a fixed amount of the list and inserts a `Fork` constructor containing another `Par` computation that will produce more of the list. The consumer, upon finding a `Fork`, calls `fork` to start production of the next chunk of the list. The `Fork` doesn't have to be at the end; for example, the list might be produced in chunks of 200 elements, with the first `Fork` being at the 100 element mark, and every 200 elements thereafter. This would mean that at any time there would be at least 100 and up to 300 elements waiting to be consumed.

I'll leave the rest of the implementation of this idea as an exercise for you to try on your own. See if you can modify `streamFromList`, `streamFold`, and `streamMap` to incorporate the `Fork` constructor. The chunk size and fork distance should be parameters to the producers (`streamFromList` and `streamMap`).

Limitations of Pipeline Parallelism

Pipeline parallelism is limited in that we can expose only as much parallelism as we have pipeline stages. It therefore tends to be less effective than data parallelism, which can expose a lot more parallelism. Still, pipeline parallelism is a useful tool to have in your toolbox.

The earlier example also exposes a limitation of the `Par` monad; we cannot produce a lazy stream from `runPar` itself. The call to `streamFold` accumulates the entire list before it returns. You can't return an `IList` from `runPar` and consume it in another `runPar`, because returning an `IVar` from `runPar` is illegal and will probably result in an error. Besides, `runPar` always runs all the forked `Par` computations to completion before returning, because this is necessary to ensure deterministic results. There is an IO version of the `Par` monad that we'll encounter in "The ParIO monad" on page 237, and you could use that for lazy streaming, although unlike the pure `Par` monad, determinism is not guaranteed when using the IO version.

Example: A Conference Timetable

In this section, we'll look at a program that finds a valid timetable for a conference.[4] The outline of the problem is this:

- The conference runs T parallel tracks, and each track has the same number of talk slots, S; hence there are $T * S$ talk slots in total. For simplicity, we assume that the talk slots all start and finish at the same time across the tracks.

- There are at most $T * S$ talks to assign to tracks and slots (if there are fewer talks than slots, we can make up the difference with dummy talks that represent empty slots).

- There are a number of attendees who have each expressed a preference for some talks they would like to see.

- The goal is to assign talks to slots and tracks so that the attendees can attend all the talks they want to see; that is, we never schedule two talks that an attendee wanted to see on two different tracks in the same slot.

Here's a small example. Suppose we have two tracks and two slots, and four talks named A, B, C, and D. There are four attendees—P, Q, R, and S—and each wants to go to two talks:

- P wants to see A and B
- Q wants to see B and C
- R wants to see C and D
- S wants to see A and D

One solution is:

Track	Slot 1	Slot 2
1	B	C
2	D	A

There are other solutions, but they are symmetrical with this one (interchange either the tracks or the slots or both).

Timetabling is an instance of a *constraint satisfaction* problem: we're finding assignments for variables (talk slots) that satisfy the constraints (attendees' preferences). The problem requires an exhaustive search, but we can be more clever than just generating all the possible assignments and testing each one. We can fill in the timetable incrementally: assign a talk to the first slot of the first track, then find a talk for the first slot

---

4. I'm avoiding the term "schedule" here because we already use it a lot in concurrent programming.

of the second track that doesn't introduce a conflict, and so on until we've filled up the first slot of all the tracks. Then we proceed to the second slot and so on until we've filled the whole timetable. This incremental approach prunes a lot of the search space because we avoid searching for solutions when the partial grid already contains a conflict.[5]

If at any point we cannot fill a slot without causing a conflict, we have to *backtrack* to the previous slot and choose a different talk instead. If we exhaust all the possibilities at the previous slot, then we have to backtrack further. So, in general, the search pattern is a tree. A fragment of the search tree for the example above is shown in Figure 4-3.

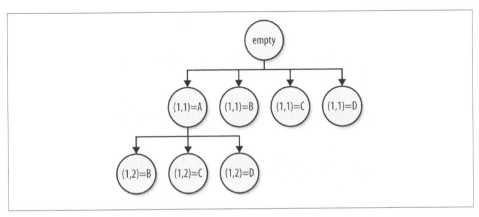

Figure 4-3. Tree-shaped search pattern for the timetabling problem

If we are interested in *all* the solutions (perhaps because we want to pick the best one according to some criteria), we have to explore the whole tree.

Algorithms that have this tree-shaped structure are often called *divide and conquer*. A divide-and-conquer algorithm is one in which the problem is recursively split into smaller subproblems that are solved separately, then combined to form the whole solution. In this case, starting from the empty timetable, we're dividing the solution space according to which talk goes in the first slot, and then by which talk goes in the second slot, and so on recursively until we fill the timetable. Divide-and-conquer algorithms have some nice properties, not least of which is that they parallelize well because the branches are independent of one another.

So let's look at how to code up a solution in Haskell. First, we need a type to represent talks; for simplicity, I'll just number them:

---

5. I should mention that even with some pruning, an exhaustive search will be impractical beyond a small number of slots. Real-world solutions to this kind of problem use heuristics.

timetable.hs

```haskell
newtype Talk = Talk Int
  deriving (Eq,Ord)

instance NFData Talk

instance Show Talk where
  show (Talk t) = show t
```

An attendee is represented by her name and the talks she wants to attend:

```haskell
data Person = Person
  { name  :: String
  , talks :: [Talk]
  }
  deriving (Show)
```

And the complete timetable is represented as a list of lists of Talk. Each list represents a single slot. So if there are four tracks and three slots, for example, the timetable will be three lists of four elements each.

```haskell
type TimeTable = [[Talk]]
```

Here's the top-level function: it takes a list of Person, a list of Talk, the number of tracks and slots, and returns a list of TimeTable:

```haskell
timetable :: [Person] -> [Talk] -> Int -> Int -> [TimeTable]
timetable people allTalks maxTrack maxSlot =
```

First, I'm going to cache some information about which talks clash with each other. That is, for each talk, we want to know which other talks cannot be scheduled in the same slot, because one or more attendees want to see both of them. This information is collected in a Map called clashes, which is built from the [Person] passed to timetable:

```haskell
clashes :: Map Talk [Talk]
clashes = Map.fromListWith union
  [ (t, ts)
  | s <- people
  , (t, ts) <- selects (talks s) ]
```

The auxiliary function selects takes a list and returns a list of pairs, one pair for each item in the input list. The first element of each pair is an element, and the second is the original list with that element removed. For efficient implementation, selects does not preserve the order of the elements. Example output:

```haskell
*Main> selects [1..3]
[(1,[2,3]),(2,[1,3]),(3,[2,1])]
```

Now we can write the algorithm itself. Remember that the algorithm is recursive: at each stage, we start with a partially filled-in timetable, and we want to determine all the possible ways of filling in the next slot and recursively generate all the solutions from those. The recursive function is called generate. Here is its type:

```
generate :: Int          -- current slot number
         -> Int          -- current track number
         -> [[Talk]]     -- slots allocated so far
         -> [Talk]       -- talks in this slot
         -> [Talk]       -- talks that can be allocated in this slot
         -> [Talk]       -- all talks remaining to be allocated
         -> [TimeTable]  -- all possible solutions
```

The first two arguments tell us where in the timetable we are, and the second two arguments are the partially complete timetable. In fact, we're filling in the slots in reverse order, but the slots are independent of one another so it makes no difference. The last two arguments keep track of which talks remain to be assigned: the first is the list of talks that we can put in the current slot (taking into account clashes with other talks already in this slot), and the second is the complete list of talks still left to assign.

The implementation of generate looks a little dense, but I'll walk through it step by step:

```
generate slotNo trackNo slots slot slotTalks talks
  | slotNo == maxSlot   = [slots]                              -- ❶
  | trackNo == maxTrack =
      generate (slotNo+1) 0 (slot:slots) [] talks talks        -- ❷
  | otherwise = concat                                         -- ❸
      [ generate slotNo (trackNo+1) slots (t:slot) slotTalks' talks' -- ❹
      | (t, ts) <- selects slotTalks                           -- ❺
      , let clashesWithT = Map.findWithDefault [] t clashes    -- ❻
      , let slotTalks' = filter (`notElem` clashesWithT) ts    -- ❼
      , let talks' = filter (/= t) talks                       -- ❽
      ]
```

❶   If we've filled in all the slots, we're done; the current list of slots is a solution.

❷   If we've filled in all the tracks for the current slot, move on to the next slot.

❸   Otherwise, we're going to fill in the next talk in this slot. The result is the concatenation of all the solutions arising from the possibilities for filling in that talk.

❺   Here we select all the possibilities for the next talk from slotTalks, binding the next talk to t.

❻   Decide which other talks clash with t.

❼   Remove from slotTalks the talks that clash with t.

❽   Remove t from talks.

❹   For each t, recursively call generate with the new partial solution.

Finally, we need to call generate with the empty timetable to start things off:

```
generate 0 0 [] [] allTalks allTalks
```

The program is equipped with some machinery to generate test data, so we can see how long it takes with a variety of inputs. Unfortunately, it turns out to be hard to find some parameters that don't either take forever or complete instantaneously, but here's one set:

```
$ ./timetable 4 3 11 10 3 +RTS -s
```

The command-line arguments set the parameters for the search: 4 slots, 3 tracks, 11 total talks, and 10 participants who each want to go to 3 talks. This takes about 1 second to calculate the number of possible timetables (about 31,000).

Adding Parallelism

This code is already quite involved, and if we try to parallelize it directly, it is likely to get more complicated. We'd prefer to separate the parallelism as far as possible from the algorithm code. With Strategies (Chapter 3), we did this by generating a lazy data structure. But this application is an example where generating a lazy data structure doesn't work very well, because we would have to return the entire search tree as a data structure.

Instead, I want to demonstrate another technique for separating the parallelism from the algorithm: building a *parallel skeleton*. A parallel skeleton is nothing more than a higher-order function that abstracts a pattern of computation. We've already seen one parallel skeleton: parMap, the function that describes data parallelism, abstracted over the function to apply in parallel. Here we need a different skeleton, which I'll call the *search* skeleton (although it's a variant of a more general divide-and-conquer skeleton).

I'll start by refactoring the algorithm into a skeleton and its instantiation, and then add parallelism to the skeleton. The type of the search skeleton is as follows:

timetable1.hs

```
search :: ( partial -> Maybe solution )    -- ❶
       -> ( partial -> [ partial ] )        -- ❷
       -> partial                           -- ❸
       -> [solution]                        -- ❹
```

The search function is polymorphic in two types: partial is the type of partial solutions, and solution is the type of complete solutions. We'll see how these are instantiated in our example shortly.

❶   The first argument to search is a function that tells whether a particular partial solution corresponds to a complete solution, and if so, what the solution is.

❷   The second argument takes a partial solution and refines it to a list of further partial solutions. It is expected that this process doesn't continue forever!

❸   To get things started, we need an initial, empty value of type partial.

❹   The result is a list of solutions.

The definition of search is quite straightforward. It's one of those functions that is almost impossible to get wrong, because the type describes exactly what it does:

```
search finished refine emptysoln = generate emptysoln
  where
    generate partial
      | Just soln <- finished partial = [soln]
      | otherwise  = concat (map generate (refine partial))
```

Now to refactor timetable to use search. The basic idea is that the arguments to generate constitute the partial solution, so we'll just package them up:

```
type Partial = (Int, Int, [[Talk]], [Talk], [Talk], [Talk])
```

The rest of the refactoring is mechanical, so I won't describe it in detail. The result is:

```
timetable :: [Person] -> [Talk] -> Int -> Int -> [TimeTable]
timetable people allTalks maxTrack maxSlot =
  search finished refine emptysoln
 where
  emptysoln = (0, 0, [], [], allTalks, allTalks)

  finished (slotNo, trackNo, slots, slot, slotTalks, talks)
    | slotNo == maxSlot = Just slots
    | otherwise         = Nothing

  clashes :: Map Talk [Talk]
  clashes = Map.fromListWith union
    [ (t, ts)
    | s <- people
    , (t, ts) <- selects (talks s) ]

  refine (slotNo, trackNo, slots, slot, slotTalks, talks)
    | trackNo == maxTrack = [(slotNo+1, 0, slot:slots, [], talks, talks)]
    | otherwise =
        [ (slotNo, trackNo+1, slots, t:slot, slotTalks', talks')
        | (t, ts) <- selects slotTalks
        , let clashesWithT = Map.findWithDefault [] t clashes
        , let slotTalks' = filter (`notElem` clashesWithT) ts
        , let talks' = filter (/= t) talks
        ]
```

The algorithm works exactly as before. All we did was pull out the search pattern as a higher-order function and call it.

Now to parallelize the search skeleton. As you might expect, the basic idea is that at each stage, we'll spawn off the recursive calls in parallel and then collect the results. Here's how to express that using the Par monad:

timetable2.hs

```
parsearch :: NFData solution
       => ( partial -> Maybe solution )
       -> ( partial -> [ partial ] )
```

```
          -> partial
          -> [solution]

parsearch finished refine emptysoln
  = runPar $ generate emptysoln
  where
    generate partial
      | Just soln <- finished partial = return [soln]
      | otherwise  = do
          solnss <- parMapM generate (refine partial)
          return (concat solnss)
```

We're using parMapM to call generate in parallel on the list of partial solutions returned by refine, and then concatenating the results. However, this doesn't work out too well; on the parameter set we used before, it adds a factor of five overhead. The problem is that as we get near the leaves of the search tree, the granularity is too fine in relation to the overhead of spawning the calls in parallel.

So we need a way to make the granularity coarser. We can't use chunking, because we don't have a flat list here; we have a tree. For tree-shaped parallelism we need to use a different technique: a *depth threshold*. The basic idea is quite simple: spawn recursive calls in parallel down to a certain depth, and below that depth use the original sequential algorithm.

Our parsearch function needs an extra parameter, namely the depth to parallelize to:

timetable3.hs

```
parsearch :: NFData solution
      => Int
      -> ( partial -> Maybe solution )    -- finished?
      -> ( partial -> [ partial ] )       -- refine a solution
      -> partial                          -- initial solution
      -> [solution]

parsearch maxdepth finished refine emptysoln
  = runPar $ generate 0 emptysoln
  where
    generate d partial | d >= maxdepth              -- ❶
      = return (search finished refine partial)
    generate d partial
      | Just soln <- finished partial = return [soln]
      | otherwise  = do
          solnss <- parMapM (generate (d+1)) (refine partial)
          return (concat solnss)
```

❶   The depth argument d increases by one each time we make a recursive call to generate. If it reaches the maxdepth passed as an argument to parsearch, then we call search (the sequential algorithm) to do the rest of the search below this point.

Using a depth of three in this case works reasonably well and gets us a speedup of about three on four cores relative to the original sequential version. Adding the skeleton unfortunately incurs some overhead, but in return it gains us some worthwhile modularity: it would have been difficult to add the depth threshold without first abstracting the skeleton.

Here are the main points to take away from this example:

- Tree-shaped (*divide and conquer*) computations parallelize well.
- You can abstract the parallel pattern as a *skeleton* using higher-order functions.
- To control the granularity in a tree-shaped computation, add a *depth threshold*, and use the sequential version of the algorithm below a certain depth.

Example: A Parallel Type Inferencer

In this section, we will parallelize a type inference engine, such as you might find in a compiler for a functional language. The purpose of this example is to demonstrate two things: one, that parallelism can be readily applied to program analysis problems, and two, that the dataflow model works well even when the structure of the parallelism is entirely dependent on the input and cannot be predicted beforehand.

The outline of the problem is as follows: given a list of bindings of the form x = e for a variable x and expression e, infer the types for each of the variables. Expressions consist of integers, variables, application, lambda expressions, let expressions, and arithmetic operators (+, -, *, /).

We can test the type inference engine on a few simple examples. Load it in GHCi (from the directory *parinfer* in the sample code):

```
$ ghci parinfer.hs
```

The function test typechecks an expression. Simple arithmetic expressions have type Int:

```
*Main> test "1 + 2"
Int
```

We can use lambda expressions, let expressions, and higher-order functions, just like in Haskell:

```
*Main> test "\\x -> x"
a0 -> a0
*Main> test "\\x -> x + 1"
Int -> Int
*Main> test "\\g -> \\h -> g (h 3)"
(a2 -> a3) -> (Int -> a2) -> a3
```

(Note that in order to get the backslash character in a Haskell String, we need to use
"\\".)

When the type inferencer is run as a standalone program, it typechecks a file of bindings, and infers a type for each one. For simplicity, we assume the list of bindings is ordered and nonrecursive; any variable used in an expression has to be defined earlier in the list. Later bindings may also shadow earlier ones.

For example, consider the following set of bindings for which we want to infer types:

```
f = ...
g = ... f ...
h = ... f ...
j = ... g ... h ...
```

I'm using the notation "... f ..." to stand for an expression involving f. The specific expression isn't important here, only that it mentions f.

We could proceed in a linear fashion through the list of bindings: first inferring the type for f, then the type for g, then the type for h, and so on. However, if we look at the dataflow graph for this set of bindings (Figure 4-4), we can see that there is some parallelism.

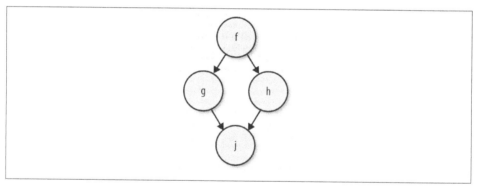

Figure 4-4. Flow of types between f, g, h, j

Clearly we can infer the types of g and h in parallel, once the type of f is known. When viewed this way, we can see that type inference is a natural fit for the dataflow model; we can consider each binding to be a node in the graph, and the edges of the graph carry inferred types from bindings to usage sites in the program.

Building a dataflow graph for the type inference problem allows parallelism to be automatically extracted from the type inference process. The actual amount of parallelism present depends entirely on the structure of the input program, however. An input program in which every binding depends on the previous one in the list would have no parallelism to extract. Fortunately, most programs aren't like that—usually there is a decent amount of parallelism implicit in the dependency structure.

Note that we're not necessarily exploiting *all* the available parallelism here. There might be parallelism available within the inference of individual bindings. However, to try to parallelize too deeply might cause granularity problems, and parallelizing the outer level is likely to gain the most reward.

The type inference engine that I'm using for this example is a rather ancient piece of code that I modified to add parallelism.[6] The changes to add parallelism were quite modest.[7]

The types from the inference engine that we will need to work with are as follows:

```
type VarId = String -- Variables
data Term     -- Terms in the input program
data Env      -- Environment, mapping VarId to PolyType
data PolyType -- Polymorphic types
```

In programming language terminology, an environment is a mapping that assigns some meaning to the variables of an expression. A type inference engine uses an environment to assign types to variables; this is the purpose of the Env type. When we typecheck an expression, we must supply an Env that gives the types of the variables that the expression mentions. An Env is created using makeEnv:

```
makeEnv :: [(VarId,PolyType)] -> Env
```

To determine which variables we need to populate the Env with, we need a way to extract the free (unbound) variables of an expression; this is what the freeVars function does:

```
freeVars :: Term -> [VarId]
```

The underlying type inference engine for expressions takes a Term and an Env that supplies the types for the free variables of the Term and delivers a PolyType:

```
inferTopRhs :: Env -> Term -> PolyType
```

While the sequential part of the inference engine uses an Env that maps VarIds to PolyTypes, the parallel part of the inference engine will use an environment that maps VarIds to IVar PolyType, so that we can fork the inference engine for a given binding, and then wait for its result later.[8] The environment for the parallel type inferencer is called TopEnv:

---

6. This code was authored by Philip Wadler and found in the nofib benchmark suite of Haskell programs.

7. I did, however, take the liberty of modernizing the code in various ways, although that wasn't strictly necessary.

8. We are ignoring the possibility of type errors here; in a real implementation, the IVar would probably contain an Either type representing either the inferred type or an error.

```
type TopEnv = Map VarId (IVar PolyType)
```

All that remains is to write the top-level loop. We'll do this in two stages. First, a function to infer the type of a single binding:

```
inferBind :: TopEnv -> (VarId,Term) -> Par TopEnv
inferBind topenv (x,u) = do
  vu <- new                                              -- ❶
  fork $ do                                              -- ❷
    let fu = Set.toList (freeVars u)                     -- ❸
    tfu <- mapM (get . fromJust . flip Map.lookup topenv) fu   -- ❹
    let aa = makeEnv (zip fu tfu)                        -- ❺
    put vu (inferTopRhs aa u)                            -- ❻
  return (Map.insert x vu topenv)                        -- ❼
```

❶ Create an IVar, vu, to hold the type of this binding.

❷ Fork the computation that does the type inference.

❸ The inputs to this type inference are the types of the variables mentioned in the expression u. Hence we call freeVars to get those variables.

❹ For each of the free variables, look up its IVar in the topenv, and then call get on it. Hence this step will wait until the types of all the free variables are available before proceeding.

❺ Build an Env from the free variables and their types.

❻ Infer the type of the expression u, and put the result in the IVar we created at the beginning.

❼ Back in the parent, return topenv extended with x mapped to the new IVar vu.

Next we use inferBind to define inferTop, which infers types for a list of bindings:

```
inferTop :: TopEnv -> [(VarId,Term)] -> Par [(VarId,PolyType)]
inferTop topenv0 binds = do
  topenv1 <- foldM inferBind topenv0 binds                    -- ❶
  mapM (\(v,i) -> do t <- get i; return (v,t)) (Map.toList topenv1) -- ❷
```

❶ Use foldM (from Control.Monad) to perform inferBind over each binding, accumulating a TopEnv that will contain a mapping for each of the variables.

❷ Wait for all the type inference to happen, and collect the results. Hence we turn the TopEnv back into a list and call get on all of the IVars.

This parallel implementation works quite nicely. To demonstrate it, I've constructed a synthetic input for the type checker, a fragment of which is given below (the full version is in the file *parinfer/benchmark.in*).

```
id = \x->x ;
```

```
a = \f -> f id id ;
a = \f -> f a a ;
a = \f -> f a a ;
...
a = let f = a in \x -> x ;

b = \f -> f id id ;
b = \f -> f b b ;
b = \f -> f b b ;
...
b = let f = b in \x -> x ;

c = \f -> f id id ;
c = \f -> f c c ;
c = \f -> f c c ;
...
c = let f = c in \x -> x ;

d = \f -> f id id ;
d = \f -> f d d ;
d = \f -> f d d ;
...
d = let f = d in \x -> x ;
```

There are four sequences of bindings that can be inferred in parallel. The first sequence is the set of bindings for a (each successive binding for a shadows the previous one), then identical sequences named b, c, and d. Each binding in a sequence depends on the previous one, but the sequences are independent of one another. This means that our parallel typechecking algorithm should automatically infer types for the a, b, c, and d bindings in parallel, giving a maximum speedup of 4.

With one processor, the result should be something like this:

```
$ ./parinfer <benchmark.in +RTS -s
...
  Total   time    4.71s (  4.72s elapsed)
```

The result with two processors represents a speedup of 1.96:

```
$ ./parinfer <benchmark.in +RTS -s -N2
...
  Total   time    4.79s (  2.41s elapsed)
```

With three processors, the result is:

```
$ ./parinfer <benchmark.in +RTS -s -N3
...
  Total   time    4.92s (  2.42s elapsed)
```

This is almost exactly the same as with two processors! But this is to be expected: there are four independent problems, so the best we can do is to overlap the first three and then run the final one. Thus the program will take the same amount of time as with two processors, where we could overlap two problems at a time. Adding the fourth processor allows all four problems to be overlapped, resulting in a speedup of 3.66:

```
$ ./parinfer <benchmark.in +RTS -s -N4
...
  Total   time    5.10s (  1.29s elapsed)
```

Using Different Schedulers

The Par monad is implemented as a library in Haskell, so aspects of its behavior can be changed without changing GHC or its runtime system. One way in which this is useful is in changing the scheduling strategy; certain scheduling strategies are better suited to certain patterns of execution.

The monad-par library comes with two schedulers: the "Trace" scheduler and the "Direct" scheduler, where the latter is the default. In general the Trace scheduler performs slightly worse than the Direct scheduler, but not always; it's worth trying both with your code to see which gives the better results.

To choose one or the other, just import the appropriate module. For example, to use the Trace scheduler instead of the Direct scheduler:

```
import Control.Monad.Par.Scheds.Trace
   -- instead of Control.Monad.Par
```

Remember that you need to make this change in *all* the modules of your program that import Control.Monad.Par.

The Par Monad Compared to Strategies

I've presented two different parallel programming models, each with advantages and disadvantages. In reality, though, both approaches are suitable for a wide range of tasks; most Parallel Haskell benchmarks achieve broadly similar results when coded with either Strategies or the Par monad. So which to choose is to some extent a matter of personal preference. However, there are a number of trade-offs that are worth bearing in mind, as these might tip the balance one way or the other for your code:

- As a general rule of thumb, if your algorithm naturally produces a lazy data structure, then writing a `Strategy` to evaluate it in parallel will probably work well. If not, then it can be more straightforward to use the `Par` monad to express the parallelism.

- The `runPar` function itself is relatively expensive, whereas `runEval` is free. So when using the `Par` monad, you should usually try to thread the `Par` monad around to all the places that need parallelism to avoid needing multiple `runPar` calls. If this is inconvenient, then `Eval` or Strategies might be a better choice. In particular, nested calls to `runPar` (where a `runPar` is evaluated during the course of executing another `Par` computation) usually give poor results.

- Strategies allow a separation between algorithm and parallelism, which can allow more reuse and a cleaner specification of parallelism. However, using a parallel skeleton works with both approaches.

- The `Par` monad has more overhead than the `Eval` monad. At the present time, `Eval` tends to perform better at finer granularities, due to the direct runtime system support for sparks. At larger granularities, `Par` and `Eval` perform approximately the same.

- The `Par` monad is implemented entirely in a Haskell library (the `monad-par` package), and is thus easily modified. There is a choice of scheduling strategies (see "Using Different Schedulers" on page 82).

- The `Eval` monad has more diagnostics in ThreadScope. There are graphs that show different aspects of sparks: creation rate, conversion rate, and so on. The `Par` monad is not currently integrated with ThreadScope.

- The `Par` monad does not support speculative parallelism in the sense that `rpar` does ("GC'd Sparks and Speculative Parallelism" on page 48); parallelism in the `Par` monad is always executed.

CHAPTER 5

Data Parallel Programming with Repa

The techniques we've seen in the previous chapters are great for parallelizing code that uses ordinary Haskell data structures like lists and Maps, but they don't work as well for data-parallel algorithms over large arrays. That's because large-scale array computations demand very good raw sequential performance, which we can get only by operating on arrays of unboxed data. We can't use Strategies to parallelize operations over unboxed arrays, because they need lazy data structures (boxed arrays would be suitable, but not unboxed arrays). Similarly, Par doesn't work well here either, because in Par the data is passed in IVars.

In this chapter, we're going to see how to write efficient numerical array computations in Haskell and run them in parallel. The library we're going to use is called *Repa*, which stands for REgular PArallel arrays.[1] The library provides a range of efficient operations for creating arrays and operating on arrays in parallel.

The Repa package is available on Hackage. If you followed the instructions for installing the sample code dependencies earlier, then you should already have it, but if not you can install it with cabal install:

```
$ cabal install repa
```

In this chapter, I'm going to use GHCi a lot to illustrate the behavior of Repa; trying things out in GHCi is a great way to become familiar with the types and operations that Repa provides. Because Repa provides many operations with the same names as Prelude functions (e.g., map), we usually import Data.Array.Repa with a short module alias:

```
> import Data.Array.Repa as Repa
```

This way, we can refer to Repa's map function as Repa.map.

---

1. Note that we're using Repa version 3.2 here; 3.0 had a somewhat different API.

Arrays, Shapes, and Indices

Everything in Repa revolves around arrays. A computation in Repa typically consists of computing an array in parallel, perhaps using other arrays as inputs. So we'll start by looking at the type of arrays, how to build them, and how to work with them.

The `Array` type has three parameters:

```
data Array r sh e
```

The `e` parameter is the type of the elements, for example `Double`, `Int`, or `Word8`. The `r` parameter is the *representation type*, which describes how the array is represented in memory; I'll come back to this shortly. The `sh` parameter describes the *shape* of the array; that is, the number of dimensions it has.

Shapes are built out of two type constructors, Z and :.:

```
data Z = Z
data tail :. head = tail :. head
```

The simplest shape, Z, is the shape of an array with no dimensions (i.e., a scalar), which has a single element. If we add a dimension, `Z :. Int`, we get the shape of an array with a single dimension indexed by `Int`, otherwise known as a vector. Adding another dimension gives `Z :. Int :. Int`, the shape of a two-dimensional array, or matrix. New dimensions are added on the right, and the `:.` operator associates left, so when we write `Z :. Int :. Int`, we really mean `(Z :. Int) :. Int`.

The Z and `:.` symbols are both type constructors and value constructors, which can be a little confusing at times. For example, the data value `Z :. 3` has type `Z :. Int`. The data value form is used in Repa to mean either "shapes" or "indices." For example, `Z :. 3` can be either the shape of three-element vectors, or the index of the fourth element of a vector (indices count from zero).

Repa supports only `Int`-typed indices. A few handy type synonyms are provided for the common shape types:

```
type DIM0 = Z
type DIM1 = DIM0 :. Int
type DIM2 = DIM1 :. Int
```

Let's try a few examples. A simple way to build an array is to use `fromListUnboxed`:

```
fromListUnboxed :: (Shape sh, Unbox a) => sh -> [a] -> Array U sh a
```

The `fromListUnboxed` function takes a shape of type `sh` and a list of elements of type `a`, and builds an array of type `Array U sh a`. The `U` is the representation and stands for Unboxed: this array will contain unboxed elements. Don't worry about the `Shape` and `Unbox` type classes. They are just there to ensure that we use only the appropriate shape constructors (Z and `:.`) and supported element types, respectively.

Let's build a 10-element vector of Int and fill it with the numbers 1...10. We need to pass a shape argument, which will be Z:.10 for a 10-element vector:

```
> fromListUnboxed (Z :. 10) [1..10]

<interactive>:15:1:
    No instance for (Shape (Z :. head0))
      arising from a use of `fromListUnboxed'
    The type variable `head0' is ambiguous
    Possible fix: add a type signature that fixes these type variable(s)
    Note: there is a potential instance available:
      instance Shape sh => Shape (sh :. Int)
        -- Defined in `Data.Array.Repa.Index'
    Possible fix: add an instance declaration for (Shape (Z :. head0))
    In the expression: fromListUnboxed (Z :. 10) [1 .. 10]
    In an equation for `it': it = fromListUnboxed (Z :. 10) [1 .. 10]
```

Oops! This illustrates something that you will probably encounter a lot when working with Repa: a type error caused by insufficient type information. In this case, the integer 10 in Z :. 10 is overloaded, so we have to say explicitly that we mean Int. There are many ways to give GHC the extra bit of information it needs; one way is to add a type signature to the whole expression, which has type Array U DIM1 Int:

```
> fromListUnboxed (Z :. 10) [1..10] :: Array U DIM1 Int
AUnboxed (Z :. 10) (fromList [1,2,3,4,5,6,7,8,9,10])
```

Similarly, we can make a two-dimensional array, with 3 rows of 5 columns, and fill it with the elements 1 to 15:

```
> fromListUnboxed (Z :. 3 :. 5) [1..15] :: Array U DIM2 Int
AUnboxed ((Z :. 3) :. 5) (fromList [1,2,3,4,5,6,7,8,9,10,11,12,13,14,15])
```

Conceptually, the array we created is this:

```
1   2   3   4   5
6   7   8   9   10
11  12  13  14  15
```

But internally, the array is stored as a single vector (after all, computer memory is one-dimensional). We can see the vector in the result of the call to fromListUnboxed; it contains the same elements that we initialized the array with.

The shape of the array is there to tell Repa how to interpret the operations on it. For example, if we ask for the element at index Z:.2:.1 in an array with shape Z:.3:.5, we'll get the element at position 2 * 5 + 1 in the vector. We can try it using the ! operator, which extracts an element from an array. The type of ! is:

```
(!) :: (Shape sh, Source r e) => Array r sh e -> sh -> e
```

Let's get the element at position Z:.2:.1 from our example matrix:

```
> let arr = fromListUnboxed (Z :. 3 :. 5) [1..15] :: Array U DIM2 Int
> arr ! (Z:.2:.1)
12
```

The element 12 is therefore 2 rows down and 1 column across. As I mentioned earlier, indices count from zero in Repa.

Internally, Repa is using the function toIndex to convert an index to an Int offset, given a shape:

```
toIndex :: Shape sh => sh -> sh -> Int
```

For example:

```
> toIndex (Z:.3:.5 :: DIM2) (Z:.2:.1 :: DIM2)
11
```

Because the layout of an array in memory is the same regardless of its shape, we can even change the shape without copying the array:

```
> reshape (Z:.5:.3) arr ! (Z:.2:.1 :: DIM2)
8
```

With the shape Z:.5:.3, the index Z:.2:.1 corresponds to the element at $2 * 3 + 1 = 7$, which has value 8.

Here are a couple of other operations on shapes that often come in handy:

```
rank :: Shape sh => sh -> Int  -- number of dimensions
size :: Shape sh => sh -> Int  -- number of elements
```

To retrieve the shape of an array, we can use extent:

```
extent :: (Shape sh, Source r e) => Array r sh e -> sh
```

For example:

```
> extent arr
(Z :. 3) :. 5
> rank (extent arr)
2
> size (extent arr)
15
```

Operations on Arrays

We can map a function over an array using Repa's map function:

```
Repa.map :: (Shape sh, Source r a)
         => (a -> b) -> Array r sh a -> Array D sh b
```

We can see from the type that map returns an array with the representation D. The D representation stands for Delayed; this means that the array has not been computed yet. A delayed array is represented by a function from indices to elements.

We can apply map to an array, but there's no way to print out the result:

```
> let a = fromListUnboxed (Z :. 10) [1..10] :: Array U DIM1 Int
> Repa.map (+1) a

<interactive>:26:1:
    No instance for (Show (Array D DIM1 Int))
      arising from a use of `print'
    Possible fix:
      add an instance declaration for (Show (Array D DIM1 Int))
    In a stmt of an interactive GHCi command: print it
```

As its name suggests, a delayed array is not an array *yet*. To turn it into an array, we have to call a function that allocates the array and computes the value of each element. The computeS function does this for us:

```
computeS :: (Load r1 sh e, Target r2 e) => Array r1 sh e -> Array r2 sh e
```

The argument to computeS is an array with a representation that is a member of the Load class, whereas its result is an array with a representation that is a member of the Target class. The most important instances of these two classes are D and U respectively; that is, computeS turns a delayed array into a concrete unboxed array.[2].

Applying computeS to the result of map gives us an unboxed array:

```
> computeS (Repa.map (+1) a) :: Array U DIM1 Int
AUnboxed (Z :. 10) (fromList [2,3,4,5,6,7,8,9,10,11])
```

You might be wondering why there is this extra complication—why doesn't map just produce a new array? The answer is that by representing the result of an array operation as a delayed array, a sequence of array operations can be performed without ever building the intermediate arrays; this is an optimization called *fusion*, and it's critical to achieving good performance with Repa. For example, if we composed two maps together:

```
> computeS (Repa.map (+1) (Repa.map (^2) a)) :: Array U DIM1 Int
AUnboxed (Z :. 10) (fromList [2,5,10,17,26,37,50,65,82,101])
```

The intermediate array between the two maps is not built, and in fact if we compile this rather than running it in GHCi, provided the optimization option -O is enabled, it will compile to a single efficient loop over the input array.

Let's see how it works. The fundamental way to get a delayed array is fromFunction:

```
fromFunction :: sh -> (sh -> a) -> Array D sh a
```

---

2. There are other array representations that aren't covered in this chapter; for more details, see the Repa documentation

The `fromFunction` operation creates a delayed array. It takes the shape of the array and a function that specifies the elements. For example, we can make a delayed array that represents the vector of integers 0 to 9 like this:

```
> let a = fromFunction (Z :. 10) (\(Z:.i) -> i :: Int)
> :t a
a :: Array D (Z :. Int) Int
```

Delayed arrays support indexing, just like manifest arrays:

```
> a ! (Z:.5)
5
```

Indexing a delayed array works by just calling the function that we supplied to `fromFunction` with the given index.

We need to apply `computeS` to make the delayed array into a manifest array:

```
> computeS a :: Array U DIM1 Int
AUnboxed (Z :. 10) (fromList [0,1,2,3,4,5,6,7,8,9])
```

The `computeS` function creates the array and for each of the indices of the array, it calls the function stored in the delayed array to find the element at that position.

The `map` function, along with many other operations on arrays, can be specified in terms of `fromFunction`. For example, here is a definition of `map`:

```
> let mymap f a = fromFunction (extent a) (\ix -> f (a ! ix))
> :t mymap
mymap
  :: (Shape sh, Source r e) =>
     (e -> a) -> Array r sh e -> Array D sh a
```

It works just like the real `map`:

```
> computeS (mymap (+1) a) :: Array U DIM1 Int
AUnboxed (Z :. 10) (fromList [1,2,3,4,5,6,7,8,9,10])
```

What happens if we compose two `map`s together? The result would be a delayed array containing a function that indexes into another delayed array. So we're building up a nested function that defines the array elements, rather than intermediate arrays. Furthermore, Repa is carefully engineered so that at compile time the nested function call is optimized away as far as possible, yielding very efficient code.

Example: Computing Shortest Paths

In "Example: Shortest Paths in a Graph" on page 61, we looked at an implementation of the Floyd-Warshall algorithm for computing the lengths of shortest paths in a sparse weighted directed graph. Here, we'll investigate how to code up the algorithm over *dense* graphs, using Repa.

For reference, here is the pseudocode definition of the algorithm:

```
shortestPath :: Graph -> Vertex -> Vertex -> Vertex -> Weight
shortestPath g i j 0 = weight g i j
shortestPath g i j k = min (shortestPath g i j (k-1))
                           (shortestPath g i k (k-1) + shortestPath g k j (k-1))
```

We implement this by first computing all the shortest paths for k == 0, then k == 1, and so on up to the maximum vertex in the graph.

For the dense version, we're going to use an adjacency matrix; that is, a two-dimensional array indexed by pairs of vertices, where each element is the length of the path between the two vertices. Here is our representation of graphs:

fwdense.hs

```
type Weight = Int
type Graph r = Array r DIM2 Weight
```

The implementation of the shortest paths algorithm is as follows:

```
shortestPaths :: Graph U -> Graph U
shortestPaths g0 = go g0 0                                     -- ❶
  where
    Z :. _ :. n = extent g0                                    -- ❷

    go !g !k | k == n    = g                                   -- ❸
             | otherwise =
                 let g' = computeS (fromFunction (Z:.n:.n) sp) -- ❹
                 in  go g' (k+1)                               -- ❺
      where
        sp (Z:.i:.j) = min (g ! (Z:.i:.j)) (g ! (Z:.i:.k) + g ! (Z:.k:.j)) -- ❻
```

❷ The number of vertices in the graph, n, is found by pattern-matching on the shape of the input graph, which we get by calling extent.

❶ We need to loop over the vertices, with k taking values from 0 up to n - 1. This is done with a local recursive function go, which takes the current graph g and k as arguments. The initial value for g is g0, the input graph, and the initial value for k is 0.

❸ The first case in go applies when we have looped over all the vertices, and k == n. The result is the current graph, g.

❹ Here is the interesting case. We're going to build a new adjacency matrix, g', for this step using fromFunction. The shape of the array is Z:.n:.n, the same as the input, and the function to compute each element is sp (discussed later).

To manifest the new graph, we call computeS. Do we have to call computeS for each step, or could we wait until the end? If we don't manifest the graph at each step, then we will be calling a nest of k functions every time we index into the current graph, g, which is exactly what this dynamic-programming solution seeks to avoid. So we *must* manifest the graph at each step.

❺ Recursively call go to continue with the next step, passing the new graph we just computed, g', and the next value of k.

❻ The sp function computes the value of each element in the new matrix and is a direct translation of the pseudocode: the shortest path between i and j is the minimum of the current shortest path, and the shortest path that goes from i to k and then to j, all of which we get by indexing into the current graph, g.

The code is quite readable and somewhat shorter than the sparse version of the algorithm we saw before. However, there are a couple of subtleties that might not be obvious, but are nevertheless important for making the code run quickly:

- I deliberately used an explicit recursive function, go, rather than something like foldl', even though the latter would lead to shorter code. The optimizations in Repa work much better when all the code is visible to the compiler, and calling out to library functions can sometimes hide details from GHC and prevent optimizations. There are no hard and fast rules here; I experimented with both the explicit version and the foldl' version, and found the explicit loop faster.

- There are bang-patterns on the arguments to go. This is good practice for iterative loops like this one and helps Repa to optimize the loop.

Let's go ahead and compile the program and try it out on a 500-vertex graph:

```
> ghc fwdense.hs -O2 -fllvm
[1 of 1] Compiling Main              ( fwdense.hs, fwdense.o )
Linking fwdense ...
> ./fwdense 500 +RTS -s
31250125000
  1,077,772,040 bytes allocated in the heap
     31,516,280 bytes copied during GC
     10,334,312 bytes maximum residency (171 sample(s))
      2,079,424 bytes maximum slop
             32 MB total memory in use (3 MB lost due to fragmentation)

                                  Tot time (elapsed)  Avg pause  Max pause
  Gen  0       472 colls,     0 par    0.01s   0.01s     0.0000s    0.0005s
```

```
Gen  1          171 colls,     0 par   0.03s    0.03s     0.0002s    0.0063s

INIT   time    0.00s  (  0.00s elapsed)
MUT    time    1.46s  (  1.47s elapsed)
GC     time    0.04s  (  0.04s elapsed)
EXIT   time    0.00s  (  0.00s elapsed)
Total  time    1.50s  (  1.50s elapsed)
```

Note that I added a couple of optimization options: -O2 turns up GHC's optimizer, and
-fllvm enables GHC's LLVM backend, which significantly improves the performance
of Repa code; on my machine with this particular example, I see a 40% improvement
from -fllvm.[3]

Parallelizing the Program

Now to make the program run in parallel. To compute an array in parallel, Repa provides
a variant of the computeS operation, called computeP:

```
computeP :: (Monad m, Source r2 e, Target r2 e, Load r1 sh e)
         => Array r1 sh e
         -> m (Array r2 sh e)
```

Whereas computeS computes an array sequentially, computeP uses the available cores
to compute the array in parallel. It knows the size of the array, so it can divide the work
equally amongst the cores.

The type is almost the same as computeS, except that computeP takes place in a monad.
It works with any monad, and it doesn't matter which monad is used because the purpose
of the monad is only to ensure that computeP operations are performed in sequence and
not nested. Hence we need to modify our code so that the go function is in a monad,
which entails a few small changes. Here is the code:

```
shortestPaths :: Graph U -> Graph U
shortestPaths g0 = runIdentity $ go g0 0                    -- ❶
  where
    Z :. _ :. n = extent g0

    go !g !k | k == n    = return g                        -- ❷
             | otherwise = do
                 g' <- computeP (fromFunction (Z:.n:.n) sp)  -- ❸
                 go g' (k+1)
      where
        sp (Z:.i:.j) = min (g ! (Z:.i:.j)) (g ! (Z:.i:.k) + g ! (Z:.k:.j))
```

❶   We need to use a monad, so the Identity monad will do.

---

3. You might not have LLVM installed on your computer, in which case the -fllvm option will not work. Don't
   worry: Repa works perfectly well without it. The code will just be slower.

❷   Remember to `return` the result, as we're now in a monad.

❸   Instead of `let` to bind `g'`, we use `do` and monadic bind and replace `computeS` with `computeP`. There are no differences to the `fromFunction` call or the `sp` function.

To run it in parallel, we'll need to add the `-threaded` option when compiling. Let's see how it performs:

```
> ghc -O2 fwdense1 -threaded -fllvm  -fforce-recomp
[1 of 1] Compiling Main             ( fwdense1.hs, fwdense1.o )
Linking fwdense1 ...
> ./fwdense1 500 +RTS -s
31250125000
...
  Total   time    1.89s (  1.91s elapsed)
```

There's some overhead for using `computeP`, which here seems to be about 27%. That's quite high, but we can recoup it by using more cores. With four cores:

```
> ./fwdense1 500 +RTS -s -N4
31250125000
...
  Total   time    2.15s (  0.57s elapsed)
```

That equates to a 2.63 speedup against the sequential version, for almost zero effort. Not bad!

Monads and computeP

Did we really need to thread a monad through the go function? Strictly speaking, the answer is no, because you can always replace `computeS` with (`runIdentity` . `computeP`), but this can lead to trouble. To illustrate what can go wrong, let's compute two arrays with `computeP`, where the second will depend on the first. The first is just a vector of `Int`:

```
> let arr = fromFunction (Z:.5) (\(Z:.i) -> i :: Int)
> let parr = runIdentity $ computeP arr :: Array U DIM1 Int
```

And the second is a copy of the first, using `fromFunction` again:

```
> let arr2 = fromFunction (Z:.5) (\ix -> parr ! ix)
```

Now, when we try to compute the second array using `computeP`, we get:

```
> runIdentity $ computeP arr2 :: Array U DIM1 Int
Data.Array.Repa: Performing nested parallel computation sequentially.
  You've probably called the 'compute' or 'copy' function while another
  instance was already running. This can happen if the second version
  was suspended due to lazy evaluation. Use 'deepSeqArray' to ensure
  that each array is fully evaluated before you 'compute' the next one.
```

A call to `computeP` cannot refer to another array calculated with `computeP`, unless the inner `computeP` has already been evaluated. Here, we didn't evaluate it; we just bound it with `let`, using `runIdentity` to satisfy the `Monad` requirement.

The monad requirement in `computeP` is there to help us avoid this problem, because `computeP` ensures that the result is fully evaluated in the monad. In GHCi, we can use the `IO` monad:

```
> let arr = fromFunction (Z:.5) (\(Z:.i) -> i :: Int)
> parr <- computeP arr :: IO (Array U DIM1 Int)
> let arr2 = fromFunction (Z:.5) (\ix -> parr ! ix)
> computeP arr2 :: IO (Array U DIM1 Int)
AUnboxed (Z :. 5) (fromList [0,1,2,3,4])
```

So this is the rule of thumb: if your program makes multiple calls to `computeP`, try to ensure that they are performed in the same monad.

Folding and Shape-Polymorphism

Folds are an important class of operations over arrays; they are the operations that perform a collective operation over all the elements of an array to produce a single result, such as summing the array or finding its maximum element. For example, the function `sumAllS` calculates the sum of all the elements in an array:

```
sumAllS
  :: (Num a, Shape sh, Source r a, Unbox a, Elt a)
  => Array r sh a
  -> a
```

For an array of elements of type `a` that supports addition (the `Num` constraint), `sumAllS` produces a single result that is the sum of all the elements:

```
> let arr = fromListUnboxed (Z :. 10) [1..10] :: Array U DIM1 Int
> sumAllS arr
55
```

But sometimes we don't want to fold over the whole array. There are occasions where we need to fold over just one dimension. For example, in the shortest paths example, suppose we wanted to take the resulting matrix of path lengths and find for each vertex the furthest distance we would have to travel from that vertex to any other vertex in the graph.

Our graph may have some nodes that are not connected, and in that case we represent the distance between them by a special large value called `inf` (the value of `inf` doesn't matter as long as it is larger than all the path lengths in the graph). For the purposes of finding the maximum distance to other nodes, we'll ignore nodes that are not reachable and hence have path length `inf`. So the function to compute the maximum of two path lengths is as follows:

```
maxDistance :: Weight -> Weight -> Weight
maxDistance x y
  | x == inf  = y
  | y == inf  = x
  | otherwise = max x y
```

Now we want to fold `maxDistance` over just one dimension of our two-dimensional adjacency matrix. There is a function called `foldS` that does just that; here is its type:

```
foldS :: (Shape sh, Source r a, Elt a, Unbox a)
      => (a -> a -> a)              -- ❶
      -> a                          -- ❷
      -> Array r (sh :. Int) a      -- ❸
      -> Array U sh a               -- ❹
```

❶   The function to fold.

❷   The unitary value of type a.

❸   The input array. Note that the shape is (sh :. Int), which means that this is an array of some shape sh with one more dimension.

❹   The output array has shape sh; that is, one dimension fewer than the input array. For example, if we pass in an array of shape Z:.Int:.Int, sh is Z:.Int. The fold takes place over the inner dimension of the array, which we normally think of as the *rows*. Each row is reduced to a single value.

The *fwdense.hs* program has a small test graph of six vertices:

```
> extent testGraph
(Z :. 6) :. 6
```

If we use `foldS` to fold `maxDistance` over the matrix of shortest paths, we obtain the maximum distance from each vertex to any other vertex:

```
> foldS maxDistance inf (shortestPaths testGraph)
AUnboxed (Z :. 6) (fromList [20,19,31,18,15,21])
```

And if we fold once more, we'll find the longest distance between any two nodes (for which a path exists) in the graph:

```
> foldS maxDistance inf (foldS maxDistance inf (shortestPaths testGraph))
AUnboxed Z (fromList [31])
```

Note that the result this time is an array with zero dimensions, otherwise known as a scalar.

A function named `foldP` allows us to fold in parallel:

```
foldP :: (Shape sh, Source r a, Elt a, Unbox a, Monad m)
      => (a -> a -> a)
      -> a
      -> Array r (sh :. Int) a
      -> m (Array U sh a)
```

For the same reasons as `computeP`, `foldP` is performed in an arbitrary monad. The arguments are the same as for `foldS`.

 The function argument used with `foldP` must be *associative*. That is, the function f must satisfy f x (f y z) == f (f x y) z. This is because unlike `foldS`, `foldP` doesn't necessarily fold the function over the array elements in strict left-to-right order; it folds different parts of the array in parallel and then combines the results from those parts using the folding function.

Note that strictly speaking, although mathematical addition is associative, floating-point addition is not, due to rounding errors. However, we tend to ignore this detail when using `foldP` because a small amount of nondeterminism in the floating point result is normally acceptable.

Example: Image Rotation

Repa is a great tool for coding image manipulation algorithms, which tend to be naturally parallel and involve a lot of data. In this section, we'll write a program to rotate an image about its center by a specified number of degrees.

For reading and writing image data, Repa provides an interface to the *DevIL* library, which is a cross-platform C library for image manipulation. *DevIL* supports reading and writing various common image formats, including PNG and JPG. The library is wrapped by the Haskell package `repa-devil`, which provides a convenient Haskell API to *DevIL*. The two operations we'll be using are `readImage` and `writeImage`:

```
readImage  :: FilePath -> IL Image
writeImage :: FilePath -> Image -> IL ()
```

Where the `Image` type defines various in-memory image representations:

```
data Image
  = RGBA (Array F DIM3 Word8)
  | RGB  (Array F DIM3 Word8)
  | BGRA (Array F DIM3 Word8)
  | BGR  (Array F DIM3 Word8)
  | Grey (Array F DIM2 Word8)
```

A color image is represented as a three-dimensional array. The first two dimensions are the Y and X axes, and the last dimension contains the three color channels and optionally an alpha channel. The first four constructors of `Image` correspond to different orderings of the color channels and the presence or not of an alpha channel. The last option, `Grey`, is a grayscale image with one byte per pixel.

Which one of these is returned by readImage depends on the type of image file being read. For example, a color JPEG image returns data in RGB format, but a PNG image returns in RGBA format.

You may have noticed one unfamiliar aspect to these array types: the F representation type. This indicates that the array data is held in foreign memory; that is, it was allocated by C code. Apart from being allocated by C rather than Haskell, the F representation is identical to U.

Note that readImage and writeImage are in the IL monad. The purpose of the IL monad is to ensure that the *DevIL* library is initialized properly. This is done by runIL:

```
runIL :: IL a -> IO a
```

It's perfectly fine to have multiple calls to runIL; the library will be initialized only once.

Our program will take three arguments: the number of degrees to rotate the image by, the input filename, and the output filename, respectively:

```
main :: IO ()
main = do
    [n, f1,f2] <- getArgs
    runIL $ do
      (RGB v) <- readImage f1                                    -- ❶
      rotated <- computeP $ rotate (read n) v :: IL (Array F DIM3 Word8) -- ❷
      writeImage f2 (RGB rotated)                                -- ❸
```

❶ Read the image data from the file f1 (the second command-line argument).

❷ The function rotate, which we will define shortly, returns a delayed array representing the rotated image. We call computeP here to calculate the new array in parallel. In the earlier examples, we used computeP to produce arrays with U representation, but here we're producing an array with F representation. This is possible because computeP is overloaded on the desired output representation; this is the purpose of the Target type class.

❸ Finally, write the new image to the file f2.

Next we'll write the function rotate, which actually calculates the rotated image data. First, we have a decision to make: what should the size of the rotated image be? We have the option of producing a smaller image than the input, and discarding any pixels that fall outside the boundaries after rotation, or to adjust the image size to contain the rotated image, and fill in the empty areas with something else (e.g., black). I'll opt, somewhat arbitrarily, to keep the output image size the same as the input and fill in the empty areas with black. Please feel free to modify the program to do something more sensible.

```
rotate :: Double -> Array F DIM3 Word8 -> Array D DIM3 Word8
rotate deg g = fromFunction (Z :. y :. x :. k) f        -- ❶
```

```
where
    sh@(Z :. y :. x :. k)    = extent g

    !theta = pi/180 * deg                    -- ❷

    !st = sin theta                          -- ❸
    !ct = cos theta

    !cy = fromIntegral y / 2 :: Double        -- ❹
    !cx = fromIntegral x / 2 :: Double

    f (Z :. i :. j :. k)                      -- ❺
      | inShape sh old = g ! old              -- ❻
      | otherwise      = 0                    -- ❼
      where
        fi = fromIntegral i - cy              -- ❽
        fj = fromIntegral j - cx

        i' = round (st * fj + ct * fi + cy)   -- ❾
        j' = round (ct * fj - st * fi + cx)

        old = Z :. i' :. j' :. k              -- ❿
```

The formula to rotate a point (x,y) by an angle θ about the origin is given by:

$$x' = y \sin\theta + x \cos\theta$$

$$y' = y \cos\theta + x \sin\theta$$

However, we want to rotate our image about the center, but the origin is the upper-left corner. Hence we need to adjust the points to be relative to the center of the image before translation and adjust them back afterward.

❶ We're creating a delayed array, represented by the function f. The dimensions of the array are the same as the input array, which we get by calling extent just below.

❷ Convert the angle by which to rotate the image from degrees to radians.

❸ Because we'll need the values of sin theta and cos theta twice each, we defined them once here.

❹ cy and cx are the y- and x-coordinates, respectively, of the center of the image.

❺ The function f, which gives the value of the new image at position i, j, k (where k here is between 0 and 2, corresponding to the RGB color channels).

❻ First, we need to check whether the old pixel (the pixel we are rotating into this position) is within the bounds of the original image. The function inShape does this check for us:

```
inShape :: Shape sh => sh -> sh -> Bool
```

If the old pixel is within the image, then we return the value at that position in the old image.

❼ If the rotated position in the old image is out of bounds, then we return zero, giving a black pixel at this position in the new image.

❽ fi and fj are the *y* and *x* values of this point relative to the center of the image, respectively.

❾ i' and j' are the coordinates of the pixel in the old image that will be rotated to this position in the new image, given by the previous formulae for st and ct.

❿ Finally, old is the index of the pixel in the old image.

To see the program working, we first need an image to rotate: Figure 5-1.

Figure 5-1. Image in need of rotation

Running the program like so results in the straightened image shown in Figure 5-2:

```
$ ./rotateimage 4 wonky.jpg straight.jpg
```

Figure 5-2. Straightened image

Let's check the performance of the program:

```
$ rm straight.jpg
$ ./rotateimage 4 wonky.jpg straight.jpg +RTS -s
...
  Total    time    0.69s  (  0.69s elapsed)
```

And see how much we can gain by running it in parallel, on four cores:

```
$ ./rotateimage 4 wonky.jpg straight.jpg +RTS -s -N4
...
  Total    time    0.76s  (  0.24s elapsed)
```

The result is a speedup of 2.88. However, this program spends 0.05s of its time reading and writing the image file (measured by modifying the program to omit the rotation step), and if we factor this into the results, we obtain a speedup for the parallel portion of the program of 3.39.

Summary

Repa provides a convenient framework for describing array operations and has some significant benefits:

- Intermediate arrays are automatically eliminated when array operations are composed (*fusion*).

- Operations like `computeP` and `foldP` automatically parallelize using the available cores.

There are a couple of gotchas to bear in mind:

- Repa relies heavily on GHC's optimizer and is quite sensitive to things like strictness annotations and `INLINE` pragmas. A good rule of thumb is to use both of these liberally. You might also need to use simpler code and fewer library functions so that GHC can see all of your code and optimize it.

- Don't forget to add the `-fllvm` option if your computer supports it.

There's much more to Repa that we haven't covered. For example, Repa has support for stencil convolutions: a common class of image-processing algorithms in which a transformation on each pixel is calculated as some function of the surrounding pixels. For certain kinds of stencil functions that are known at compile time, Repa can generate specialized code that runs extremely fast.

To learn more, take a look at the full Repa documentation on Hackage (*http://hackage.haskell.org/package/repa*).

CHAPTER 6
GPU Programming with Accelerate

The most powerful processor in your computer may not be the CPU. Modern graphics processing units (GPUs) usually have something on the order of 10 to 100 times more raw compute power than the general-purpose CPU. However, the GPU is a very different beast from the CPU, and we can't just run ordinary Haskell programs on it. A GPU consists of a large number of parallel processing units, each of which is much less powerful than one core of your CPU, so to unlock the power of a GPU we need a highly parallel workload. Furthermore, the processors of a GPU all run exactly the same code in lockstep, so they are suitable only for data-parallel tasks where the operations to perform on each data item are identical.

In recent years GPUs have become less graphics-specific and more suitable for performing general-purpose parallel processing tasks. However, GPUs are still programmed in a different way from the CPU because they have a different instruction set architecture. A special-purpose compiler is needed to compile code for the GPU, and the source code is normally written in a language that resembles a restricted subset of C. Two such languages are in widespread use: NVidia's CUDA and OpenCL. These languages are very low-level and expose lots of details about the workings of the GPU, such as how and when to move data between the CPU's memory and the GPU's memory.

Clearly, we would like to be able to make use of the vast computing power of the GPU from Haskell without having to write code in CUDA or OpenCL. This is where the Accelerate library comes in: Accelerate is an embedded domain-specific language (EDSL) for programming the GPU. It allows us to write Haskell code in a somewhat stylized form and have it run directly on the GPU. For certain tasks, we can obtain orders of magnitude speedup by using Accelerate.

During the course of this chapter, I'll be introducing the various concepts of Accelerate, starting with the basic data types and operations and progressing to full-scale examples that run on the GPU.

As with Repa in the previous chapter, I'll be illustrating many of the Accelerate operations by typing expressions into GHCi. Accelerate comes with an interpreter, which means that for experimenting with Accelerate code, you don't need a machine with a GPU. To play with examples yourself, first make sure the accelerate package is installed:

```
$ cabal install accelerate
```

The accelerate package provides the basic infrastructure, which includes the Data. Array. Accelerate module for constructing array computations, and Data.Array.Accelerate.Interpreter for interpreting them. To actually run an Accelerate computation on a GPU, you will also need a supported GPU card and the accelerate-cuda package; I'll cover that later in "Running on the GPU" on page 115.

When you have the accelerate package installed, you can start up GHCi and import the necessary modules:

```
$ ghci
Prelude> import Data.Array.Accelerate as A
Prelude A> import Data.Array.Accelerate.Interpreter as I
Prelude A I>
```

As we'll see, Accelerate shares many concepts with Repa. In particular, array shapes and indices are the same, and Accelerate also has the concept of shape-polymorphic operations like fold.

Overview

I mentioned earlier that Accelerate is an embedded domain-specific language for programming GPUs. More specifically, it is a deeply embedded DSL. This means that programs are written in Haskell syntax using operations of the library, but the method by which the program runs is different from a conventional Haskell program. A program fragment that uses Accelerate works like this:

- The Haskell code generates a data structure in an internal representation that the programmer doesn't get to see.

- This data structure is then compiled into GPU code using the accelerate-cuda package and run directly on the GPU. When you don't have a GPU, the accelerate package *interprets* the code instead, using Accelerate's built-in interpreter. Both methods give the same results, but of course running on the GPU should be far faster.

Both steps happen while the Haskell program is running; there's no extra compile step, apart from compiling the Haskell program itself.

By the magic of Haskell's overloading and abstraction facilities, the Haskell code that you write using Accelerate usually looks much like ordinary Haskell code, even though it generates another program rather than actually producing the result directly.

While reading this chapter, you probably want to have a copy of the Accelerate API documentation (*http://hackage.haskell.org/package/accelerate/*) at hand.

Arrays and Indices

As with Repa, Accelerate is a framework for programming with arrays. An Accelerate computation takes arrays as inputs and delivers one or more arrays as output. The type of Accelerate arrays has only two parameters, though:

```
data Array sh e
```

Here, e is the element type, and sh is the shape. There is no representation type. Even though Accelerate does have delayed arrays internally and compositions of array operations are fused in much the same way as in Repa, arrays are not explicitly tagged with a representation type.

Shapes and indices use the same data types as Repa (for more details see "Arrays, Shapes, and Indices" on page 86):

```
data Z = Z
data tail :. head = tail :. head
```

And there are some convenient type synonyms for common shapes:

```
type DIM0 = Z
type DIM1 = DIM0 :. Int
type DIM2 = DIM1 :. Int
```

Because arrays of dimensionality zero and one are common, the library provides type synonyms for those:

```
type Scalar e = Array DIM0 e
type Vector e = Array DIM1 e
```

You can build arrays and experiment with them in ordinary Haskell code using fromList:

```
fromList :: (Shape sh, Elt e) => sh -> [e] -> Array sh e
```

As we saw with Repa, we have to be careful to give GHC enough type information to fix the type of the indices (to Int), and the same is true in Accelerate. Let's build a 10-element vector using fromList:

```
> fromList (Z:.10) [1..10] :: Vector Int
Array (Z :. 10) [1,2,3,4,5,6,7,8,9,10]
```

Similarly, we can make a two-dimensional array, with three rows of five columns:

```
> fromList (Z:.3:.5) [1..] :: Array DIM2 Int
Array (Z :. 3 :. 5) [1,2,3,4,5,6,7,8,9,10,11,12,13,14,15]
```

The operation for indexing one of these arrays is indexArray:

```
> let arr = fromList (Z:.3:.5) [1..] :: Array DIM2 Int
> indexArray arr (Z:.2:.1)
12
```

(There is also a ! operator that performs indexing, but unlike indexArray it can only be used in the context of an Accelerate computation, which we'll see shortly.)

One thing to remember is that in Accelerate, arrays cannot be nested; it is impossible to build an array of arrays. This is because arrays must be able to be mapped directly into flat arrays on the GPU, which has no support for nested arrays.

We can, however, have arrays of tuples. For example:

```
> fromList (Z:.2:.3) (Prelude.zip [1..] [1..]) :: Array DIM2 (Int,Int)
Array (Z :. 2 :. 3) [(1,1),(2,2),(3,3),(4,4),(5,5),(6,6)]
```

Internally, Accelerate will translate an array of tuples into a tuple of arrays; this is done entirely automatically, and we don't need to worry about it. Arrays of tuples are a very useful structure, as we shall see.

Running a Simple Accelerate Computation

So far, we have been experimenting with arrays in the context of ordinary Haskell code; we haven't constructed an actual Accelerate computation over arrays yet. An Accelerate computation takes the form run *E*, where:

```
run :: Arrays a => Acc a -> a
```

The expression *E* has type Acc a, which means "an accelerated computation that delivers a value of type a." The Arrays class allows a to be either an array or a tuple of arrays. A value of type Acc a is really a data structure (we'll see in a moment how to build it), and the run function evaluates the data structure to produce a result. There are two versions of run: one exported by Data.Array.Accelerate.Interpreter that we will be using for experimentation and testing, and another exported by Data.Array.Accelerate. CUDA (in the accelerate-cuda package) that runs the computation on the GPU.

Let's try a very simple example. Starting with the 3×5 array of Int from the previous section, let's add one to every element:

```
> let arr = fromList (Z:.3:.5) [1..] :: Array DIM2 Int
> run $ A.map (+1) (use arr)
Array (Z :. 3 :. 5) [2,3,4,5,6,7,8,9,10,11,12,13,14,15,16]
```

Breaking this down, first we call A.map, which is the map function from Data.Array. Accelerate; recall that we used import Data.Array.Accelerate as A earlier. We have to use the qualified name, because there are two map functions in scope: A.map and Prelude.map.

Here is the type of A.map:

```
A.map :: (Shape ix, Elt a, Elt b)
      => (Exp a -> Exp b)
      -> Acc (Array ix a)
      -> Acc (Array ix b)
```

A few things will probably seem unusual about this type. First let's look at the second argument. This is the array to map over, but rather than just an Array ix a, it is an Acc (Array ix a)—that is, an array in the Accelerate world rather than the ordinary Haskell world. We need to somehow turn our Array DIM2 Int into an Acc (Array DIM2 Int). This is what the use function is for:

```
use :: Arrays arrays => arrays -> Acc arrays
```

The use function is the way to take arrays from Haskell and inject them into an Accelerate computation. This might actually involve copying the array from the computer's main memory into the GPU's memory.

The first argument to A.map has type Exp a -> Exp b. Here, Exp is a bit like Acc. It represents a computation in the world of Accelerate, but whereas Acc is a computation delivering an array, Exp is a computation delivering a single value.

In the example we passed (+1) as the first argument to map. This expression is overloaded in Haskell with type Num a => a -> a, and we're accustomed to seeing it used at types like Int -> Int and Double -> Double. Here, however, it is being used at type Exp Int -> Exp Int; this is possible because Accelerate provides an instance for Num (Exp a), so expressions built using integer constants and overloaded Num operations work just fine in the world of Exp.[1]

Here's another example, which squares every element in the array:

```
> run $ A.map (^2) (use arr)
Array (Z :. 3 :. 5) [1,4,9,16,25,36,49,64,81,100,121,144,169,196,225]
```

We can inject values into the Accelerate world with functions such as use (and some more that we'll see shortly), but the only way to get data *out* of an Accelerate computation is to run it with run, and then the result becomes available to the caller as an ordinary Haskell value.

---

1. This comes with a couple of extra constraints, which we won't go into here.

Type Classes: Elt, Arrays, and Shape

There are a few type classes that commonly appear in the operations from `Data.Array.Accelerate`. The types are restricted to a fixed set, and aside from this we don't need to know anything more about them; indeed, Accelerate hides the methods from the public API. Briefly, these are the three type classes you will encounter most often:

`Elt`
> The class of types that may be array elements. Includes all the usual numeric types, as well as indices and tuples. In types of the form `Exp e`, the `e` is often required to be an instance of `Elt`. Note in particular that arrays are not an instance of `Elt`; this is the mechanism by which Accelerate enforces that arrays cannot be nested.

`Arrays`
> This type class includes arrays and tuples of arrays. In `Acc a`, the `a` must always be an instance of the type class `Arrays`.

`Shape`
> The class of shapes and indices. This class includes only `Z` and `:.` and is used to ensure that values used as shapes and indices are constructed from these two types.

See the Accelerate documentation for a full list of the instances of each class.

Scalar Arrays

Sometimes we want to use a single value in a place where the API only allows an array; this is quite common in Accelerate because most operations are over arrays. For example, the result of `run` contains only arrays, not scalars, so if we want to return a single value, we have to wrap it in an array first. The `unit` operation is provided for this purpose:

```
unit :: Elt e => Exp e -> Acc (Scalar e)
```

Recall that `Scalar` is a type synonym for `Array DIM0`; an array with zero dimensions has only one element. Now we can return a single value from `run`:

```
> run $ unit (3::Exp Int)
Array (Z) [3]
```

The dual to `unit` is `the`, which extracts a single value from a `Scalar`:

```
the :: Elt e => Acc (Scalar e) -> Exp e
```

Indexing Arrays

The `!` operator indexes into an array:

```
(!) :: (Shape ix, Elt e) => Acc (Array ix e) -> Exp ix -> Exp e
```

Unlike the indexArray function that we saw earlier, the ! operator works in the Accelerate world; the array argument has type Acc (Array ix e), and the index is an Exp ix. So how do we get from an ordinary index like Z:.3 to an Exp (Z:.Int)? There is a handy function index1 for exactly this purpose:

```
index1 :: Exp Int -> Exp (Z :. Int)
```

So now we can index into an array. Putting these together in GHCi:

```
> let arr = fromList (Z:.10) [1..10] :: Array DIM1 Int
> run $ unit (use arr ! index1 3)
Array (Z) [4]
```

Creating Arrays Inside Acc

We saw earlier how to create arrays using fromList and then inject them into the Acc world with use. This is not a particularly efficient way to create arrays. Even if the compiler is clever enough to optimize away the intermediate list, the array data will still have to be copied over to the GPU's memory. So it's usually better to create arrays inside Acc. The Accelerate library provides a few ways to create arrays inside Acc; the simplest one is fill:

```
fill :: (Shape sh, Elt e) => Exp sh -> Exp e -> Acc (Array sh e)
```

The fill operation creates an array of the specified shape in which all elements have the same value. We can create arrays in which the elements are drawn from a sequence by using enumFromN and enumFromStepN:

```
enumFromN     :: (Shape sh, Elt e, IsNum e)
              => Exp sh -> Exp e -> Acc (Array sh e)

enumFromStepN :: (Shape sh, Elt e, IsNum e)
              => Exp sh -> Exp e -> Exp e -> Acc (Array sh e)
```

In enumFromN, the first argument is the shape and the second is the value of the first element. For example, enumFromN (index1 N) M is the same as use (fromList (Z:.N) [M..]).

The enumFromStepN function is the same, except that we can specify the increment between the element values. For instance, to create a two-dimensional array of shape three rows of five columns, where the elements are drawn from the sequence [15,14..]:

```
> run $ enumFromStepN (index2 3 5) 15 (-1) :: Array DIM2 Int
Array (Z :. 3 :. 5) [15,14,13,12,11,10,9,8,7,6,5,4,3,2,1]
```

Note that we used index2, the two-dimensional version of index1 that we saw earlier, to create the shape argument.

A more general way to create arrays is provided by generate:

```
generate :: (Shape ix, Elt a)
         => Exp ix -> (Exp ix -> Exp a)
         -> Acc (Array ix a)
```

This time, the values of the elements are determined by a user-supplied function from Exp ix to Exp a; that is, the function that will be applied to each index in the array to determine the element value at that position. This is exactly like the fromFunction operation we used in Repa, except that here we must supply a function in the Exp world rather than an arbitrary Haskell function.

For instance, to create a two-dimensional array in which every element is given by the sum of its x and y coordinates, we can use generate:

```
> run $ generate (index2 3 5) (\ix -> let Z:.y:.x = unlift ix in x + y)
Array (Z :. 3 :. 5) [0,1,2,3,4,1,2,3,4,5,2,3,4,5,6]
```

Let's look in more detail at the function argument:

```
\ix -> let Z:.y:.x = unlift ix in x + y
```

The function as a whole must have type Exp DIM2 -> Exp Int, and hence ix has type Exp DIM2. We need to extract the x and y values from the index, which means we need to deconstruct the Exp DIM2. The function unlift does this; in general, you should think of unlift as a way to take apart a structured value inside an Exp. It works for tuples and indices. In the previous example, we're using unlift at the following type:[2]

```
unlift :: Exp (Z :. Int :. Int) -> Z :. Exp Int :. Exp Int
```

The result is a DIM2 value in the Haskell world, so we can pattern match against Z:.x:.y to extract the x and y values, both of type Exp Int. Then x + y gives us the sum of x and y as an Exp Int, by virtue of the overloaded + operator.

There is a dual to unlift, unsurprisingly called lift, which does the opposite transformation. In fact, the index2 function that we used in the generate example earlier is defined in terms of lift:

```
index2 :: Exp Int -> Exp Int -> Exp DIM2
index2 i j = lift (Z :. i :. j)
```

This use of lift has the following type:

```
lift :: Z :. Exp Int :. Exp Int -> Exp (Z :. Int :. Int)
```

The lift and unlift functions are essential when we're working with indices in Accelerate, and as we'll see later, they're useful for working with tuples as well.

---

2. The unlift function is actually a method of the Unlift class, which has instances for indices (of any dimensionality) and various sizes of tuples. See the Accelerate documentation for details.

Zipping Two Arrays

The `zipWith` function combines two arrays to produce a third array by applying the supplied function to corresponding elements of the input arrays:

```
zipWith :: (Shape ix, Elt a, Elt b, Elt c)
        => (Exp a -> Exp b -> Exp c)
        -> Acc (Array ix a) -> Acc (Array ix b)
        -> Acc (Array ix c)
```

The first argument is the function to apply to each pair of elements, and the second and third arguments are the input arrays. For example, zipping two arrays with (+):

```
> let a = enumFromN (index2 2 3) 1 :: Acc (Array DIM2 Int)
> let b = enumFromStepN (index2 2 3) 6 (-1) :: Acc (Array DIM2 Int)
> run $ A.zipWith (+) a b
Array (Z :. 2 :. 3) [7,7,7,7,7,7]
```

Here we zipped together two arrays of identical shape, but what happens if the shapes are different? The type of `zipWith` requires that the input arrays have identical dimensionality, but the sizes of the dimensions might be different. For example, we'll use the same 2×3 array as before, but zip it with a 3×5 array containing elements [10, 20..]:

```
> let a = enumFromN (index2 2 3) 1 :: Acc (Array DIM2 Int)
> let b = enumFromStepN (index2 3 5) 10 10 :: Acc (Array DIM2 Int)
> run $ A.zipWith (+) a b
Array (Z :. 2 :. 3) [11,22,33,64,75,86]
```

What happened is that `zipWith` used the overlapping intersection of the two arrays. With two-dimensional arrays, you can visualize it like this: lay one array on top of the other, with their upper-left-hand corners at the same point, and pair together the elements that coincide. The final array has the shape of the overlapping portion of the two arrays.

Constants

We saw earlier that simple integer literals and numeric operations are automatically operations in Exp by virtue of being overloaded. But what if we already have an Int value and we need an Exp Int? This is what the function `constant` is for:

```
constant :: Elt t => t -> Exp t
```

Note that `constant` works only for instances of Elt, which you may recall is the class of types allowed to be array elements, including numeric types, indices, and tuples of Elts.

Example: Shortest Paths

As our first full-scale example, we'll again tackle the Floyd-Warshall shortest paths algorithm. For details of the algorithm, please see the Repa example in "Example: Computing Shortest Paths" on page 90; the algorithm here will be identical, except that we're going to run it on a GPU using Accelerate to see how much faster it goes.

Here are the type of graphs, represented as adjacency matrices:

fwaccel.hs

```
type Weight = Int32
type Graph = Array DIM2 Weight
```

The algorithm is a sequence of steps, each of which takes a value for k and a Graph as input and produces a new Graph. First, we'll write the code for an individual step before we see how to put multiple steps together. Here is the code for a step:

```
step :: Acc (Scalar Int) -> Acc Graph -> Acc Graph
step k g = generate (shape g) sp                        -- ❶
  where
    k' = the k                                          -- ❷

    sp :: Exp DIM2 -> Exp Weight
    sp ix = let
              (Z :. i :. j) = unlift ix                 -- ❸
            in
              A.min (g ! (index2 i j))                  -- ❹
                    (g ! (index2 i k') + g ! (index2 k' j))
```

❶ The step function takes two arguments: k, which is the iteration number, and g, which is the graph produced by the previous iteration. In each step, we're computing the lengths of the shortest paths between each two elements, using only vertices up to k. The graph from the previous iteration, g, gives us the lengths of the shortest paths using vertices up to k - 1. The result of this step is a new Graph, produced by calling the generate function. The new array has the same shape as g, and the elements of the array are determined by the function sp, defined in the where clause.

❷ The k argument is passed in as a scalar array; the sidebar explains why. To extract the value from the array, we call the.

❸ The sp function takes the index of an element in the array and returns the value of the element at that position. We need to unlift the input index to extract the two components, i and j.

❹ This is the core of the algorithm; to determine the length of the shortest path between i and j, we take the minimum of the previous shortest path from i to j, and the path that goes from i to k and then from k to j. All of these lookups in the g graph are performed using the ! operator, and using index2 to construct the indices.

Passing Inputs as Arrays

Why did we pass in the k value as an Acc (Scalar Int) rather than a plain Int? After all, we could use constant to convert an Int into an Exp Int that we could use with index2. The answer is quite subtle, and to understand it we first need to know a little more about how Accelerate works. When the program runs, the Accelerate library evaluates the expression passed to run to make a series of CUDA fragments (called *kernels*). Each kernel takes some arrays as inputs and produces arrays as outputs. In our example, each call to step will produce a kernel, and when we compose a sequence of step calls together, we get a series of kernels. Each kernel is a piece of CUDA code that has to be compiled and loaded onto the GPU; this can take a while, so Accelerate remembers the kernels it has seen before and tries to reuse them.

Our goal with step is to make a kernel that will be reused. If we don't reuse the same kernel for each step, the overhead of compiling new kernels will ruin the performance.

We can look at the code that Accelerate sees when it evaluates the argument to run by evaluating an Acc expression in GHCi. Here's what a typical call to step evaluates to:

```
> step (unit (constant 2)) (use (fromList (Z:.3:.3) [1..9]))
let a0 = use ((Array (Z :. 3 :. 3) [1,2,3,4,5,6,7,8,9]))
in let a1 = unit 2
    in generate
        (shape a0)
        (\x0 -> ...)
```

I've omitted the innards of the generate argument for space, but by all means try it yourself. The important thing to notice here is the line let a1 = unit 2; this is the scalar array for the k argument to step, and it is outside the call to generate. The generate function is what turns into the CUDA kernel, and to arrange that we get the same CUDA kernel each time we need the arguments to generate to remain constant.

Now see what happens if we change step so that it takes an Int as an argument instead. I've replaced the Acc (Scalar Int) with Int, and changed k' = the k to k' = constant k.

```
> step 2 (use (fromList (Z:.3:.3) [1..9]))
let a0 = use ((Array (Z :. 3 :. 3) [1,2,3,4,5,6,7,8,9]))
in generate
    (shape a0)
```

```
(\x0 -> min (let x1 = 2
            in ... ))
```

Previously, the code created by k was defined outside the generate call, but now the definition let x1 = 2 is embedded inside the call. Hence each generate call will have a different k value embedded in it, which will defeat Accelerate's caching of CUDA kernels.

The rule of thumb is that if you're running a sequence of array operations inside Acc, make sure that the things that change are always passed in as arrays and not embedded in the code as constants.

How can you tell if you get it wrong? One way is to look at the code as we just did. Another way is to use the debugging options provided by the accelerate-cuda package, which are described briefly in "Debugging the CUDA Backend" on page 116.

Now that we have the step function, we can write the wrapper that composes the sequence of step calls together:

```
shortestPathsAcc :: Int -> Acc Graph -> Acc Graph
shortestPathsAcc n g0 = foldl1 (>->) steps g0          -- ❶
  where
  steps :: [ Acc Graph -> Acc Graph ]                  -- ❷
  steps = [ step (unit (constant k)) | k <- [0 .. n-1] ] -- ❸
```

❷   First we construct a list of the steps, where each takes a Graph and delivers a Graph.

❸   The list of steps is constructed by applying step to each value of k in the sequence 0 .. n-1, wrapping the k values up as scalar arrays using unit and constant.

❶   To put the sequence together, Accelerate provides a special operation designed for this task:

```
(>->) :: (Arrays a, Arrays b, Arrays c)
      => (Acc a -> Acc b) -> (Acc b -> Acc c) -> Acc a -> Acc c
```

This is called the pipeline operator, because it is used to connect two Acc computations together in a pipeline, where the output from the first is fed into the input of the second. We could achieve this with simple function composition, but the advantage of using the >-> operator is that it tells Accelerate that there is no sharing between the two computations, and any intermediate arrays used by the first computation can be garbage-collected when the second begins. Without this operator, it is possible to fill up memory when running algorithms with many iterations. So our shortestPathsAcc function connects together the sequence of step calls by left-folding with >-> and then passes g0 as the input to the pipeline.

Now that we have defined the complete computation, we can write a function that wraps run around it:

```
shortestPaths :: Graph -> Graph
shortestPaths g0 = run (shortestPathsAcc n (use g0))
  where
    Z :. _ :. n = arrayShape g0
```

We can try the program on test data, using the Accelerate interpreter:

```
> shortestPaths testGraph
Array (Z :. 6 :. 6) [0,16,999,13,20,20,19,0,999,5,4,9,11,27,0,24,31,31,18,3,
999,0,7,7,15,4,999,1,0,8,11,17,999,14,21,0]
```

Running on the GPU

To run the program on a real GPU, you'll need a supported GPU card and some additional software. Consult the Accelerate documentation to help you get things set up. Then install the accelerate-cuda package:

```
$ cabal install accelerate-cuda -fdebug
```

I've enabled debugging support here with the -fdebug flag, which lets us pass some extra options to the program to see what the GPU is doing.

To use Accelerate's CUDA support, we need to use:

```
import Data.Array.Accelerate.CUDA
```

in place of:

```
import Data.Array.Accelerate.Interpreter
```

A version of the shortest paths program that has this is in fwaccel-gpu.hs. Compile it in the usual way:

```
$ ghc -O2 fwaccel.hs -threaded
```

The program includes a benchmarking wrapper that generates a large graph over which to run the algorithm. Let's run it on a graph with 2,000 nodes:[3]

```
$ ./fwaccel 2000 +RTS -s
...
  Total   time   14.71s ( 16.25s elapsed)
```

For comparison, I tried the Repa version of this program on a graph of the same size, using seven cores on the same machine:[4]

---

3. These results were obtained on an Amazon EC2 Cluster GPU instance that had an NVidia Tesla card. I used CUDA version 4.

4. Using all eight cores was slower than using seven.

```
$ ./fwdense1 2000 +RTS -s -N7
...
   Total   time   259.78s  ( 40.13s elapsed)
```

So the Accelerate program running on the GPU is significantly faster than Repa. Moreover, about 3.5s of the runtime of the Accelerate program is taken up by initializing the
GPU on this machine, which we can see by running the program with a small input
size.

Debugging the CUDA Backend

When the accelerate-cuda package is compiled with -fdebug, there are a few extra
debugging options available. These are the most useful ones:

-dverbose
   Prints some information about the type and capabilities of the GPU being used.

-ddump-cc
   Prints information about CUDA kernels as they are compiled and run. Using this
   option will tell you whether your program is generating the number of kernels that
   you were expecting.

For a more complete list, see the *accelerate-cuda.cabal* file in the accelerate-cuda
package sources.

Example: A Mandelbrot Set Generator

In this second example, we'll build a Mandelbrot set generator that runs on the GPU.
The end result will be the picture in Figure 6-1. Generating an image of the Mandelbrot
set is a naturally parallel process—each pixel is independent of the others—but there
are some aspects to this problem that make it an interesting example to program using
Accelerate. In particular, we'll see how to use conditionals and to work with arrays of
tuples.

Figure 6-1. Mandelbrot set picture generated on the GPU

The Mandelbrot set is a mathematical construction over the *complex plane*, which is the two-dimensional plane of complex numbers. A particular point is said to be in the set if, when the following equation is repeatedly applied, the magnitude of z (written as $|z|$) does not diverge to infinity:

$$z_{(n+1)} = c + z_n^2$$

where c is the point on the plane (a complex number), and $z_0 = c$.

In practice, we iterate the equation for a fixed number of times, and if it has not diverged at that point, we declare the point to be in the set. Furthermore, to generate a pretty picture, we remember the iteration at which each point diverged and map the iteration values to a color gradient.

We know that $|z|$ will definitely diverge if it is greater than 2. The magnitude of a complex number $x + iy$ is given by $\sqrt{(x^2 + y^2)}$, so we can simplify the condition by squaring both sides, giving us this condition for divergence: $x^2 + y^2 > 4$.

Let's express this using Accelerate. First, we want a type for complex numbers. Accelerate lets us work with tuples, so we can represent complex numbers as pairs of floating point numbers. Not all GPUs can work with Doubles, so for the best compatibility we'll use Float:

mandel/mandel.hs

```
type F           = Float
type Complex     = (F,F)
type ComplexPlane = Array DIM2 Complex
```

We'll be referring to Float a lot, so the F type synonym helps to keep things readable.

The following function, next, embodies the main Mandelbrot formula: it computes the next value of *z* for a given point *c*.

```
next :: Exp Complex -> Exp Complex -> Exp Complex
next c z = c `plus` (z `times` z)
```

We can't use the normal + and * operations here, because there is no instance of Num for Exp Complex. In other words, Accelerate doesn't know how to add or multiply our complex numbers, so we have to define these operations ourselves. First, plus:

```
plus :: Exp Complex -> Exp Complex -> Exp Complex
plus a b = ...
```

To sum two complex numbers, we need to sum the components. But how can we access the components? We cannot pattern match on Exp Complex. There are a few different ways to do it, and we'll explore them briefly. Accelerate provides operations for selecting the components of pairs in Exp, namely:

```
fst :: (Elt a, Elt b) => Exp (a, b) -> Exp a
snd :: (Elt a, Elt b) => Exp (a, b) -> Exp b
```

So we could write plus like this:

```
plus :: Exp Complex -> Exp Complex -> Exp Complex
plus a b = ...
  where
    ax = A.fst a
    ay = A.snd a
    bx = A.fst b
    by = A.snd b
```

But how do we construct the result? We want to write something like (ax+bx, ay+by), but this has type (Exp F, Exp F), whereas we want Exp (F,F). Fortunately the lift function that we saw earlier performs this transformation, so the result is:

```
plus :: Exp Complex -> Exp Complex -> Exp Complex
plus a b = lift (ax+bx, ay+by)
  where
    ax = A.fst a
    ay = A.snd a
    bx = A.fst b
    by = A.snd b
```

In fact, we could do a little better, since `A.fst` and `A.snd` are just instances of `unlift`, and we could do them both in one go:

```
plus :: Exp Complex -> Exp Complex -> Exp Complex
plus a b = lift (ax+bx, ay+by)
  where
    (ax, ay) = unlift a
    (bx, by) = unlift b
```

Unfortunately, if you try this you will find that there isn't enough type information for GHC, so we have to help it out a bit:

```
plus :: Exp Complex -> Exp Complex -> Exp Complex
plus a b = lift (ax+bx, ay+by)
  where
    (ax, ay) = unlift a :: (Exp F, Exp F)
    (bx, by) = unlift b :: (Exp F, Exp F)
```

We can go a little further because Accelerate provides some utilities that wrap a function in `lift` and `unlift`. For a two-argument function, the right variant is called `lift2`:

```
plus :: Exp Complex -> Exp Complex -> Exp Complex
plus = lift2 f
  where f :: (Exp F, Exp F) -> (Exp F, Exp F) -> (Exp F, Exp F)
        f (x1,y1) (x2,y2) = (x1+x2,y1+y2)
```

Unfortunately, again we had to add the type signature to get it to typecheck, but it does aid readability. This is perhaps as close to "natural" as we can get for this definition: the necessary lifting and unlifting are confined to just one place.

We also need to define `times`, which follows the same pattern as `plus`, although of course this time we are multiplying the two complex numbers together:

```
times :: Exp Complex -> Exp Complex -> Exp Complex
times = lift2 f
  where f :: (Exp F, Exp F) -> (Exp F, Exp F) -> (Exp F, Exp F)
        f (ax,ay) (bx,by)   = (ax*bx-ay*by, ax*by+ay*bx)
```

So now we can compute z_{n+1} given z and c. But we need to think about the program as a whole. For each point, we need to iterate this process until divergence, and then remember the number of iterations at which divergence happened. This creates a small problem: GPUs are designed to do the *same thing* to lots of different data at the same time, whereas we want to do something different depending on whether or not a particular point has diverged. So in practice, we can't do what we would normally do in a single-threaded language and iterate each point until divergence. Instead, we must find a way to apply the same operation to every element of the array for a fixed number of iterations.

There is a conditional operation in Accelerate, with this type:

```
(?) :: Elt t => Exp Bool -> (Exp t, Exp t) -> Exp t
```

The first argument is an `Exp Bool`, and the second argument is a pair of expressions. If the Boolean evaluates to true, the result is the first component of the pair; otherwise it is the second.

However, as a rule of thumb, using conditionals in GPU code is considered "bad" because conditionals cause *SIMD divergence*. This means that when the GPU hits a conditional instruction, it first runs all the threads that take the true branch and then runs the threads that take the false branch. Of course if you have nested conditionals, the amount of parallelism rapidly disappears.

We can't avoid *some* kind of conditional in the Mandelbrot example, but we can make sure there is only a bounded amount of divergence by having just one conditional per iteration and a fixed number of iterations. The trick we'll use is to keep a pair (z,i) for every array element, where i is the iteration at which that point diverged. So at each iteration, we do the following:

- Compute `z' = next c z`.
- If it is greater than four, the result is `(z,i)`.
- Otherwise, the result is `(z',i+1)`

The implementation of this sequence is the `iter` function, defined as follows:

```
iter :: Exp Complex -> Exp (Complex,Int) -> Exp (Complex,Int)
iter c p =
  let
     (z,i) = unlift p :: (Exp Complex, Exp Int)    -- ❶
     z' = next c z                                 -- ❷
  in
  (dot z' >* 4.0) ?                                -- ❸
    ( p                                            -- ❹
    , lift (z', i+1)                               -- ❺
    )
```

❶ The first thing to do is `unlift p` so we can access the components of the pair.

❷ Next, we compute `z'` by calling `next`.

❸ Now that we have `z'` we can do the conditional test using the `?` operator. The `dot` function computes $x^2 + y^2$ where x and y are the components of z; it follows the same pattern as `plus` and `times` so I've omitted its definition.

❹ If the condition evaluates to true, we just return the original `p`.

❺ In the false case, then we return the new `z'` and `i+1`.

The algorithm needs two arrays: one array of `c` values that will be constant throughout the computation, and a second array of `(z,i)` values that will be recomputed by each iteration. Our arrays are two-dimensional arrays indexed by pixel coordinates because the aim is to generate a picture from the iteration values at each pixel.

The initial complex plane of c values is generated by a function genPlane:

```
genPlane :: F -> F
         -> F -> F
         -> Int
         -> Int
         -> Acc ComplexPlane
```

Its definition is rather long so I've omitted it here, but essentially it is a call to generate ("Creating Arrays Inside Acc" on page 109).

From the initial complex plane we can generate the initial array of (z,i) values, which is done by initializing each z to the corresponding c value and i to zero. In the code, this can be found in the mkinit function.

Now we can put the pieces together and write the code for the complete algorithm:

```
mandelbrot :: F -> F -> F -> F -> Int -> Int -> Int
           -> Acc (Array DIM2 (Complex,Int))

mandelbrot x y x' y' screenX screenY max_depth
  = iterate go zs0 !! max_depth           -- ❶
  where
    cs  = genPlane x y x' y' screenX screenY -- ❷
    zs0 = mkinit cs                         -- ❸

    go :: Acc (Array DIM2 (Complex,Int))
       -> Acc (Array DIM2 (Complex,Int))
    go = A.zipWith iter cs                  -- ❹
```

❷   cs is our static complex plane generated by genPlane.

❸   zs0 is the initial array of (z,i) values.

❹   The function go performs one iteration, producing a new array of (z,i), and it is expressed by zipping iter over both cs and the current array of (z,i).

❶   To perform all the iterations, we simply call the ordinary list function iterate:

```
iterate :: (a -> a) -> a -> [a]
```

and take the element at position depth, which corresponds to the go function having been applied depth times. Note that in this case, we don't want to use the pipeline operator >-> because the iterations share the array cs.

The complete program has code to produce an output file in PNG format, by turning the Accelerate array into a Repa array and then using the repa-devil library that we saw in "Example: Image Rotation" on page 97. To compile the program, install the `accelerate` and `accelerate-cuda` packages as before, and then:

```
$ ghc -O2 -threaded mandel.hs
```

Then generate a nice big image (again, this is running on an Amazon EC2 Cluster GPU instance):

```
$ rm out.png; ./mandel --size=4000 +RTS -s
...
  Total   time    8.40s ( 10.56s elapsed)
```

PART II

Concurrent Haskell

Concurrent Haskell is the collective name for the facilities that Haskell provides for programming with multiple threads of control. Unlike parallel programming, where the goal is to make the program run faster by using more CPUs, the goal in concurrent programming is usually to write a program with multiple interactions. These interactions might be with the user via a user interface of some kind, with other systems, or indeed between different subsystems within the same program. Concurrency allows us to write a program in which each of these interactions is described separately but all happen at the same time. As we shall see, concurrency is a powerful tool for structuring programs with multiple interactions.

In many application areas today, some kind of concurrency is a necessity. A typical user-facing application will have an interface that must remain responsive while the application is downloading data from the network or calculating some results. Often these applications may be interacting with multiple servers over the network at the same time; a web browser, for example, will have many concurrent connections open to the sites that the user is browsing, while all the time maintaining a responsive user interface. Server-side applications also need concurrency in order to manage multiple client interactions simultaneously.

Haskell takes the view that concurrency is a useful abstraction because it allows each interaction to be programmed separately, resulting in greater modularity. Abstractions should not be too expensive because then we won't use them—hence GHC provides lightweight threads so that concurrency can be used for a wide range of applications, without needing to worry about the overhead.

Haskell's philosophy is to provide a set of very simple but general features that you can use to build higher-level functionality. So while the built-in functionality may seem quite sparse, in practice it is general enough to implement elaborate abstractions. Furthermore, because these abstractions are not built in, you can make your own choices about which programming model to adopt, or to program down to the low-level interfaces for performance.

Therefore, to learn Concurrent Haskell, we can start from the low-level interfaces and then explore how to combine them and build on top to create higher-level abstractions, which is exactly the approach taken in this book. The aim is that by building up the implementations of higher-level abstractions using the low-level features, the higher-level abstractions will be more accessible and less mysterious than if we had just described an API. Furthermore, by seeing examples of how to build higher-level abstractions, you should be able to go away and build your own variations or entirely new libraries.

Haskell does not take a stance on which concurrent programming model is best: actors, shared memory, and transactions are all supported, for example. (Conversely, Haskell *does* take a stance on parallel programming; we strongly recommend that you use one of the deterministic programming models from Part I for parallel programming.) Haskell provides all of these concurrent programming models and more—but this flexibility is a double-edged sword. The advantage is that you can choose from a wide range of tools and pick the one best suited to the task at hand, but the disadvantage is that it can be hard to decide which tool is best for the job. Hopefully by demonstrating a series of examples using each of the programming models that Haskell provides, this book will help you develop an intuition for which tool to pick for your own projects.

In the following chapters we're going on a tour of Concurrent Haskell, starting with the basics of threads and communication in Chapter 7 through Chapter 10, moving on to some higher-level abstractions in Chapter 11, and then we'll look at how to build multithreaded network applications in Chapter 12. Chapter 13 deals with using Concurrent Haskell to achieve parallelism, and in Chapter 14 we look at writing distributed programs that run on multiple computers. Finally, Chapter 15 will present some techniques for debugging and performance-tuning and talk about the interaction between Concurrent Haskell and foreign code.

CHAPTER 7

Basic Concurrency: Threads and MVars

The fundamental action in concurrency is forking a new thread of control. In Concurrent Haskell, this is achieved with the forkIO operation:

```
forkIO :: IO () -> IO ThreadId
```

The forkIO operation takes a computation of type IO () as its argument; that is, a computation in the IO monad that eventually delivers a value of type (). The computation passed to forkIO is executed in a new thread that runs concurrently with the other threads in the system. If the thread has effects, those effects will be interleaved in an indeterminate fashion with the effects from other threads.

To illustrate the interleaving of effects, let's try a simple example with two threads, one that repeatedly prints the letter A while the other repeatedly prints B:

fork.hs

```
import Control.Concurrent
import Control.Monad
import System.IO

main = do
  hSetBuffering stdout NoBuffering          -- ❶
  forkIO (replicateM_ 100000 (putChar 'A')) -- ❷
  replicateM_ 100000 (putChar 'B')          -- ❸
```

❶ Put the output Handle into nonbuffered mode, so that we can see the interleaving more clearly.

❷ Create a thread to print the character A 100,000 times.

❸ In the main thread, print B 100,000 times.

Try running the program; it should produce output similar to this:

```
AAAAAAAAABABABABABABABABABABABABABABABABABABABABAB
ABABABABABABABABABABABABABABABABABABABABABABABABAB
ABABABABABABABABABABABABABABABABABABABABABABABABAB
ABABABABABABABABABABABABABABABABABABABABABABABABAB
```

The output might have a different pattern, depending on the particular version of GHC that you use to run the test. In this case, we sometimes see strings of a single letter and sometimes a regular alternation between the two letters. Strings of a single letter are to be expected; the runtime system runs one thread for a "time slice" and then switches to the other thread.[1] But why do we see sequences where each thread only gets a chance to output a single letter before switching? The threads in this example are contending for a single resource, the stdout Handle, so the behavior is affected by how contention for this resource is managed by the runtime system. We'll see later how GHC's fairness policy gives rise to the ABABABA behavior seen here.

A Simple Example: Reminders

The following program illustrates the creation of threads in a program that implements timed reminders. The user enters a number of seconds, and after the specified time has elapsed, the program prints a message and emits a beep.[2] Any number of reminders can be active simultaneously.

We'll need an operation that waits for some time to elapse:

```
threadDelay :: Int -> IO ()
```

The function threadDelay takes an argument representing a number of microseconds and waits for that amount of time before returning.

reminders.hs

```
import Control.Concurrent
import Text.Printf
import Control.Monad

main =
  forever $ do
    s <- getLine        -- ❶
    forkIO $ setReminder s -- ❷

setReminder :: String -> IO ()
setReminder s  = do
  let t = read s :: Int
  printf "Ok, I'll remind you in %d seconds\n" t
```

---

1. The length of the time slice is typically 1/50 of a second, but it can be set manually; the options for doing this will be discussed later in "RTS Options to Tweak" on page 284.

2. We regret that the audio functionality is available only on certain platforms.

```
    threadDelay (10^6 * t)                   -- ❸
    printf "%d seconds is up! BING!\BEL\n" t -- ❹
```

The program works by creating a thread for each new request for a reminder:

❶   Waits for input from the user.

❷   Creates a new thread to handle this reminder.

❸   The new thread, after printing a confirmation message, waits for the specified number of seconds using threadDelay.

❹   Finally, when threadDelay returns, the reminder message is printed.

For example:

```
$ ./reminders
2
Ok, I'll remind you in 2 seconds
3
Ok, I'll remind you in 3 seconds
4
Ok, I'll remind you in 4 seconds
2 seconds is up! BING!
3 seconds is up! BING!
4 seconds is up! BING!
```

Let's extend this example to allow the user to terminate the program by entering exit instead of a number. We need to modify only the main function:

reminders2.hs

```
main = loop
  where
    loop = do
      s <- getLine
      if s == "exit"
        then return ()
        else do forkIO $ setReminder s
                loop
```

Instead of forever, we now use a recursive loop, and we choose to return from the loop if the string entered was "exit"; otherwise, we create a new thread as before and loop again. Returning from the loop causes main itself to return, which ends the program.

Now we can terminate the program, even if there are outstanding reminders:

```
$ ./reminders2
2
Ok, I'll remind you in 2 seconds
3
Ok, I'll remind you in 3 seconds
2 seconds is up! BING!
```

```
exit
$
```

This tells us something important about how threads work in Haskell: *the program terminates when main returns, even if there are other threads still running.* The other threads simply stop running and cease to exist after main returns.

Why does Haskell make this design decision, when in many cases it would be more useful to wait for all the concurrent threads to finish before terminating the program? Haskell's approach is to give you the simplest possible interface that allows you to program whatever behavior you need, and waiting for threads is an additional service that can be implemented using the facilities provided by Concurrent Haskell. Higher-level interfaces can be provided by libraries. If you don't like the behavior provided by a certain library, you can always modify it or write your own.

In "MVar as a Simple Channel: A Logging Service" on page 130, we'll see one way to wait for a thread to terminate. In Chapter 8, we will build a more general interface for waiting for threads, which will be developed further in the following chapters.

Communication: MVars

So far, we have learned how to create threads, but they can't talk to each other. In this section we'll introduce MVar, the basic communication mechanism provided by Concurrent Haskell.

The API for MVar is as follows:

```
data MVar a  -- abstract

newEmptyMVar :: IO (MVar a)
newMVar      :: a -> IO (MVar a)
takeMVar     :: MVar a -> IO a
putMVar      :: MVar a -> a -> IO ()
```

An MVar can be thought of as a box that is either empty or full. The newEmptyMVar operation creates a new empty box, and newMVar creates a new full box containing the value passed as its argument. The takeMVar operation removes the value from a full MVar and returns it, but waits (or *blocks*) if the MVar is currently empty. Symmetrically, the putMVar operation puts a value into the MVar but blocks if the MVar is already full.

The following sequence of small examples should help to illustrate how MVars work. First, this program passes a single value from one thread to another:

mvar1.hs

```
main = do
  m <- newEmptyMVar
  forkIO $ putMVar m 'x'
```

```
  r <- takeMVar m
  print r
```

The MVar is empty when it is created, the child thread puts the value x into it, and the main thread takes the value and prints it. If the main thread calls takeMVar before the child thread has put the value, no problem: takeMVar blocks until the value is available.

This second example passes *two* values from the child thread to the main thread:

mvar2.hs

```
main = do
  m <- newEmptyMVar
  forkIO $ do putMVar m 'x'; putMVar m 'y'
  r <- takeMVar m
  print r
  r <- takeMVar m
  print r
```

The output when we run the program will be 'x' followed by 'y'. An MVar can be used in this way as a simple channel between two threads, or even between many writers and a single reader. We will see a realistic example of this use case shortly.

What happens if a thread blocks in takeMVar but there is no other thread to perform the corresponding putMVar? For example:

mvar3.hs

```
main = do
  m <- newEmptyMVar
  takeMVar m
```

If we run the program, we should see this:

```
$ ./mvar3
mvar3: thread blocked indefinitely in an MVar operation
```

The runtime system detects that the takeMVar operation in the main thread is blocked forever and throws a special exception called BlockedIndefinitelyOnMVar. In practice, this means that if you accidentally write a program that contains a deadlock, in many cases the program will fail with an exception rather than just hanging, which is useful for debugging. We'll return to cover deadlock detection in more detail in "Detecting Deadlock" on page 278.

The MVar is a fundamental building block that generalizes many different communication and synchronization patterns, and over the next few sections we shall see examples of these various use cases. To summarize the main ways in which an MVar can be used:

- An MVar is a *one-place channel*, which means that it can be used for passing messages between threads, but it can hold at most one message at a time.

- An MVar is a *container for shared mutable state*. For example, a common design pattern in Concurrent Haskell, when several threads need read and write access to some state, is to represent the state value as an ordinary immutable Haskell data structure stored in an MVar. Modifying the state consists of taking the current value with takeMVar (which implicitly acquires a lock), and then placing a new value back in the MVar with putMVar (which implicitly releases the lock again).

  Sometimes the mutable state is not a Haskell data structure; it might be stored in C code or on the filesystem, for example. In such cases, we can use an MVar with a dummy value such as () to act as a lock on the external state, where takeMVar acquires the lock and putMVar releases it again.[3]

- An MVar is a *building block* for constructing larger concurrent Datastructures.

The next three sections give examples of each of these use cases in turn.

MVar as a Simple Channel: A Logging Service

A logging service is a thread to which the rest of the program can send messages, and it is the job of the logger to record those messages somewhere. For example, the logger might just print the messages to the screen, or store them in a file, or perhaps forward them over the network to a separate machine that collects logs from multiple sources.

Logging is usually a fire-and-forget activity. We care that the log messages from any given thread come out in the right order, but we don't need to wait until the logger has actually recorded each message before we go on to do something else. Therefore, running the logging service in a separate thread means that logging can take place concurrently with other activity in the system, which means that we can overlap the input/output performed by the logger with other activity in the program.

In this section, we implement a simple logging service in Concurrent Haskell using an MVar for communication. The logging service will have the following API:

```
data Logger

initLogger :: IO Logger
logMessage :: Logger -> String -> IO ()
logStop    :: Logger -> IO ()
```

There is an abstract data type called Logger that represents a handle to the logging service, and a new logging service is created by calling initLogger. The handle is required to perform a logging action—having Logger be a value that we pass around rather than a globally known top-level value is good practice; it means we could have multiple loggers, for example.

---

3. It works perfectly well the other way around, too; just be sure to be consistent about the policy.

There are two operations that we can perform: logMessage takes a String and logs it, and logStop causes the logging service to terminate. The latter operation is important because if we want to shut down the program, we need to be sure that the logging service has finished processing any outstanding requests. Recall from "A Simple Example: Reminders" on page 126 that when the main thread exits, the program terminates immediately rather than waiting for other threads to terminate first. Hence logStop has an extra requirement: it must not return until the logging service has processed all outstanding requests and stopped.

The implementation is given in the following code fragments. First, the data type Logger:

logger.hs

```
data Logger = Logger (MVar LogCommand)

data LogCommand = Message String | Stop (MVar ())
```

The Logger is just an MVar that we use as a channel for communication with the logging thread. Requests are made by placing a LogCommand in the MVar, and the logging thread will process requests one at a time by taking them from the MVar.

There are two kinds of requests that we can make, and so LogCommand is a data type with two constructors. The first, Message, is straightforward; it simply contains a String that we want to log. The second, Stop, obviously represents the message requesting that the logging thread terminate, but it contains a field of type MVar (). This enables the sender of the Stop message to wait for a reply from the logging thread that indicates it has finished. We'll see how this works in a moment.

The initLogger function creates a new logging service:

```
initLogger :: IO Logger
initLogger = do
  m <- newEmptyMVar
  let l = Logger m
  forkIO (logger l)
  return l
```

This is straightforward: just create an empty MVar for the channel and fork a thread to perform the service. The thread will run the function logger, which is defined as follows:

```
logger :: Logger -> IO ()
logger (Logger m) = loop
  where
   loop = do
     cmd <- takeMVar m
     case cmd of
       Message msg -> do
         putStrLn msg
         loop
       Stop s -> do
```

```
            putStrLn "logger: stop"
            putMVar s ()
```

The logger is implemented with a recursive `loop`. The `loop` function retrieves the next `LogCommand` from the `MVar` and inspects it. If it is a `Message`, this simple logger just prints the message using `putStrLn` and recursively invokes `loop`. If it is a `Stop` command, the logger emits a log message to say that it is stopping, replies to the initiator of the `Stop` by putting the unit value `()` into the `MVar` from the `Stop` command, and then returns without calling `loop` again, which causes the logger thread to exit.

Next we have the implementation of `logMessage`, which is the function that a client uses to log a message.

```
logMessage :: Logger -> String -> IO ()
logMessage (Logger m) s = putMVar m (Message s)
```

This is simple. Just put a `Message` command in the `MVar`. Next up, `logStop`:

```
logStop :: Logger -> IO ()
logStop (Logger m) = do
  s <- newEmptyMVar
  putMVar m (Stop s)
  takeMVar s
```

We have to create an empty `MVar` to hold the response and then send a `Stop` command to the logger containing the new empty `MVar`. After sending the command, we call `takeMVar` on the new `MVar` to wait for the response. After the logging thread has processed the `Stop` command, it puts `()` into this `MVar`, which allows the `takeMVar` to continue and `logStop` to return.

We can test our logger with a simple `main` function:

logger.hs

```
main :: IO ()
main = do
  l <- initLogger
  logMessage l "hello"
  logMessage l "bye"
  logStop l
```

If we run the program, we should see this:

```
$ ./logger
hello
bye
logger: stop
```

Does this logger achieve what we set out to do? The `logMessage` function can return immediately provided the `MVar` is already empty, and then the logger will proceed concurrently with the caller of `logMessage`. However, if there are multiple threads trying to log messages at the same time, it seems likely that the logging thread would not be able to process the messages fast enough and most of the threads would get blocked in logMessage while waiting for the MVar to become empty. This is because the MVar is only a one-place channel. If it could hold more messages, we would gain greater concurrency when multiple threads need to call logMessage simultaneously. In "MVar as a Building Block: Unbounded Channels" on page 135, we will see how to use MVar to build fully buffered channels.

MVar as a Container for Shared State

Concurrent programs often need to share some state between multiple threads. Furthermore, we usually need to be able to perform complex operations on the state, in a way that makes these operations appear atomic from the point of view of the other threads. Other threads should not be able to observe intermediate states during a complex operation, nor should they be able to initiate their own operations while another operation is in progress.

Traditional imperative languages achieve this using "locks," whereby to operate on the state (including reading it) a thread must acquire a lock, perform the operation, and then release the lock. Only one thread is allowed to hold the lock at any given time, so the acquisition of a lock must block until the lock is available.

MVar provides the combination of a lock and a mutable variable in Haskell. To acquire the lock, we take the MVar, whereas, to update the variable and release the lock, we put the MVar.[4]

The following example models a phone book as a piece of mutable state that may be concurrently modified and inspected by multiple threads. First, we define the types:

phonebook.hs

```
type Name        = String
type PhoneNumber = String
type PhoneBook   = Map Name PhoneNumber

newtype PhoneBookState = PhoneBookState (MVar PhoneBook)
```

A PhoneBook is a mapping from names to phone numbers represented by Haskell's Map type from the Data.Map library. To make this into a piece of shared mutable state, all we need to do is wrap it in an MVar. Here, we have made a new type called PhoneBookState to contain the MVar. This is simply good practice. If we were to make this interface into

---

4. It is worth noting that while MVar is somewhat easier to use than locks in an imperative language, some of the same problems that plague locks also affect MVar, such as the potential to cause accidental deadlock by taking locks in the wrong order. Fortunately, there are solutions to these problems, which we will discuss in Chapter 10.

a library, the `PhoneBookState` type could be exported abstractly so that clients could not see or depend on its implementation.

Making a new `PhoneBookState` is straightforward:

```
new :: IO PhoneBookState
new = do
  m <- newMVar Map.empty
  return (PhoneBookState m)
```

Now to implement `insert`, the operation that allows a thread to insert a new entry in the phone book:

```
insert :: PhoneBookState -> Name -> PhoneNumber -> IO ()
insert (PhoneBookState m) name number = do
  book <- takeMVar m
  putMVar m (Map.insert name number book)
```

We call `takeMVar` to get the current `PhoneBook`, which has the effect of locking the state against concurrent updates. Any other thread attempting to update the state will now block in `takeMVar`. Then, `putMVar` simultaneously unlocks the state and updates it with the new value, which we construct by calling `Map.insert` to insert the new entry into the phone book.

Next, we'll create a `lookup` operation that allows us to query the phone book for a particular name:

```
lookup :: PhoneBookState -> Name -> IO (Maybe PhoneNumber)
lookup (PhoneBookState m) name = do
  book <- takeMVar m
  putMVar m book
  return (Map.lookup name book)
```

Note that we need to put back the state after taking it; otherwise, the state would remain locked after `lookup` returns.

Now we can test our data structure with a simple `main` function that inserts a few entries in a phone book and then does a couple of `lookup`s:

phonebook.hs

```
main = do
  s <- new
  sequence_ [ insert s ("name" ++ show n) (show n) | n <- [1..10000] ]
  lookup s "name999" >>= print
  lookup s "unknown" >>= print
```

We should see the following:

```
$ ./phonebook
Just "999"
Nothing
```

This example illustrates an important principle for managing state in Concurrent Haskell programs. We can take *any* pure immutable data structure such as `Map` and turn it into mutable shared state by simply wrapping it in an `MVar`.

Using immutable data structures in a mutable wrapper has further benefits. Note that in the `lookup` operation, we simply grabbed the current value of the state and then the complex `Map.lookup` operation takes place outside of the `takeMVar`/`putMVar` sequence. This is good for concurrency, because it means the lock is held only for a very short time. This is possible only because the value of the state is immutable. If the data structure were mutable, we would have to hold the lock while operating on it.[5]

The effect of lazy evaluation here is important to understand. The `insert` operation had this line:

```
putMVar m (Map.insert name number book)
```

This places in the `MVar` the *unevaluated* expression `Map.insert name number book`. There are both good and bad consequences to this. The benefit is that we don't have to wait for `Map.insert` to finish before we can unlock the state; as in `lookup`, the state is only locked very briefly. However, if we were to do many `insert` operations consecutively, the `MVar` would build up a large chain of unevaluated expressions, which could create a space leak. As an alternative, we might try:

```
putMVar m $! Map.insert name number book
```

The `$!` operator is like the infix apply operator `$`, but it evaluates the argument strictly before applying the function. The effect is to reverse the two consequences of the lazy version noted previously. Now we hold the lock until `Map.insert` has completed, but there is no risk of a space leak. To get brief locking *and* no space leaks, we need to use a trick:

```
let book' = Map.insert name number book
putMVar m book'
seq book' (return ())
```

With this sequence, we're storing an unevaluated expression in the `MVar`, but it is evaluated immediately after the `putMVar`. The lock is held only briefly, but now the thunk is also evaluated so we avoid building up a long chain of thunks.

MVar as a Building Block: Unbounded Channels

One of the strengths of `MVars` is to provide a useful building block from which larger abstractions can be constructed. Here, we will use `MVars` to construct an unbounded buffered channel that supports the following basic interface:

---

5. The other option is to use a lock-free algorithm, which is enormously complex and difficult to get right.

```
data Chan a

newChan   :: IO (Chan a)
readChan  :: Chan a -> IO a
writeChan :: Chan a -> a -> IO ()
```

This channel implementation is available in the Haskell module `Control.Concurrent.Chan`. The structure of the implementation is represented diagrammatically in Figure 7-1, where each bold box represents an `MVar` and the lighter boxes are ordinary Haskell data structures.

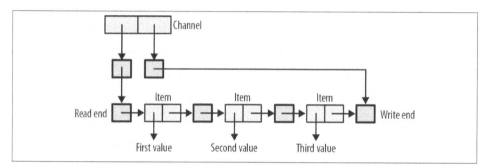

Figure 7-1. Structure of the buffered channel implementation

The current contents of the channel are represented as a `Stream`, defined like this:

chan.hs

```
type Stream a = MVar (Item a)
data Item a   = Item a (Stream a)
```

A `Stream` represents the sequence of values currently stored in the channel. Each element is an `MVar` containing an `Item`, which contains the value and the rest of the `Stream`. The end of the `Stream` is represented by an empty `MVar` called the *hole*, into which the next value to be written to the channel will be placed.

The channel needs to track both ends of the `Stream`, because values read from the channel are taken from the beginning, and values written are added to the end. Hence a channel consists of two pointers called the *read* and the *write* pointer, respectively, both represented by `MVar`s:

```
data Chan a
 = Chan (MVar (Stream a))
        (MVar (Stream a))
```

The read pointer always points to the next item to be read from the channel, and the write pointer points to the *hole* into which the next item written will be placed.

To construct a new channel, we must first create an empty `Stream`, which is just a single empty `MVar`, and then the `Chan` constructor with `MVar`s for the read and write ends, both pointing to the empty `Stream`:

```
newChan :: IO (Chan a)
newChan = do
  hole   <- newEmptyMVar
  readVar  <- newMVar hole
  writeVar <- newMVar hole
  return (Chan readVar writeVar)
```

To add a new element to the channel we must make an `Item` with a new hole, fill in the current hole to point to the new item, and adjust the write-end of the `Chan` to point to the new hole:

```
writeChan :: Chan a -> a -> IO ()
writeChan (Chan _ writeVar) val = do
  newHole <- newEmptyMVar
  oldHole <- takeMVar writeVar
  putMVar oldHole (Item val newHole)
  putMVar writeVar newHole
```

To remove a value from the channel, we must follow the read end of the `Chan` to the first `MVar` of the stream, take that `MVar` to get the `Item`, adjust the read end to point to the next `MVar` in the stream, and finally return the value stored in the `Item`:

```
readChan :: Chan a -> IO a
readChan (Chan readVar _) = do
  stream <- takeMVar readVar          -- ❶
  Item val tail <- takeMVar stream    -- ❷
  putMVar readVar tail                -- ❸
  return val
```

Consider what happens if the channel is empty. The first `takeMVar` (❶) will succeed, but the second `takeMVar` (❷) will find an empty hole, and so will block. When another thread calls `writeChan`, it will fill the hole, allowing the first thread to complete its `takeMVar`, update the read end (❸) and finally return.

If multiple threads concurrently call `readChan`, the first one will successfully call `takeMVar` on the read end, but the subsequent threads will all block at this point until the first thread completes the operation and updates the read end. If multiple threads call `writeChan`, a similar thing happens: the write end of the `Chan` is the synchronization point, allowing only one thread at a time to add an item to the channel. However, the read and write ends, being separate `MVar`s, allow concurrent `readChan` and `writeChan` operations to proceed without interference.

This implementation allows a nice generalization to *multicast* channels without changing the underlying structure. The idea is to add one more operation:

```
dupChan :: Chan a -> IO (Chan a)
```

This creates a duplicate Chan with the following semantics:

- The new Chan begins empty.
- Subsequent writes to either Chan are read from both; that is, reading an item from one Chan does not remove it from the other.

This implementation seems to fit the bill:

```
dupChan :: Chan a -> IO (Chan a)
dupChan (Chan _ writeVar) = do
  hole <- readMVar writeVar
  newReadVar <- newMVar hole
  return (Chan newReadVar writeVar)
```

I'm using readMVar here, which is defined thus:[6]

```
readMVar :: MVar a -> IO a
readMVar m = do
  a <- takeMVar m
  putMVar m a
  return a
```

After a dupChan, we have two channels that share a single writeVar, so items written to one channel will appear in both. However, the channels have separate readVars, so reading an item from one of the channels will not cause the item to be removed from the other channel.

Sadly, this implementation of dupChan does not work. Can you see the problem? The definition of dupChan itself is not at fault, but combined with the definition of readChan given earlier, it does not implement the required semantics. The problem is that readChan does not replace the contents of a hole after having read it, so if readChan is called to read values from both the channel returned by dupChan and the original channel, the second call will block. The fix is to change a takeMVar to readMVar in the implementation of readChan:

chan2.hs

```
readChan :: Chan a -> IO a
readChan (Chan readVar _) = do
  stream <- takeMVar readVar
  Item val tail <- readMVar stream        -- ❶
  putMVar readVar tail
  return val
```

---

6. readMVar is a standard operation provided by the Control.Concurrent module.

---

❶ Returns the Item back to the Stream, where it can be read by any duplicate channels created by dupChan.

Before we leave the topic of channels, consider one more extension to the interface that was described as an "easy extension" and left as an exercise in the original paper on Concurrent Haskell:

```
unGetChan :: Chan a -> a -> IO ()
```

The operation unGetChan pushes a value back on the read end of the channel. Leaving aside for a moment the fact that the interface does not allow the atomic combination of readChan and unGetChan (which would appear to be an important use case), let us consider how to implement unGetChan. The straightforward implementation is as follows:

```
unGetChan :: Chan a -> a -> IO ()
unGetChan (Chan readVar _) val = do
  newReadEnd <- newEmptyMVar          -- ❶
  readEnd <- takeMVar readVar         -- ❷
  putMVar newReadEnd (Item val readEnd) -- ❸
  putMVar readVar newReadEnd          -- ❹
```

❶ Creates a new hole to place at the front of the Stream.

❷ Takes the current read end, giving us the current front of the stream.

❸ Places a new Item in the new hole.

❹ Replaces the read end with a pointer to our new item.

Simple testing will confirm that the implementation works. However, consider what happens when the channel is empty, a readChan is already waiting in a blocked state, and another thread calls unGetChan. The desired semantics is that unGetChan succeeds, and readChan should return with the new element. What actually happens in this case is deadlock. The thread blocked in readChan will be holding the read end MVar, and so unGetChan will also block in takeMVar trying to take the read end. There is no known implementation of unGetChan based on this representation of Chan that has the desired semantics.

The lesson here is that programming larger structures with MVar can be much trickier than it appears. As we shall see shortly, life gets even more difficult when we consider exceptions. Fortunately there is an alternative to MVar that avoids some of these problems, which we will describe in Chapter 10.

Despite the difficulties with scaling MVars up to larger abstractions, MVars do have some nice properties, as we shall see in the next section.

Fairness

We would like our concurrent programs to be executed with some degree of *fairness*. At the very least, no thread should be starved of CPU time indefinitely, and ideally each thread should be given an equal share of the CPU.

GHC uses a simple round-robin scheduler. It does guarantee that no thread is starved indefinitely, although it does not ensure that every thread gets an exactly equal share of the CPU. In practice, though, the scheduler is reasonably fair in this respect. The MVar implementation also provides an important fairness guarantee:

No thread can be blocked indefinitely on an MVar unless another thread holds that MVar indefinitely.

In other words, if a thread *T* is blocked in takeMVar and there are regular putMVar operations on the same MVar, it is guaranteed that at some point thread *T*'s takeMVar will return. In GHC, this guarantee is implemented by keeping blocked threads in a FIFO queue attached to the MVar, so eventually every thread in the queue will get to complete its operation as long as there are other threads performing regular putMVar operations (an equivalent guarantee applies to threads blocked in putMVar when there are regular takeMVars). Note that it is not enough to merely *wake up* the blocked thread because another thread might run first and take (respectively put) the MVar, causing the newly woken thread to go to the back of the queue again, which would invalidate the fairness guarantee. The implementation must therefore wake up the blocked thread *and* perform the blocked operation in a single atomic step, which is exactly what GHC does.

Recall our example from the beginning of Chapter 7 where we had two threads, one printing As and the other printing Bs, and the output was sometimes a perfect alternation between the two: ABABABABABABABAB. This is an example of the fairness guarantee in practice. The stdout handle is represented by an MVar, so when both threads attempt to call takeMVar to operate on the handle, one of them wins and the other becomes blocked. When the winning thread completes its operation and calls putMVar, the scheduler wakes up the blocked thread *and* completes its blocked takeMVar, so the original winning thread will immediately block when it tries to reacquire the handle. Hence this leads to perfect alternation between the two threads. The only way that the alternation pattern can be broken is if one thread is descheduled while it is not holding the MVar. Indeed, this does happen from time to time as a result of preemption, and we see the occasional long string of a single letter in the output. Currently, GHC doesn't try to avoid getting into this situation, but it is possible that in the future it might implement a tweak to the scheduling policy, perhaps by yielding the CPU immediately after unblocking another thread.

A consequence of the fairness implementation is that, when multiple threads are blocked in takeMVar and another thread does a putMVar, *only one of the blocked threads becomes unblocked*. This "single wakeup" property is a particularly important performance characteristic when a large number of threads are contending for a single MVar. As we shall see later, it is the fairness guarantee—together with the single wakeup property—that keeps MVars from being completely subsumed by software transactional memory.

CHAPTER 8

Overlapping Input/Output

We can use MVar and threads to do asynchronous I/O, where "asynchronous" in this context means that the I/O is performed in the background while we do other tasks.

Suppose we want to download some web pages concurrently and wait for them all to download before continuing. We will use the following function to download a web page:

```
getURL :: String -> IO ByteString
```

This function is provided by the module GetURL in *GetURL.hs*, which is a small wrapper around the API provided by the HTTP package.

Let's use forkIO and MVar to download two web pages at the same time:

geturls1.hs

```
import Control.Concurrent
import Data.ByteString as B
import GetURL

main = do
  m1 <- newEmptyMVar                                        -- ❶
  m2 <- newEmptyMVar                                        -- ❷

  forkIO $ do                                               -- ❸
    r <- getURL "http://www.wikipedia.org/wiki/Shovel"
    putMVar m1 r

  forkIO $ do                                               -- ❹
    r <- getURL "http://www.wikipedia.org/wiki/Spade"
    putMVar m2 r

  r1 <- takeMVar m1                                         -- ❺
  r2 <- takeMVar m2                                         -- ❻
  print (B.length r1, B.length r2)                         -- ❼
```

❶ ❷ Create two new empty `MVars` to hold the results.

❸ Fork a new thread to download the first URL; when the download is complete, the result is placed in the `MVar m1`.

❹ Do the same for the second URL, placing the result in `m2`.

❺ In the main thread, this call to `takeMVar` waits for the result from `m1`.

❻ Similarly, wait for the result from `m2` (we could do these in either order).

❼ Finally, print out the length in bytes of each downloaded page.

This code is rather verbose. We could shorten it by using various existing higher-order combinators from the Haskell library, but a better approach would be to extract the common pattern as a new abstraction. We want a way to perform an action *asynchronously* and later wait for its result. So let's define an interface that does that, using `forkIO` and `MVar`:

```
data Async a = Async (MVar a)

async :: IO a -> IO (Async a)
async action = do
  var <- newEmptyMVar
  forkIO (do r <- action; putMVar var r)
  return (Async var)

wait :: Async a -> IO a
wait (Async var) = readMVar var
```

First, we define an `Async` data type that represents an asynchronous action that has been started. Its implementation is just an `MVar` that will contain the result. Again, we are creating a new data type so as to hide implementation details from clients, and indeed later in this chapter we will need to extend the `Async` type with more information.

It is important to use `readMVar` in `wait`, because this allows multiple `wait` calls to be made for the same `Async`. If we had used a simple `takeMVar`, the second and subsequent calls to `wait` would deadlock. Multiple calls to `wait` for the same `Async` might arise if we are programming in a dataflow style, as in a program that creates a single `Async` and then two further `Asyncs` that both wait for the result of the first one. In this sense, `Async` is behaving rather like `IVar` from the `Par` monad (Chapter 4), although here, the individual operations are side-effecting `IO` operations rather than pure computations and there is no guarantee of determinism.

Now we can use the `Async` interface to clean up our web page downloading example:

geturls2.hs

```
main = do
  a1 <- async (getURL "http://www.wikipedia.org/wiki/Shovel")
```

```
a2 <- async (getURL "http://www.wikipedia.org/wiki/Spade")
r1 <- wait a1
r2 <- wait a2
print (B.length r1, B.length r2)
```

Much nicer! To elaborate upon this slightly, we can make a small wrapper called timeDownload that downloads a URL and reports how much data was downloaded and how long it took, and then apply this to a list of URLs using async:

geturls3.hs

```
sites = ["http://www.google.com",
         "http://www.bing.com",
         "http://www.yahoo.com",
         "http://www.wikipedia.com/wiki/Spade",
         "http://www.wikipedia.com/wiki/Shovel"]

timeDownload :: String -> IO ()
timeDownload url = do
  (page, time) <- timeit $ getURL url    -- ❶
  printf "downloaded: %s (%d bytes, %.2fs)\n" url (B.length page) time

main = do
  as <- mapM (async . timeDownload) sites  -- ❷
  mapM_ wait as                            -- ❸
```

❶ To time the getURL call, we use an auxiliary function timeit (defined in *TimeIt.hs*).

❷ mapM maps a function over a list in a monad; in this case, the IO monad. The function we are mapping over the list is the composition of async and timeDownload. That is, for each URL in the list, we will create an Async that calls timeDownload for that URL. The result of the mapM call is the list of Asyncs created, which we bind to as.

❸ Then we wait for each of the Asyncs to complete. Notice that in this example, each Async is returning only a () token when it completes, rather than the web page contents as in the earlier examples. Hence we're using mapM_, a variant of mapM that ignores the result of applying the function to each list element and returns ().

The program produces output like this:

```
downloaded: http://www.google.com (14524 bytes, 0.17s)
downloaded: http://www.bing.com (24740 bytes, 0.18s)
downloaded: http://www.wikipedia.com/wiki/Spade (62586 bytes, 0.60s)
downloaded: http://www.wikipedia.com/wiki/Shovel (68897 bytes, 0.60s)
downloaded: http://www.yahoo.com (153065 bytes, 1.11s)
```

Our little `Async` API captures a common pattern that occurs with concurrent programming, but so far we have ignored one crucial detail: error handling. To deal with errors, we will need to understand how exceptions work in Haskell, and so the next section will review Haskell's exception-handling support before we return to the question of error handling in "Error Handling with Async" on page 151.

Exceptions in Haskell

The Haskell 98 and 2010 standards provide a limited form of exceptions in the IO monad. The IO exception mechanism has been extended by the `Control.Exception` module that comes with GHC to include exceptions generated by purely functional code (e.g., `error` and pattern-matching failure), and to define an extensible hierarchy of exception types. The result of this incremental development is that there are some inconsistencies in the APIs as the Haskell 98/2010 interfaces are gradually replaced by the new, more general APIs.

Haskell has no special syntax or built-in semantics for exception handling; everything is done with library functions. Thus, the idioms for exception catching in particular may look a little strange. The tradeoff is that we are able to build higher-level exception handling combinators that embody more powerful abstractions, as we shall see shortly.

In Haskell, exceptions are thrown by the `throw` function:

```
throw :: Exception e => e -> a
```

Two things to note here:

- `throw` takes a value of any type that is an instance of the `Exception` type class.
- `throw` returns the unrestricted type variable `a`, so it can be called from anywhere.

The `Exception` type class is provided by the `Control.Exception` module and is defined as follows:

```
class (Typeable e, Show e) => Exception e where
  -- ...
```

Its methods are not important here (see the documentation for details), but the important principle is that any type that is an instance of both `Typeable` and `Show` can be an `Exception`.[1]

One common type used as an exception is `ErrorCall`:

---

1. An introduction to `Typeable` is beyond the scope of this book; please refer to the documentation for the module `Data.Typeable`.

```
newtype ErrorCall = ErrorCall String
    deriving (Typeable)

instance Show ErrorCall where { ... }

instance Exception ErrorCall
```

For example, we can throw an `ErrorCall` like so:

```
throw (ErrorCall "oops!")
```

In fact, the function `error` from the `Prelude` does exactly this and is defined as:

```
error :: String -> a
error s = throw (ErrorCall s)
```

I/O operations in Haskell also throw exceptions to indicate errors, and these are usually values of the `IOException` type. Operations to build and inspect `IOException` can be found in the `System.IO.Error` library.

Exceptions in Haskell can be caught, but *only in the IO monad*. The basic exception-catching function is `catch`:

```
catch :: Exception e => IO a -> (e -> IO a) -> IO a
```

The `catch` function takes two arguments:

- The `IO` operation to perform, of type `IO a`
- An exception handler of type `e -> IO a`, where `e` must be an instance of the `Exception` class

The behavior is as follows: the `IO` operation in the first argument is performed, and if it throws an exception *of the type expected by the handler*, `catch` executes the handler, passing it the exception value that was thrown. So a call to `catch` catches only exceptions of a particular type, determined by the argument type of the exception handler.

To demonstrate this, we will need a new exception type. Let's make our own in GHCi.[2] First some setup:

```
> import Prelude hiding (catch) -- not needed for GHC 7.6.1 and later
> import Control.Exception
> import Data.Typeable
> :set -XDeriveDataTypeable
```

Remember that to make a type an instance of `Exception`, it must also be an instance of `Show` and `Typeable`. To enable automatic derivation for `Typeable`, we need to turn on the `-XDeriveDataTypeable` flag.

---

2. For this example to work in GHCi, you will need at least GHC 7.4.1

In GHC 7.4.x and earlier, the Prelude exports a function called catch, which is similar to Control.Exception.catch but restricted to IOExceptions. If you're using exceptions with GHC 7.4.x or earlier, you should use the following:

```
import Control.Exception
import Prelude hiding (catch)
```

Note that this code still works with GHC 7.6.1 and later, because it is now a warning, rather than an error, to mention a nonexistent identifier in a hiding clause.

Now we define a new type and make it an instance of Exception:

```
> data MyException = MyException deriving (Show, Typeable)
> instance Exception MyException
```

Then we check that we can throw it:

```
> throw MyException
*** Exception: MyException
```

OK, now to catch it. The catch function is normally used infix, like this: action `catch` \e -> handler.

If we try to call catch without adding any information about the type of exception to catch, we will get an ambiguous type error from GHCi:

```
> throw MyException `catch` \e -> print e

<interactive>:10:33:
    Ambiguous type variable `a0' in the constraints:
      (Show a0) arising from a use of `print' at <interactive>:10:33-37
      (Exception a0)
        arising from a use of `catch' at <interactive>:10:19-25
    Probable fix: add a type signature that fixes these type variable(s)
    In the expression: print e
    In the second argument of `catch', namely `\ e -> print e'
    In the expression: throw MyException `catch` \ e -> print e
```

So we need to add an extra type signature to tell GHCi which type of exceptions we wanted to catch:

```
> throw MyException `catch` \e -> print (e :: MyException)
MyException
```

The exception was successfully thrown, caught by the catch function, and printed by the exception handler. If we throw a different type of exception, it won't be caught by this handler:

```
> throw (ErrorCall "oops") `catch` \e -> print (e :: MyException)
*** Exception: oops
```

What if we wanted to catch *any* exception? In fact, it is possible to do this because the exception types form a hierarchy, and at the top of the hierarchy is a type called SomeException that includes all exception types. Therefore, to catch any exception, we can write an exception handler that catches the SomeException type:

```
> throw (ErrorCall "oops") `catch` \e -> print (e :: SomeException)
oops
```

Writing an exception handler that catches all exceptions is useful in only a couple of cases, though:

- Testing and debugging, as in the above example
- Performing some cleanup, before re-throwing the exception

Catching SomeException and then continuing is not good practice in production code, because for obvious reasons it isn't a good idea to ignore unknown error conditions.

The catch function is not the only way to catch exceptions. Sometimes it is more convenient to use the try variant instead:

```
try :: Exception e => IO a -> IO (Either e a)
```

For example:

```
> try (readFile "nonexistent") :: IO (Either IOException String)
Left nonexistent: openFile: does not exist (No such file or directory)
```

Another variant of catch is handle, which is just catch with its arguments reversed:

```
handle :: Exception e => (e -> IO a) -> IO a -> IO a
```

This is particularly useful when the exception handler is short but the action is long. In this case, we can use a pattern like this:

```
handle (\e -> ...) $ do
   ...
```

It is often useful to be able to perform some operation if an exception is raised and then re-throw the exception. For this, the onException function is provided:

```
onException :: IO a -> IO b -> IO a
```

This is straightforwardly defined using catch:

```
onException io what
   = io `catch` \e -> do _ <- what
                         throwIO (e :: SomeException)
```

To re-throw the exception here we used throwIO, which is a variant of throw for use in the IO monad:

```
throwIO :: Exception e => e -> IO a
```

It is always better to use throwIO rather than throw in the IO monad because throwIO guarantees strict ordering with respect to other IO operations, whereas throw does not.

We end this short introduction to exceptions in Haskell with two very useful functions, bracket and finally:

```
bracket :: IO a -> (a -> IO b) -> (a -> IO c) -> IO c

finally :: IO a -> IO b -> IO a
```

These are two of the higher-level abstractions mentioned earlier. The bracket function allows us to set up an exception handler to reliably deallocate a resource or perform some cleanup operation. For example, suppose we want to create a temporary file on the file system, perform some operation on it, and have the temporary file reliably removed afterward—even if an exception occurred during the operation. We could use bracket like so:

```
bracket (newTempFile "temp")
        (\file -> removeFile file)
        (\file -> ...)
```

In a call bracket a b c, the first argument a is the operation that allocates the resource (in this case, creating the temporary file), the second argument b deallocates the resource again (in this case, deleting the temporary file), and the third argument c is the operation to perform. Both b and c take the result of a as an argument. In this case, that means they have access to the name of the temporary file that was created.

The bracket function is readily defined using the pieces we already have:

```
bracket :: IO a -> (a -> IO b) -> (a -> IO c) -> IO c
bracket before after during = do
  a <- before
  c <- during a `onException` after a
  after a
  return c
```

This definition suffices for now, but note that later in Chapter 9, we will revise it to add safety in the presence of thread cancellation.

The finally function is a special case of bracket:

```
finally :: IO a -> IO b -> IO a
finally io after = do
  io `onException` after
  after
```

Again, we will be revising this definition later.

Error Handling with Async

If we run the geturls2 example with the network cable unplugged, we see something like this:

```
$ ./geturls2
geturls2: connect: does not exist (No route to host)
geturls2: connect: does not exist (No route to host)
geturls2: thread blocked indefinitely in an MVar operation
```

What happens is that the two calls to getURL fail with an exception, as they should. This exception propagates to the top of the thread that async created, where it is caught by the default exception handler that every forkIO thread gets. The default exception handler prints the exception to stderr, and then the thread terminates. So in geturls2, we see two network errors printed. But now, because these threads have not called putMVar to pass a result back to the main thread, the main thread is still blocked in takeMVar. When the child threads exit after printing their error messages, the main thread is then deadlocked. The runtime system notices this and sends it the BlockedIndefinitelyOnMVar exception, which leads to the third error message, shown earlier.

This explains what we saw, but clearly this behavior is not what we want: the program is deadlocked after the error rather than exiting gracefully or handling it. The natural behavior would be for the error to be made available to the thread that calls wait because that way the caller can find out whether the asynchronous computation returned an error or a result and act accordingly. Moreover, a particularly convenient behavior is for wait to simply propagate the exception in the current thread so that in the common case the programmer need not write any error-handling code at all.

To implement this, we need to elaborate on Async slightly:

geturls4.hs

```
data Async a = Async (MVar (Either SomeException a)) -- ❶

async :: IO a -> IO (Async a)
async action = do
  var <- newEmptyMVar
  forkIO (do r <- try action; putMVar var r)  -- ❷
  return (Async var)

waitCatch :: Async a -> IO (Either SomeException a) -- ❸
waitCatch (Async var) = readMVar var

wait :: Async a -> IO a -- ❹
wait a = do
  r <- waitCatch a
  case r of
```

```
Left e  -> throwIO e
Right a -> return a
```

❶ Where previously we had `MVar a`, now we have `MVar (Either SomeException a)`. If the `MVar` contains `Right a`, then the operation completed successfully and returned value a; whereas if it contains `Left e`, then the operation threw the exception e.

❷ The `action` is now wrapped in `try`, which returns `Either SomeException a`—exactly the type we need to put into the `MVar`. Earlier, we cautioned that catching `SomeException` is often not a good idea, but this is one case where it is fine because we are catching exceptions in one thread with the intention of propagating them to another thread, and we want the behavior to be the same for *all* exceptions.

❸ Now we will provide two ways to wait for the result of an `Async`. The first, `waitCatch`, returns `Either SomeException a` so the caller can handle the error immediately.

❹ The second way to wait for a result is `wait`, which has the same type as before. However, now, if `wait` finds that the `Async` resulted in an exception, the exception is re-thrown by `wait` itself. This implements the convenient error-propagating behavior mentioned previously.

Using this new `Async` layer, our `geturls` example now fails more gracefully (see *geturls4.hs* for the complete code):

```
$ ./geturls4
geturls4: connect: timeout (Connection timed out)
[3]    25198 exit 1     ./geturls4
$
```

The program exited with an error code after the first failure, rather than deadlocking as before.

The basic `Async` API is the same as before—`async` and `wait` have the same types—but now it has error-handling built in, and it is much harder for the programmer to accidentally forget to handle errors. The only way to ignore an error is to ignore the result as well.

Merging

Suppose we want to wait for one of several different events to occur. For example, when downloading multiple URLs, we want to perform some action as soon as the first one has downloaded.

The pattern for doing this with MVar is that each of the separate actions must put its results into the same MVar, so that we can then call takeMVar to wait for the first such event to occur. Here is the *geturls3.hs* example from Chapter 8, modified to wait for the *first* URL to complete downloading and then to report which one it was.

geturls5.hs

```
sites = ["http://www.google.com",
         "http://www.bing.com",
         "http://www.yahoo.com",
         "http://www.wikipedia.com/wiki/Spade",
         "http://www.wikipedia.com/wiki/Shovel"]

main :: IO ()
main = do
  m <- newEmptyMVar
  let
    download url = do
        r <- getURL url
        putMVar m (url, r)

  mapM_ (forkIO . download) sites

  (url, r) <- takeMVar m
  printf "%s was first (%d bytes)\n" url (B.length r)
  replicateM_ (length sites - 1) (takeMVar m)
```

Here, we create a single MVar and then fork a thread for each of the URLs to download. Each thread writes its result into the same MVar, where the result is now a pair of the URL and its contents. The main thread takes the first result from the MVar, announces which URL was the quickest to download, and then waits for the rest of the results to arrive.

```
$ ./geturls5
http://www.google.com was first (10483 bytes)
$
```

While this pattern works, it can be a little inconvenient to arrange it so that all the events feed into the same MVar. For example, suppose we want to extend our Async API to allow waiting for either of two Asyncs simultaneously, returning the result of the first one to succeed or propagating the exception if either Async fails. The function we want is waitEither, with this type:

```
waitEither :: Async a -> Async b -> Async (Either a b)
```

Note that because the input Asyncs have already been created, we are too late to tell them to put their results into the same MVar. Instead, we have to create two *new* threads to collect the results of each Async and merge them into a new MVar:

geturls6.hs

```
waitEither :: Async a -> Async b -> IO (Either a b)
waitEither a b = do
  m <- newEmptyMVar
  forkIO $ do r <- try (fmap Left  (wait a)); putMVar m r
  forkIO $ do r <- try (fmap Right (wait b)); putMVar m r
  wait (Async m)
```

To get the right error-handling behavior, waitEither uses wait to grab each result wrapped in a try to catch any exceptions and then puts each result into the newly created MVar m. Then we make a new Async from m and wait for the result of that.

We can generalize waitEither to wait for a list of Asyncs, returning the result from the first one to complete:

```
waitAny :: [Async a] -> IO a
waitAny as = do
  m <- newEmptyMVar
  let forkwait a = forkIO $ do r <- try (wait a); putMVar m r
  mapM_ forkwait as
  wait (Async m)
```

Now, waitAny can be used to rewrite *geturls5.hs* using Async:

geturls6.hs

```
main :: IO ()
main = do
  let
    download url = do
        r <- getURL url
        return (url, r)

  as <- mapM (async . download) sites

  (url, r) <- waitAny as
  printf "%s was first (%d bytes)\n" url (B.length r)
  mapM_ wait as
```

The code for waitAny is quite short and does the job, but it is slightly annoying to have to create an extra thread per Async for this simple operation. Threads might be cheap, but we ought to be able to merge multiple sources of events more directly. Later in Chapter 10, we will see how software transactional memory allows a neater and more efficient implementation of waitAny.

CHAPTER 9

Cancellation and Timeouts

In an interactive application, it is often important for one thread to *interrupt* the execution of another thread after the occurrence of some particular condition. Some examples of this kind of behavior include the following:

- When the user clicks the "stop" button in a web browser, the browser may need to interrupt several activities, such as a thread downloading the page, a thread rendering the page, and a thread running scripts.

- A server application typically wants to give a client a set amount of time to issue a request before closing its connection, so as to avoid letting dormant connections use up resources.

- An application that has a thread running a user interface and a separate thread performing some compute-intensive task (say, generating a visualization of some data) needs to interrupt the computation when the user changes the parameters via the user interface.

The crucial design decision in supporting cancellation is whether the intended victim should have to poll for the cancellation condition or whether the thread is immediately cancelled in some way. This is a tradeoff:

1. If the thread has to poll, then there is a danger that the programmer may forget to poll regularly enough, and the thread will become unresponsive, perhaps permanently so. Unresponsive threads lead to hangs and deadlocks, which are particularly unpleasant from a user's perspective.

2. If cancellation happens asynchronously, critical sections that modify state need to be protected from cancellation. Otherwise, cancellation may occur mid-update, leaving some data in an inconsistent state.

In fact, the choice is really between doing only (1) or doing both (1) and (2), because if (2) is the default, protecting a critical section amounts to switching to polling behavior for the duration of the critical section.

In most imperative languages, it is unthinkable for (2) to be the default, because so much code modifies state. Haskell has a distinct advantage in this area because most code is purely functional, so it can be safely aborted or suspended and later resumed without affecting correctness. Moreover, our hand is forced: by definition, purely functional code cannot poll for the cancellation condition, so it must be cancellable by default.

Therefore, fully asynchronous cancellation is the only sensible default in Haskell, and the design problem reduces to deciding how cancellation is handled by code in the IO monad.

Asynchronous Exceptions

Exceptions are already a fact of life in the IO monad, and the usual idioms for writing IO monad code include using functions like bracket and finally to acquire and release resources in a reliable way (see "Exceptions in Haskell" on page 146). We would like bracket to work even if a thread is cancelled, so cancellation should behave like an exception. However, there's a fundamental difference between the kind of exception thrown by openFile when the file does not exist, for example, and an exception that may arise *at any time* because the user pressed the "stop" button. We call the latter kind an *asynchronous* exception because it is asynchronous from the point of view of the "victim"; they didn't ask for it. Conversely, exceptions thrown using the normal throw and throwIO are called *synchronous* exceptions.

To initiate an asynchronous exception, Haskell provides the throwTo primitive, which throws an exception from one thread to another:

```
throwTo :: Exception e => ThreadId -> e -> IO ()
```

As with synchronous exceptions, the type of the exception must be an instance of the Exception class. The ThreadId is a value returned by a previous call to forkIO, and may refer to a thread in any state: running, blocked, or finished (in the latter case, throwTo is a no-op).

To illustrate the use of throwTo, we now elaborate on the example from "Error Handling with Async" on page 151, in which we downloaded several web pages concurrently, to allow the user to hit 'q' at any time to stop the downloads.

First, we will extend our Async mini-API to allow cancellation. We add one operation:

```
cancel :: Async a -> IO ()
```

This cancels an existing Async. If the operation has already completed, then cancel has no effect.

To implement `cancel`, we need the `ThreadId` of the thread running the Async, so we must store that in the Async type along with the `MVar` that holds the result. Hence the Async type now looks like:

```
data Async a = Async ThreadId (MVar (Either SomeException a))
```

Given this, the implementation of `cancel` just throws an exception to the thread:

```
cancel :: Async a -> IO ()
cancel (Async t var) = throwTo t ThreadKilled
```

The `ThreadKilled` exception is provided by the `Control.Exception` library and is typically used for cancelling threads in this way.)

For the example, we will need `waitCatch`, which has the same implementation it had in "Error Handling with Async" on page 151. What happens if we call `waitCatch` on an Async that has been cancelled? In that case, `cancel` throws the `ThreadKilled` exception to the thread, so `waitCatch` will return `Left ThreadKilled`.

The remaining piece of the implementation is the `async` operation, which must now store the `ThreadId` returned by `forkIO` in the Async constructor:

```
async :: IO a -> IO (Async a)
async action = do
  m <- newEmptyMVar
  t <- forkIO (do r <- try action; putMVar m r)
  return (Async t m)
```

Now we can change the `main` function of the example to support cancelling the downloads:

geturlscancel.hs

```
main = do
  as <- mapM (async . timeDownload) sites          -- ❶

  forkIO $ do                                       -- ❷
    hSetBuffering stdin NoBuffering
    forever $ do
      c <- getChar
      when (c == 'q') $ mapM_ cancel as

  rs <- mapM waitCatch as                           -- ❸
  printf "%d/%d succeeded\n" (length (rights rs)) (length rs) -- ❹
```

❶   Starts the downloads as before.

❷   Forks a new thread that repeatedly reads characters from the standard input and if a q is found, calls `cancel` on all the Asyncs.

❸   Waits for all the results (complete or cancelled).

❹ Emits a summary with a count of how many of the operations completed successfully. If we run the sample and hit q fast enough, we see something like this:

```
downloaded: http://www.google.com (14538 bytes, 0.17s)
downloaded: http://www.bing.com (24740 bytes, 0.22s)
q2/5 finished
```

Note that this works even though the program is sitting atop a large and complicated HTTP library that provides no direct support for either cancellation or asynchronous I/O. Haskell's support for cancellation is modular in this respect; most library code needs to do nothing to support it, although there are some simple and unintrusive rules that need to be followed when dealing with state, as we shall see in the next section.

Masking Asynchronous Exceptions

As we mentioned earlier, the danger with fully asynchronous exceptions is that one might fire while we are in the middle of updating some shared state, leaving the data in an inconsistent state, and with a high probability of leading to mayhem later. Hence, we certainly need a way to control the delivery of asynchronous exceptions during critical sections. But we must tread carefully: a natural idea is to provide operations to turn off asynchronous exception delivery and turn it on again, but this is not what we really need.

Consider the following problem: a thread wishes to call takeMVar, perform an operation depending on the value of the MVar, and finally put the result of the operation in the MVar. The code must be responsive to asynchronous exceptions, but it should be safe. If an asynchronous exception arrives after the takeMVar but before the final putMVar, the MVar should not be left empty. Instead, the original value should be restored.

If we code this problem using the facilities we've seen so far, we might end up with something like the following function problem, which takes two arguments—m, an MVar to modify, and f, a function that takes the current value of the MVar—and computes a new value in the IO monad.

```
problem :: MVar a -> (a -> IO a) -> IO ()
problem m f = do
  a <- takeMVar m                            -- ❶
  r <- f a `catch` \e -> do putMVar m a; throw e  -- ❷
  putMVar m r                                -- ❸
```

There are at least two points where, if an asynchronous exception strikes, the invariant will be violated. If an exception strikes between ❶ and ❷ or between ❷ and ❸, the MVar will be left empty. In fact, there is no way to shuffle around the exception handlers to ensure the MVar is always left full. To fix this problem, Haskell provides the mask combinator:[1]

```
mask :: ((IO a -> IO a) -> IO b) -> IO b
```

The mask operation defers the delivery of asynchronous exceptions for the duration of its argument. The type might look a bit confusing, but bear with me. First, I'll show an example of mask in use and then explain how it works:[2]

```
problem :: MVar a -> (a -> IO a) -> IO ()
problem m f = mask $ \restore -> do
  a <- takeMVar m
  r <- restore (f a) `catch` \e -> do putMVar m a; throw e
  putMVar m r
```

mask is applied to a *function*, which takes as its argument a function restore. The restore function can be used to restore the delivery of asynchronous exceptions to its present state during execution of the argument to mask. If we imagine shading the entire argument to mask except for the expression (f a), asynchronous exceptions cannot be raised in the shaded portions.

This solves the problem that we had previously because now an exception can be raised only while (f a) is working, and we have an exception handler to catch any exceptions in that case. But a new problem has been introduced: takeMVar might block for a long time, but it is inside the mask so the thread will be unresponsive during that time. Furthermore, there's no good reason to mask exceptions during takeMVar; it would be safe for exceptions to be raised right up until the point where takeMVar returns. Hence, this is exactly the behavior that Haskell defines for takeMVar: a small number of operations, including takeMVar, are designated as *interruptible*. Interruptible operations may receive asynchronous exceptions even inside mask.

What justifies this choice? Think of mask as "switching to polling mode" for asynchronous exceptions. Inside a mask, asynchronous exceptions are no longer asynchronous, but they can still be raised by certain operations. In other words, asynchronous exceptions become *synchronous* inside mask.

---

1. Historical note: the original presentation of asynchronous exceptions used a pair of combinators, block and unblock, here, but mask was introduced in GHC 7.0.1 to provide a more modular behavior and to avoid using the overloaded term "block."

2. For simplicity here, we are using a slightly less general version of mask than the real one in the Control. Exception library.

All operations that may block indefinitely are designated as interruptible.[3] This turns out to be the ideal behavior in many situations, as in the previous problem example.

The observant reader may spot a new flaw. The putMVar function can also block indefinitely, so the definition of interruptible includes putMVar, and therefore the problem function above is still unsafe because an asynchronous exception could be raised by either putMVar.

However, thanks to a subtlety in the precise definition of interruptibility, we are still safe. An interruptible operation may receive an asynchronous exception only *if it actually blocks*. In the case of problem above, we know the MVar is definitely empty when we call putMVar, so putMVar cannot block, which means that it is not interruptible.

How do we know that the MVar is definitely empty? Strictly speaking, we don't, because another thread might call putMVar on the same MVar after the takeMVar call in problem. The guarantee therefore relies on the MVar being operated in a consistent way, where every operation consists of takeMVar followed by putMVar. This is a common requirement for many MVar operations—a particular use of MVar comes with a protocol that operations must follow or risk a deadlock.

When you really need to call an interruptible function but can't afford the possibility that an asynchronous exception might be raised, there is a last resort:

```
uninterruptibleMask :: ((IO a -> IO a) -> IO b) -> IO b
```

This works just like mask, except that interruptible operations may not receive asynchronous exceptions. Be very careful with uninterruptibleMask; accidental misuse may leave your application unresponsive. Every instance of uninterruptibleMask should be treated with the utmost suspicion.

---

3. An exception is foreign calls; see "Asynchronous Exceptions and Foreign Calls" on page 288.

For debugging, it is sometimes handy to be able to find out whether the current thread is in the mask state or not. The Control. Exception library provides a useful function for this purpose:

```
getMaskingState :: IO MaskingState
```

```
data MaskingState
  = Unmasked
  | MaskedInterruptible
  | MaskedUninterruptible
```

The getMaskingState function returns one of the following constructors:

Unmasked
: The current thread is not inside mask or uninterruptibleMask.

MaskedInterruptible
: The current thread is inside mask.

MaskedUninterruptible
: The current thread is inside uninterruptibleMask.

We can provide higher-level combinators to insulate programmers from the need to use mask directly. For example, the earlier problem function has general applicability when working with MVars and is provided under the name modifyMVar_ in the Control. Concurrent.MVar library:

```
modifyMVar_ :: MVar a -> (a -> IO a) -> IO ()
```

There is also a variant that allows the operation to return a separate result in addition to the new contents of the MVar:

```
modifyMVar :: MVar a -> (a -> IO (a, b)) -> IO b
```

Here's a simple example of modifyMVar, used to implement the classic "compare-and-swap" operation:

```
casMVar :: Eq a => MVar a -> a -> a -> IO Bool
casMVar m old new =
  modifyMVar m $ \cur ->
    if cur == old
        then return (new,True)
        else return (cur,False)
```

The casMVar function takes an MVar, an old value, and a new value. If the current contents of the MVar are equal to old, then it is replaced by new and cas returns True; otherwise it is left unmodified and cas returns False.

Working on multiple MVars is possible by nesting calls to modifyMVar. For example, here is a function that modifies the contents of two MVars safely:

modifytwo.hs

```
modifyTwo :: MVar a -> MVar b -> (a -> b -> IO (a,b)) -> IO ()
modifyTwo ma mb f =
  modifyMVar_ mb $ \b ->
    modifyMVar ma $ \a -> f a b
```

If this blocks in the inner `modifyMVar` and an exception is raised, then the outer `modifyMVar_` will restore the contents of the `MVar` it took.

 When taking two or more `MVar`s, always take them in the same order. Otherwise, your program is likely to deadlock. We'll discuss this problem in more detail in Chapter 10.

The bracket Operation

We saw the `bracket` function earlier; in fact, `bracket` is defined with `mask` to make it safe in the presence of asynchronous exceptions:

```
bracket :: IO a -> (a -> IO b) -> (a -> IO c) -> IO c
bracket before after thing =
  mask $ \restore -> do
    a <- before
    r <- restore (thing a) `onException` after a
    _ <- after a
    return r
```

The IO actions passed in as `before` and `after` are performed inside `mask`. The `bracket` function guarantees that if `before` returns, `after` will be executed in the future. It is normal for `before` to contain a blocking operation; if an exception is raised while `before` is blocked, then no harm is done. But `before` should perform only *one* blocking operation. An exception raised by a second blocking operation would not result in `after` being executed. If you need to perform two blocking operations, the right way is to nest calls to `bracket`, as we did with `modifyMVar`.

Something else to watch out for here is using blocking operations in `after`. If you need to do this, then be aware that your blocking operation is interruptible and might receive an asynchronous exception.

Asynchronous Exception Safety for Channels

In most `MVar` code, we can use operations like `modifyMVar_` instead of `takeMVar` and `putMVar` to make our code safe in the presence of asynchronous exceptions. For example, consider the buffered channels that we defined in "MVar as a Building Block: Unbounded Channels" on page 135. As defined, the operations are not safe in the presence of asynchronous exceptions. For example, `readChan` was defined like this:

```
readChan :: Chan a -> IO a
readChan (Chan readVar _) = do
  stream <- takeMVar readVar
  Item val new <- readMVar stream
  putMVar readVar new
  return val
```

If an asynchronous exception occurs after the first `takeMVar`, then the `readVar` will be left empty and subsequent readers of the `Chan` will deadlock. To make it safe, we could use `modifyMVar`:

chan3.hs

```
readChan :: Chan a -> IO a
readChan (Chan readVar _) = do
  modifyMVar readVar $ \stream -> do
    Item val tail <- readMVar stream
    return (tail, val)
```

However, this isn't enough on its own. Remember that `readMVar` is defined like this:

```
readMVar :: MVar a -> IO a
readMVar m = do
  a <- takeMVar m
  putMVar m a
  return a
```

So it is possible that an exception arrives between the `takeMVar` and the `putMVar` in `readMVar`, which would leave the `MVar` empty. Hence we also need to use a safe `readMVar` here. There are a few approaches that work. One would be to use `modifyMVar` again to restore the original value. Another approach is to use a variant of `modifyMVar`:

```
withMVar :: MVar a -> (a -> IO b) -> IO b
```

This is like `modifyMVar` but does not change the contents of the `MVar`, and so would be more direct for the purposes of `readMVar`.

The simplest approach, and the one used by the `Control.Concurrent.MVar` library itself, is just to protect `readMVar` with a `mask`:

```
readMVar :: MVar a -> IO a
readMVar m =
  mask_ $ do
    a <- takeMVar m
    putMVar m a
    return a
```

Here `mask_` is like `mask`, but it doesn't pass a `restore` function. We can get away with this simple definition because unlike `modifyMVar`, there is no operation to perform between the `takeMVar` and `putMVar`, and so no exception handler is required.

With `writeChan`, we have to be a little careful. Here is the original definition:

```
writeChan :: Chan a -> a -> IO ()
writeChan (Chan _ writeVar) val = do
  newHole <- newEmptyMVar
  oldHole <- takeMVar writeVar
  putMVar oldHole (Item val newHole)
  putMVar writeVar newHole
```

To make the code exception-safe, our first thought might be to try this:

```
wrongWriteChan :: Chan a -> a -> IO ()
wrongWriteChan (Chan _ writeVar) val = do
  newHole <- newEmptyMVar
  modifyMVar_ writeVar $ \oldHole -> do
    putMVar oldHole (Item val newHole)   -- ❶
    return newHole                        -- ❷
```

But that doesn't work because an asynchronous exception could strike between ❶ and ❷. This would leave the old_hole full and writeVar pointing to it, which violates the invariants of the data structure. Hence we need to prevent that possibility too, and the simplest way is just to mask_ the whole sequence:

```
writeChan :: Chan a -> a -> IO ()
writeChan (Chan _ writeVar) val = do
  newHole <- newEmptyMVar
  mask_ $ do
    oldHole <- takeMVar writeVar
    putMVar oldHole (Item val newHole)
    putMVar writeVar newHole
```

Note that the two putMVars are both guaranteed not to block, so they are not interruptible.

Timeouts

A useful illustration of programming with asynchronous exceptions is to write a function that can impose a time limit on a given action. We want to provide the timeout wrapper as a combinator of the following type:

```
timeout :: Int -> IO a -> IO (Maybe a)
```

Where timeout *t* *m* has the following behavior:

1. timeout *t* *m* behaves exactly like fmap Just *m*, if *m* returns a result or raises an exception (including an asynchronous exception) within *t* microseconds.

2. Otherwise, *m* is sent an asynchronous exception of the form Timeout *u*. Timeout is a new data type that we define, and *u* is a unique value of type Unique, distinguishing this particular instance of timeout from any other. The call to timeout then returns Nothing.

The implementation is not expected to implement real-time semantics, so in practice the timeout will only approximate the requested *t* microseconds. Note that (1) requires that *m* is executed in the context of the current thread because *m* could call myThreadId, for example. Also, another thread throwing an exception to the current thread with throwTo will expect to interrupt *m*. It should be possible to *nest* timeouts, with the expected behavior.

The code for timeout, shown below, was taken from the library System.Timeout (with some cosmetic changes for presentation here). The implementation is tricky to get right. The basic idea is to fork a new thread that will wait for *t* microseconds and then call throwTo to throw the Timeout exception back to the original thread; that much seems straightforward enough. If the operation completes within the time limit, then we must ensure that this thread never throws its Timeout exception, so timeout must kill the thread before returning.

timeout.hs

```
timeout t m
    | t < 0     = fmap Just m                              -- ❶
    | t == 0    = return Nothing                           -- ❷
    | otherwise = do
        pid <- myThreadId                                  -- ❸
        u <- newUnique                                     -- ❹
        let ex = Timeout u                                 -- ❺
        handleJust                                         -- ❻
            (\e -> if e == ex then Just () else Nothing) -- ❼
            (\_ -> return Nothing)                         -- ❽
            (bracket (forkIO $ do threadDelay t            -- ❾
                                  throwTo pid ex)
                     (\tid -> throwTo tid ThreadKilled)    -- ❿
                     (\_ -> fmap Just m))                  -- ⓫
```

Here is how the implementation works, line by line:

❶❷ Handle the easy cases, where the timeout is negative or zero.

❸ Find the ThreadId of the current thread.

❹❺ Make a new Timeout exception by generating a unique value with newUnique.

❻ handleJust is an exception handler, with the following type:

```
handleJust :: Exception e
           => (e -> Maybe b) -> (b -> IO a) -> IO a
           -> IO a
```

❼ The first argument to handleJust selects which exceptions to catch. We only want to catch a Timeout exception containing the unique value that we created earlier.

⑧   The second argument to `handleJust` is the exception handler, which in this case returns `Nothing` because timeout occurred.

⑨   The computation to run inside `handleJust`. Here, we fork the child thread, using `bracket` to ensure that the child thread is always killed before the `timeout` function returns. In the child thread, we wait for `t` microseconds with `threadDelay` and then throw the `Timeout` exception to the parent thread with `throwTo`.

⑩   Always kill the child thread before returning.

⑪   The body of `bracket`: run the computation `m` passed in as the second argument to `timeout` and wrap the result in `Just`.

I encourage you to verify that the implementation works by thinking through the two cases: either `m` completes and returns a value, or the child thread throws its exception while `m` is still working.

There is one other tricky case to consider: what happens if *both* the child thread and the parent thread try to call `throwTo` at the same time? Who wins?

The answer depends on the semantics of `throwTo`. In order for this implementation of `timeout` to work properly, the call to `bracket` must not be able to return while the `Timeout` exception can still be thrown; otherwise, the exception can leak. Hence, the call to `throwTo` that kills the child thread must be synchronous. Once this call returns, the child thread cannot throw its exception anymore. Indeed, this guarantee is provided by the semantics of `throwTo`. A call to `throwTo` returns only after the exception has been raised in the target thread. Hence `throwTo` may block if the child thread is currently masking asynchronous exceptions with `mask`, and because `throwTo` may block, it is therefore *interruptible* and may itself receive asynchronous exceptions.

Returning to our "who wins" question above, the answer is "exactly one of them," and that is precisely what we require to ensure the correct behavior of `timeout`.

Catching Asynchronous Exceptions

Once thrown, an asynchronous exception propagates like a normal exception and can be caught by `catch` and the other exception-handling functions from `Control.Exception`. Suppose we catch an asynchronous exception and want to perform some operation as a result, but before we can do that, *another* asynchronous exception is received by the current thread, interrupting the first exception handler. This is undesirable: if asynchronous exceptions can interrupt exception handlers, it is hard to guarantee anything about cleanup actions performed in the event of an exception, for example.

We could fix the problem by wrapping all our calls to catch with a mask and restore pair, like so:

```
mask $ \restore ->
    restore action `catch` handler
```

And indeed some of our calls to catch already look like this. But since we almost always want asynchronous exceptions masked inside an exception handler, Haskell does it automatically for you, without having to use an explicit mask. After you return from the exception handler, exceptions are unmasked again.

There is one important pitfall to be aware of here: it is easy to accidentally remain inside the implicit mask by tail-calling out of an exception handler. Here's an example program to illustrate the problem: the program takes a list of filenames on the command line and counts the number of lines in each file, ignoring files that do not exist.

catch-mask.hs

```
main = do
  fs <- getArgs
  let
    loop !n [] = return n
    loop !n (f:fs)
      = handle (\e -> if isDoesNotExistError e
                      then loop n fs
                      else throwIO e) $
          do
            getMaskingState >>= print
            h <- openFile f ReadMode
            s <- hGetContents h
            loop (n + length (lines s)) fs

  n <- loop 0 fs
  print n
```

The loop function recursively walks down the list of filenames, attempting to open and read each one, and keeping track of the total lines so far in the first argument n. For each filename, first we call handle to set up an exception handler. If the exception handler catches an exception that satisfies isDoesNotExistError (from System.IO.Error), indicating that the file we tried to open did not exist, the exception handler recursively calls loop to look at the rest of the files.

This program works, but it has a problem that is revealed by the getMaskingState call. Suppose we run the program with a couple of filenames that don't exist:

```
$ ./catch-mask xxx yyy
Unmasked
MaskedInterruptible
0
```

The first time around the loop, we are in the Unmasked state, as expected, but the second iteration of loop reports that we are now MaskedInterruptible! This is clearly suboptimal, because we didn't intend to mask asynchronous exceptions for the second loop iteration.

The problem arose because we made a recursive call to loop from the exception handler; thus the recursive call is made inside the implicit mask of handle.

A better way to code this example is to use try instead:

catch-mask2.hs

```
main = do
  fs <- getArgs
  let
     loop !n [] = return n
     loop !n (f:fs) = do
        getMaskingState >>= print
        r <- Control.Exception.try (openFile f ReadMode)
        case r of
          Left e | isDoesNotExistError e -> loop n fs
                 | otherwise              -> throwIO e
          Right h -> do
             s <- hGetContents h
             loop (n + length (lines s)) fs

  n <- loop 0 fs
  print n
```

Now there is no exception handler as such (it is hidden inside try), so the recursive call to loop is not made within a mask. Moreover, we have narrowed the scope of the exception handling to just the openFile call, which is neater than before.

However, beware! If you need to handle *asynchronous* exceptions, it's usually important for the exception handler to be inside a mask so that you don't get interrupted by another asynchronous exception before you've finished dealing with the first one. For that reason, catch or handle might be more appropriate, because you can take advantage of the built-in mask. Just be careful to return from the exception handler rather than tail-calling out of it, to avoid the problem described above.

mask and forkIO

Let's return to our Async API for a moment, and in particular the async function:

```
async :: IO a -> IO (Async a)
async action = do
  m <- newEmptyMVar
  t <- forkIO (do r <- try action; putMVar m r)
  return (Async t m)
```

In fact, there's a bug here. If this `Async` is cancelled, and the exception strikes just after the `try` but before the `putMVar`, then the thread will die without putting anything into the `MVar` and the application will deadlock when it tries to `wait` for the result of this `Async`.

We could close this hole with a `mask`, but there's another one: the exception might also arrive just *before* the `try`, with the same consequences. So how do we mask asynchronous exceptions in that small window between the thread being created and the call to `try`? Putting a call to `mask` inside the `forkIO` isn't enough. There is still a possibility that the exception might be thrown even before `mask` is called.

For this reason, `forkIO` is specified to create a thread that *inherits* the masking state of the parent thread. This means that we can create a thread that is born in the masked state by wrapping the call to `forkIO` in a `mask`, for example:

```
async :: IO a -> IO (Async a)
async action = do
  m <- newEmptyMVar
  t <- mask $ \restore ->
          forkIO (do r <- try (restore action); putMVar m r)
  return (Async t m)
```

This pattern of performing some action when a thread has completed is fairly common, so we can embody it as a variant of `forkIO`:[4]

```
forkFinally :: IO a -> (Either SomeException a -> IO ()) -> IO ThreadId
forkFinally action fun =
  mask $ \restore ->
    forkIO (do r <- try (restore action); fun r)
```

The `forkFinally` function lets us simplify `async`:

geturlscancel2.hs

```
async :: IO a -> IO (Async a)
async action = do
  m <- newEmptyMVar
  t <- forkFinally action (putMVar m)
  return (Async t m)
```

Now the API is safe. The rule of thumb is that any exception-handling function called as the first thing in a `forkIO` is better written using `forkFinally`. In particular, if you find yourself writing `forkIO (x ` `finally` ` y)`, then write `forkFinally x (\_ -> y)` instead. Better still, use the `Async` API, which handles these details for you.[5]

---

4. The `forkFinally` function is provided by `Control.Concurrent` from GHC 7.6.1.

5. The full `Async` library is available in the `async` package on Hackage.

Asynchronous Exceptions: Discussion

This chapter has been full of tricky and subtle details—such is life when dealing with exceptions that can strike at any moment. The abstractions we've covered in this chapter like timeout and Chan are certainly hard to get right, but it is worth reminding ourselves that dealing with asynchronous exceptions at this level is something that Haskell programmers rarely have to do, for a couple of reasons:

- All non-IO Haskell code is automatically safe by construction. This is the one factor that makes asynchronous exceptions feasible.

- We can use the abstractions provided, such as bracket, to acquire and release resources. These abstractions have asynchronous-exception safety built in. Similarly, when working with MVars, the modifyMVar family of operations provides built-in safety.

We find that making most IO monad code safe is straightforward, but for those cases where things get a bit complicated, a couple of techniques can simplify matters:

- Large chunks of heavily stateful code can be wrapped in a mask, which drops into polling mode for asynchronous exceptions. This is much easier to work with. The problem then boils down to finding the interruptible operations and ensuring that exceptions raised by those will not cause problems. The GHC I/O library uses this technique: every Handle operation runs entirely inside mask.

- Using software transactional memory (STM) instead of MVars or other state representations can sweep away all the complexity in one go. STM allows us to combine multiple operations in a single *atomic* unit, which means we don't have to worry about restoring state if an exception strikes in the middle. We will describe STM in Chapter 10.

In exchange for asynchronous-exception-safety, Haskell's approach to asynchronous exceptions confers some important benefits:

- Many exceptional conditions map naturally onto asynchronous exceptions. For example, stack overflow and user interrupt (e.g., Ctrl+C at the console) are mapped to asynchronous exceptions in Haskell. Hence, Ctrl+C not only aborts the program but also does so cleanly, running all the exception handlers. Haskell programmers don't have to do anything to enable this behavior.

- Computation can always be interrupted, even if it is third-party library code. (There is an exception to this, namely calls to foreign functions, which we shall discuss in "Threads and Foreign Out-Calls" on page 286).

- Threads never just die in Haskell. It is guaranteed that a thread always gets a chance to clean up and run its exception handlers.

CHAPTER 10

Software Transactional Memory

Software transactional memory (STM) is a technique for simplifying concurrent programming by allowing multiple state-changing operations to be grouped together and performed as a single atomic operation. Strictly speaking, "software transactional memory" is an implementation technique, whereas the language construct we are interested in is "atomic blocks." Unfortunately, the former term has stuck, and so the language-level facility is called STM.

STM solves a number of problems that arise with conventional concurrency abstractions, which we describe here through a series of examples. For reference throughout the following sections, the types and operations of the STM interface are:

Control.Concurrent.STM

```
data STM a -- abstract
instance Monad STM -- among other things

atomically :: STM a -> IO a

data TVar a -- abstract
newTVar   :: a -> STM (TVar a)
readTVar  :: TVar a -> STM a
writeTVar :: TVar a -> a -> STM ()

retry     :: STM a
orElse    :: STM a -> STM a -> STM a

throwSTM  :: Exception e => e -> STM a
catchSTM  :: Exception e => STM a -> (e -> STM a) -> STM a
```

Running Example: Managing Windows

Imagine a window manager that manages multiple desktops. The user can move windows from one desktop to another, while at the same time, a program can request that its own window move from its current desktop to another desktop. The window manager uses multiple threads: one to listen for input from the user, a set of threads to listen for requests from the programs running in each existing window, and one thread that renders the display to the user.

How should the program represent the state of the display? Let's assume some abstract types representing desktops and windows respectively:

```
data Desktop  -- abstract
data Window   -- abstract
```

A display consists of a number of Desktops, each of which is displaying a set of Windows. To put it another way, a display is a mapping from Desktop to a set of Window objects. The mapping changes over time, so we want to make it mutable, and the state needs to be shared among multiple threads. Hence, following the pattern from "MVar as a Container for Shared State" on page 133, we could use a Map stored in an MVar:

```
type Display = MVar (Map Desktop (Set Window))
```

This would work, but the MVar is a single point of contention. For example, the rendering thread, which needs to look only at the currently displayed desktop, could be blocked by a window on another desktop that is moving itself. This structure doesn't allow as much concurrency as we would like.

To allow operations on separate desktops to proceed without impeding each other, perhaps we can have a separate MVar for each desktop:

```
type Display = Map Desktop (MVar (Set Window))
```

Unfortunately, this approach also quickly runs into problems. Consider an operation to move a window from one desktop to another:

```
moveWindow :: Display -> Window -> Desktop -> Desktop -> IO ()
moveWindow disp win a b = do
  wa <- takeMVar ma
  wb <- takeMVar mb
  putMVar ma (Set.delete win wa)
  putMVar mb (Set.insert win wb)
 where
  ma = disp ! a
  mb = disp ! b
```

Note that we must take both MVars before we can put the results; otherwise, another thread could potentially observe the display in a state in which the window we are moving does not exist. But this raises a problem: what if there is a concurrent call to moveWindow trying to move a window in the opposite direction? Let's think through what would happen:

```
thread 1: moveWindow d w1 a b
thread 2: moveWindow d w2 b a
```

Here's one possible interleaving:

- Thread 1 takes the MVar for desktop a.
- Thread 2 takes the MVar for desktop b.
- Thread 1 tries to take the MVar for desktop b and blocks.
- Thread 2 tries to take the MVar for desktop a and blocks.

Now we have deadlock: both threads are blocked on each other, and neither can make progress. This is an instance of the classic "Dining Philosophers" problem (*http://en.wikipedia.org/wiki/Dining_philosophers_problem*).

One solution is to impose an ordering on the MVars and require that all agents take MVars in the correct order and release them in the opposite order. That is inconvenient and error-prone, though, and furthermore we have to extend our ordering to any other state that we might need to access concurrently. Large systems written in languages with locks (e.g., operating systems) are often plagued by this problem, and managing the complexity requires building an elaborate infrastructure to detect ordering violations.

Sofware transactional memory provides a way to avoid this deadlock problem without imposing a requirement for ordering on the programmer. To solve the problem using STM, we replace MVar with TVar:

```
type Display = Map Desktop (TVar (Set Window))
```

TVar stands for "transactional variable"; it is a mutable variable that can be read or written only within the special monad STM, using the operations readTVar and writeTVar:

```
readTVar  :: TVar a -> STM a
writeTVar :: TVar a -> a -> STM ()
```

A computation in the STM monad can be *performed* in the IO monad, using the atomically function:

```
atomically :: STM a -> IO a
```

When an STM computation is performed like this, it is called a *transaction* because the whole operation takes place atomically with respect to the rest of the program. No other thread can observe an intermediate state in which only some of the operations of the transaction have taken place. The STM computation passed to atomically can be arbitrarily large and can contain any number of TVar operations, but as we shall see later there are performance implications for large transactions.

To implement moveWindow using STM, we first convert all the operations to their STM equivalents, and rename the function to moveWindowSTM to indicate that it is in the STM monad:

windowman.hs

```
moveWindowSTM :: Display -> Window -> Desktop -> Desktop -> STM ()
moveWindowSTM disp win a b = do
  wa <- readTVar ma
  wb <- readTVar mb
  writeTVar ma (Set.delete win wa)
  writeTVar mb (Set.insert win wb)
 where
  ma = disp ! a
  mb = disp ! b
```

Then, we wrap this in `atomically` to make the IO-monad version `moveWindow`:

```
moveWindow :: Display -> Window -> Desktop -> Desktop -> IO ()
moveWindow disp win a b = atomically $ moveWindowSTM disp win a b
```

The code for `moveWindowSTM` is almost identical to the `MVar` version, but the behavior is quite different: the sequence of operations inside `atomically` happens indivisibly as far as the rest of the program is concerned, so the problem we encountered earlier that required taking `MVar`s in the correct order does not occur. What's more, there is no requirement that we read both `TVar`s before we write them; this would be fine, too:

```
moveWindowSTM :: Display -> Window -> Desktop -> Desktop -> STM ()
moveWindowSTM disp win a b = do
  wa <- readTVar ma
  writeTVar ma (Set.delete win wa)
  wb <- readTVar mb
  writeTVar mb (Set.insert win wb)
 where
  ma = disp ! a
  mb = disp ! b
```

So STM is far less error-prone here. The approach also scales to any number of `TVar`s, so we could easily write an operation that moves the windows from all other desktops to the current desktop, for example.

Now suppose that we want to swap two windows, moving window *W* from desktop *A* to *B*, and simultaneously *V* from *B* to *A*. With the `MVar` representation, we would have to write a special purpose operation to do this, because it has to take the `MVar`s for *A* and *B* (in the right order) and then put both `MVar`s back with the new contents. With STM, however, we can express this much more neatly by simply making two calls to `moveWindowSTM`:

windowman.hs

```
swapWindows :: Display
            -> Window -> Desktop
            -> Window -> Desktop
            -> IO ()
swapWindows disp w a v b = atomically $ do
```

```
moveWindowSTM disp w a b
moveWindowSTM disp v b a
```

This demonstrates the *composability* of STM operations: any operation of type STM a can be composed with others to form a larger atomic transaction. For this reason, STM operations are usually provided without the atomically wrapper so that clients can compose them as necessary before finally wrapping the entire operation in atomically.

 Why is STM a different monad from IO? The STM implementation relies on being able to *roll back* the effects of a transaction in the event of a conflict with another transaction (and for other reasons, as we shall see shortly). A transaction can be rolled back only if we can track exactly what effects it has, and this would not be possible if arbitrary I/O were allowed inside a transaction—we might have performed some I/O that cannot be undone, like making a noise or launching some missiles. For this reason, the STM monad permits only side effects on TVars, and the STM implementation tracks these effects to ensure the correct transaction semantics. We will discuss the implementation of STM and its performance implications in more detail in "Performance" on page 193.

This is an example of using the Haskell type system to enforce a safety invariant. We are guaranteed that every transaction is actually a transaction, because the type system prevents arbitrary side-effects from being performed in the STM monad.

So far, we covered the basic facilities of STM and showed that STM can be used to scale atomicity in a composable way. STM improves the expressibility and robustness of concurrent programs. The benefits of STM in Haskell go further, however. In the following sections, we show how STM can be used to make blocking abstractions compose, and how STM can be used to manage complexity in the presence of failure and interruption.

Blocking

An important part of concurrent programming is dealing with *blocking* when we need to wait for some condition to be true, or to acquire a particular resource. STM provides an ingenious way to do this with a single operation:

```
retry :: STM a
```

The meaning of retry is simply "abandon the current transaction and run it again." An example should help to clarify how retry works. Let's consider how to implement MVar using STM because takeMVar and putMVar need to be able to block when the MVar is empty or full, respectively.

First the data type: an MVar is always in one of two states; either it is full and contains a value, or it is empty. We model this with a TVar containing Maybe a:[1]

tmvar.hs

```
newtype TMVar a = TMVar (TVar (Maybe a))
```

To make an empty TMVar, we simply need a TVar containing Nothing:

```
newEmptyTMVar :: STM (TMVar a)
newEmptyTMVar = do
  t <- newTVar Nothing
  return (TMVar t)
```

Now to code takeTMVar, which blocks if the desired variable is empty and returns the content once the variable is set:

```
takeTMVar :: TMVar a -> STM a
takeTMVar (TMVar t) = do
  m <- readTVar t                 -- ❶
  case m of
    Nothing -> retry              -- ❷
    Just a  -> do
      writeTVar t Nothing         -- ❸
      return a
```

❶ Read the current contents of the TVar, which we inspect with a case.

❷ If the TVar contains Nothing, then the TMVar is empty, so we need to block. The retry operation says, "Run the current transaction again," which will have the desired effect: we keep rerunning the transaction until the TVar no longer contains Nothing and the other case branch is taken. Of course, we don't really want to blindly rerun the transaction over and over again, making our CPU hot for no good reason. The STM implementation knows that there is no point rerunning the transaction unless something different is likely to happen, and that can be true only if one or more of the TVars that were read by the current transaction have changed. In fact, what happens is that the current thread is *blocked* until one of the TVars that it is reading is written to, at which point the thread is unblocked again and the transaction is rerun.

❸ If the TVar contains Just a, we empty the TMVar by writing Nothing into it and then return the a.

The implementation of putMVar is straightforward:

---

1. The TMVar implementation is available from the Control.Concurrent.STM.TMVar module in the stm package.

```
putTMVar :: TMVar a -> a -> STM ()
putTMVar (TMVar t) a = do
  m <- readTVar t
  case m of
    Nothing -> do
      writeTVar t (Just a)
      return ()
    Just _   -> retry
```

So now that we have a replacement for MVar built using STM, what can we do with it? Well, STM operations are composable, so we can perform operations on multiple TMVars at the same time:

```
atomically $ do
  a <- takeTMVar ta
  b <- takeTMVar tb
  return (a,b)
```

This STM transaction succeeds when and only when both TMVars are full; otherwise it is blocked. This explains why retry must abandon the whole transaction: if the first takeTMVar succeeds but the second one retries, we do not want the effect of the first takeTMVar to take place.

This example is difficult to program with MVar because taking a single MVar is a side effect that is visible to the rest of the program, and hence cannot be easily undone if the other MVar is empty. One way to implement it is with a *third* MVar acting as a lock to control access to the other two, but then of course all other clients have to be aware of the locking protocol.

Blocking Until Something Changes

The retry operation allows us to block on arbitrary conditions. As a concrete example, we can use retry to implement the rendering thread in our window manager example. The behavior we want is this:

- One desktop is designated as having the *focus*. The focused desktop is the one displayed by the rendering thread.
- The user may request that the focus be changed at any time.
- Windows may move around and appear or disappear of their own accord, and the rendering thread must update its display accordingly.

We are supplied with a named function render which handles the business of rendering windows on the display. It should be called whenever the window layout changes:[2]

---

2. We are assuming that the actual window contents are rendered via some separate means, e.g., compositing.

```
render :: Set Window -> IO ()
```

The currently focused desktop is a piece of state that is shared by the rendering thread and some other thread that handles user input. Therefore, we represent that by a TVar:

```
type UserFocus = TVar Desktop
```

Next, we define an auxiliary function getWindows that takes the Display and the UserFocus and returns the set of windows to render in the STM monad. The implementation is straightforward: read the current focus and look up the contents of the appropriate desktop in the Display:

windowman.hs

```
getWindows :: Display -> UserFocus -> STM (Set Window)
getWindows disp focus = do
  desktop <- readTVar focus
  readTVar (disp ! desktop)
```

Finally, we can implement the rendering thread. The general plan is to repeatedly read the current state with getWindows and call render to render it, but use retry to avoid calling render when nothing has changed. Here is the code:

```
renderThread :: Display -> UserFocus -> IO ()
renderThread disp focus = do
  wins <- atomically $ getWindows disp focus    -- ❶
  loop wins                                      -- ❷
  where
  loop wins = do                                 -- ❸
    render wins                                  -- ❹
    next <- atomically $ do
              wins' <- getWindows disp focus     -- ❺
              if (wins == wins')                 -- ❻
                then retry                       -- ❼
                else return wins'                -- ❽
    loop next
```

❶   First, we read the current set of windows to display.

❷   We use this as the initial value for the loop.

❸   The loop takes the current set of windows as an argument, renders the windows, and then blocks until something changes that requires re-rendering.

❹   Each iteration calls render to display the current state and then enters a transaction to read the next state.

❺   Inside the transaction, we read the current state.

❻   We compare it to the state we just rendered.

❼   If the states are the same, then there is no need to do anything, so we call retry.

❽   If the states are different, then we return the new state, and the loop iterates with
the new state.

The effect of the retry is precisely what we need: it waits until the value read by
getWindows could possibly be different, because another thread has successfully completed a transaction that writes to one of the TVars that is read by getWindows. That
encompasses both changes to the focus (because the user switched to a different desktop), and changes to the contents of the current desktop (because a window moved,
appeared, or disappeared). Furthermore, changes to other desktops can take place
without the rendering thread being woken up.

If it weren't for STM's retry operation, we'd have to implement this complex logic
ourselves, including implementing the signals between threads that modify the state
and the rendering thread. This is anti-modular, because operations that modify the state
have to know about the observers that need to act on changes. Furthermore, it gives rise
to a common source of concurrency bugs: *lost wakeups*. If we forgot to signal the rendering thread, the display wouldn't be updated. In this case, the effects are somewhat
benign. In a more complex scenario, lost wakeups often lead to deadlocks: the woken
thread was supposed to complete an operation on which other threads are waiting.

Merging with STM

Recall that in "Merging" on page 152 we considered the problem of waiting for any event
from a set of possible events. Typically this requires the events to be merged into a single
MVar or Chan so that we can wait for the next event using takeMVar or readChan. In turn,
this means that the source of each event needs to know which MVar(s) or Chan(s) to send
it to, rather than each event being a completely independent entity.

The more general problem of taking either of two MVars requires creating two new
threads to take each MVar and put the result into a third MVar. However, even this doesn't
really solve the problem: if we wanted to take *at most* one of two MVars, then (as far as
I am aware) there is no way to do it; you just have to construct your program in a different
way so that it doesn't need to do this.

STM provides a neat solution to both of these problems in the form of an operation that
we have not yet introduced:

```
orElse :: STM a -> STM a -> STM a
```

The operation orElse a b has the following behavior:

- First, a is executed. If a returns a result, then the orElse call returns it and ends.
- If a calls retry instead, *a*'s effects are discarded_ and b is executed instead.

The orElse operator lets us combine two blocking transactions such that *one* is performed but not both. This is exactly what we need for composing several event sources, or for taking at most one of two MVars (actually TMVars, of course). The latter is coded as follows:

code/tmvar.hs

```
takeEitherTMVar :: TMVar a -> TMVar b -> STM (Either a b)
takeEitherTMVar ma mb =
  fmap Left (takeTMVar ma)
    `orElse`
  fmap Right (takeTMVar mb)
```

There are two calls to takeTMVar, with their results wrapped in Left and Right, respectively, composed together with orElse.

One thing to note is that orElse is left-biased: if both TMVars are non-empty, takeEitherTMVar will always return the contents of the first one. Whether this is problematic depends on the application. Be aware that the left-biased nature of orElse can have implications for fairness in some situations.

STM provides two complementary ways to compose blocking operations together: the ordinary monadic bind gives us "and", and orElse gives us "or".

Async Revisited

Recall in "Merging" on page 152 that we defined waitEither for the Async abstraction by forking two extra threads. STM's orElse now allows us to define waitEither much more efficiently. Furthermore, the extra flexibility of STM lets us compose Asyncs together in more interesting ways. But first, we need to rewrite the Async implementation in terms of STM, rather than MVar. The translation is straightforward: we just replace MVar with TMVar.

```
data Async a = Async ThreadId (TMVar (Either SomeException a))
```

The async function looks familiar, with only an additional atomically to wrap the call to putTMVar in the child thread:

```
async :: IO a -> IO (Async a)
async action = do
  var <- newEmptyTMVarIO
  t <- forkFinally action (atomically . putTMVar var)
  return (Async t var)
```

Here we used newEmptyTMVarIO, which is a convenient version of newEmptyTMVar in the IO monad.

The waitCatchSTM function is like waitCatch, but in the STM monad:

```
waitCatchSTM :: Async a -> STM (Either SomeException a)
waitCatchSTM (Async _ var) = readTMVar var
```

And we can define waitSTM, the version of waitCatchSTM that re-throws an exception result, in terms of waitCatchSTM:

```
waitSTM :: Async a -> STM a
waitSTM a = do
  r <- waitCatchSTM a
  case r of
    Left e  -> throwSTM e
    Right a -> return a
```

Now we can define waitEither by composing two calls to waitSTM using orElse:

```
waitEither :: Async a -> Async b -> IO (Either a b)
waitEither a b = atomically $
  fmap Left (waitSTM a)
    `orElse`
  fmap Right (waitSTM b)
```

More generally, we can wait for any number of Asyncs simultaneously. The function waitAny does this by first mapping waitSTM over a list of Asyncs and then composing the calls together by folding them with orElse:

```
waitAny :: [Async a] -> IO a
waitAny asyncs =
  atomically $ foldr orElse retry $ map waitSTM asyncs
```

In "Merging" on page 152 (*geturls6.hs*), we downloaded several URLs simultaneously and reported the first one to finish by using a version of waitAny that forked a new thread for each Async to wait for. Using the above definition of waitAny with the STM version of Async, we can now solve the same problem without forking a new thread per Async:

geturlsfirst.hs

```
main :: IO ()
main = do
  let
    download url = do
        r <- getURL url
        return (url, r)

  as <- mapM (async . download) sites

  (url, r) <- waitAny as
  printf "%s was first (%d bytes)\n" url (B.length r)
  mapM_ wait as
```

The program works as before, creating an Async to download each URL in the list. Then it calls waitAny to get the first result, reports it, and finally waits for the rest to complete.

Implementing Channels with STM

In this section, we'll implement the Chan type from "MVar as a Building Block: Un-bounded Channels" on page 135 using STM. As we'll see, using STM to implement Chan is rather less tricky than using MVars, and furthermore we are able to add complex operations that were difficult or impossible using MVars.

The STM version of Chan is called TChan, and the interface we wish to implement is as follows:[3]

```
data TChan a

newTChan   :: STM (TChan a)
writeTChan :: TChan a -> a -> STM ()
readTChan  :: TChan a -> STM a
```

This is exactly the same as Chan, except that we renamed Chan to TChan, and all the operations are in the STM monad rather than IO. The full code for the implementation is given next.

TChan.hs:

```
data TChan a = TChan (TVar (TVarList a))
                     (TVar (TVarList a))

type TVarList a = TVar (TList a)
data TList a = TNil | TCons a (TVarList a)

newTChan :: STM (TChan a)
newTChan = do
  hole <- newTVar TNil
  read <- newTVar hole
  write <- newTVar hole
  return (TChan read write)

readTChan :: TChan a -> STM a
readTChan (TChan readVar _) = do
  listHead <- readTVar readVar
  head <- readTVar listHead
  case head of
    TNil -> retry
    TCons val tail -> do
        writeTVar readVar tail
        return val

writeTChan :: TChan a -> a -> STM ()
writeTChan (TChan _ writeVar) a = do
  newListEnd <- newTVar TNil
```

---

3. The implementation is available in the module `Control.Concurrent.STM.TChan` from the `stm` package.

```
listEnd <- readTVar writeVar
writeTVar writeVar newListEnd
writeTVar listEnd (TCons a newListEnd)
```

The implementation is similar in structure to the MVar version in "MVar as a Building Block: Unbounded Channels" on page 135, so we do not describe it line by line; however, we will point out a few important details:

- All the operations are in the STM monad, so to use them they need to be wrapped in atomically (but they can also be composed; more about that later).

- The TList type needs a TNil constructor to indicate an empty list; in the MVar implementation, the empty list was represented implicitly by an empty MVar.

- Blocking in readTChan is implemented by a call to retry.

- Nowhere did we have to worry about what happens when a read executes concurrently with a write, because all the operations are atomic.

We now describe three distinct benefits of the STM implementation compared with using MVars.

More Operations Are Possible

In "MVar as a Building Block: Unbounded Channels" on page 135, we mentioned the operation unGetChan, which could not be implemented with the desired semantics using MVars. Here is its implementation with STM:

```
unGetTChan :: TChan a -> a -> STM ()
unGetTChan (TChan readVar _) a = do
   listHead <- readTVar readVar
   newHead <- newTVar (TCons a listHead)
   writeTVar readVar newHead
```

The obvious implementation does the right thing here. Other operations that were not possible with MVars are straightforward with STM; an example is isEmptyTChan, the MVar version that suffers from the same problem as unGetChan:

```
isEmptyTChan :: TChan a -> STM Bool
isEmptyTChan (TChan read _write) = do
   listhead <- readTVar read
   head <- readTVar listhead
   case head of
     TNil -> return True
     TCons _ _ -> return False
```

Composition of Blocking Operations

Because blocking STM computations can be composed together, we can build composite operations like readEitherTChan:

```
readEitherTChan :: TChan a -> TChan b -> STM (Either a b)
```

This function reads a value from either of the two TChans passed as arguments, or blocks if they are both empty. Its implementation should look familiar, being similar to takeEitherTMVar:

```
readEitherTChan :: TChan a -> TChan b -> STM (Either a b)
readEitherTChan a b =
  fmap Left (readTChan a)
    `orElse`
  fmap Right (readTChan b)
```

Asynchronous Exception Safety

Up until now, we have said nothing about how exceptions in STM behave. The STM monad supports exceptions much like the IO monad, with two operations:

```
throwSTM :: Exception e => e -> STM a
catchSTM :: Exception e => STM a -> (e -> STM a) -> STM a
```

The throwSTM operation throws an exception, and catchSTM catches exceptions and invokes a handler, just like catch in the IO monad. However, exceptions in STM are different in one vital way: in catchSTM m h, if m raises an exception, then *all of its effects are discarded*, and then the handler h is invoked. As a degenerate case, if there is no enclosing catchSTM at all, then all of the effects of the transaction are discarded and the exception is propagated out of atomically.

An example should help to demonstrate the motivation for this behavior. Imagine an STM operation readCheck defined as follows:

```
readCheck :: TChan a -> STM a
readCheck chan = do
  a <- readTChan chan
  checkValue a
```

Where checkValue is an operation that imposes some extra constraints on the value read from the channel. Now suppose checkValue raises an exception (perhaps accidentally, e.g., divide-by-zero). We would prefer it if the readTChan had not happened because an element of the channel would be lost. Furthermore, we would like readCheck to have this behavior regardless of whether there is an enclosing exception handler or not. Hence catchSTM discards the effects of its first argument in the event of an exception.

The discarding-effects behavior is even more useful in the case of *asynchronous* exceptions. If an asynchronous exception occurs during an STM transaction, the effects of the transaction are discarded, just as for a synchronous exception. So in most cases, asynchronous exception safety in STM consists of doing *absolutely nothing at all*. There are no locks to replace, so there is no need for exception handlers or bracket and no need to worry about which critical sections to protect with mask.

The implementation of TChan given earlier is entirely safe with respect to asynchronous exceptions as it stands, and moreover any compositions of these operations are also safe.

STM provides a nice way to write code that is automatically safe with respect to asynchronous exceptions, so it can be useful even for state that is not shared between threads. The only catch is that we have to use STM consistently for all our state, but having made that leap, asynchronous exception safety comes for free.

An Alternative Channel Implementation

In the previous section, we implemented a channel type that was analogous to the MVar-based Chan, in that it has a similar implementation structure and the same basic operations. However, the flexibility of STM gives us more choices in how to construct channels, and in fact if we don't need dupChan, we can implement a much more efficient channel abstraction.

The key observation is that in STM, an operation can block on any condition whatsoever. This means we can represent the channel contents by any data structure we choose. For example, even a simple list works:

TList.hs

```
newtype TList a = TList (TVar [a])

newTList :: STM (TList a)
newTList = do
  v  <- newTVar []
  return (TList v)

writeTList :: TList a -> a -> STM ()
writeTList (TList v) a = do
  list <- readTVar v
  writeTVar v (list ++ [a])

readTList :: TList a -> STM a
readTList (TList v) = do
  xs <- readTVar v
  case xs of
    []      -> retry
    (x:xs') -> do
      writeTVar v xs'
      return x
```

This is a channel abstraction with the same behavior as TChan; readTList blocks when the channel is empty, because it can detect the empty list and call retry.

There is a performance problem with this representation, though. Note that `writeTList` must add an element to the *end* of the list, which, using the standard Haskell list datatype, requires an $O(n)$ append operation.

The solution is to use a different queue data structure that supports $O(1)$ enqueue and dequeue operations. There is a folklore technique for representing a queue that has the desired property: the idea is to represent a queue as two lists, `xs` and `ys`, where the whole contents of the list is given by `xs ++ reverse ys`. That is, to take an element from the front we take it from `xs`, and to add an element to the back we add it to the front of `ys`; both of these operations are $O(1)$. But what if `xs` is empty and we need to take an element? In that case, we must reverse `ys` and let that become the new `xs`. So while most of the time, taking an element from the front is $O(1)$, occasionally it is $O(n)$. However, we know that each list element is reversed only once, so on average the complexity of both enqueue and dequeue is $O(1)$.[4]

We can use this technique to represent the channel contents. This is the code:

TQueue.hs

```
data TQueue a = TQueue (TVar [a]) (TVar [a])

newTQueue :: STM (TQueue a)
newTQueue = do
  read  <- newTVar []
  write <- newTVar []
  return (TQueue read write)

writeTQueue :: TQueue a -> a -> STM ()
writeTQueue (TQueue _read write) a = do
  listend <- readTVar write
  writeTVar write (a:listend)

readTQueue :: TQueue a -> STM a
readTQueue (TQueue read write) = do
  xs <- readTVar read
  case xs of
    (x:xs') -> do writeTVar read xs'
                  return x
    [] -> do ys <- readTVar write
             case ys of
               [] -> retry                          -- ❶
               _  -> do let (z:zs) = reverse ys  -- ❷
                        writeTVar write []
                        writeTVar read zs
                        return z
```

4. Technically, the complexity is *amortized* $O(1)$. For more details on these kinds of data structures, I recommend reading Okasaki's *Purely Functional Data Structures* (Cambridge University Press, 1999).

❶ If we are reading from the channel and the read list is empty, then we check the write list. If that is also empty, then we block.

❷ If the ys list is non-empty, then we must reverse it and make it the new xs list, and then return the first element of the new xs as the value we read from the channel.

+ There is one subtlety here: we must be careful that the reverse is done lazily, which is why we use a let rather than case here. If we were to pattern-match on the result of the reverse strictly, the STM transaction could not complete until the reverse finished (see "Performance" on page 193).

Another happy consequence of this representation choice is that we are able to use a separate TVar for each list. This means that in the common case, readers and writers can proceed independently without conflict, which is important if we use this data structure in a parallel setting.

This implementation of channels in STM outperforms both the MVar-based Chan and the TVar-based TChan. A simple benchmark program can be found in *chanbench.hs* with three different scenarios:

- Two threads, one reading from and one writing to the channel
- One thread, writing a large number of values and then reading them
- One thread, repeatedly writing and then reading a number of values

On my computer, TQueue is about the same as Chan on the first test and wins by about 20% on the second and third test.

Why is TQueue so much faster? The main reason is that the data structure representing the channel contents is much more compact and thus faster to operate on: ordinary linked lists are very cheap in Haskell, whereas operations on TVar and MVar are much more expensive.

Bounded Channels

So far, we have seen one-place channels (MVar and TMVar) and unbounded channels (Chan and TChan), but in practice we often want something between the two. The one-place channel does not allow sufficient concurrency: consider multiple writers with a single reader. If there is a burst of writing activity, most of the writers will block waiting for the reading thread to catch up, and there will be a lot of context switching as the reader services each writer in turn. The unbounded channel has a different pathology: if the reading thread cannot keep up with the writers, the size of the channel will keep growing without bound, and in the worst case we could run out of memory.

Ideally, there should be some limit on the size of the channel so that the channel can absorb bursts of writing activity without the danger that heavy writing will use too much memory.

Fortunately, STM makes it quite straightforward to build a bounded channel. All we need to do is keep track of the current capacity in the channel and arrange that writing to the channel blocks if the channel is currently full. This implementation is based on TQueue:

TBQueue.hs

```
data TBQueue a = TBQueue (TVar Int) (TVar [a]) (TVar [a]) -- ❶

newTBQueue :: Int -> STM (TBQueue a)
newTBQueue size = do
  read  <- newTVar []
  write <- newTVar []
  cap   <- newTVar size
  return (TBQueue cap read write)

writeTBQueue :: TBQueue a -> a -> STM ()
writeTBQueue (TBQueue cap _read write) a = do
  avail <- readTVar cap                        -- ❷
  if avail == 0                                -- ❸
    then retry                                 -- ❹
    else writeTVar cap (avail - 1)             -- ❺
  listend <- readTVar write
  writeTVar write (a:listend)

readTBQueue :: TBQueue a -> STM a
readTBQueue (TBQueue cap read write) = do
  avail <- readTVar cap                        -- ❻
  writeTVar cap (avail + 1)
  xs <- readTVar read
  case xs of
    (x:xs') -> do writeTVar read xs'
                  return x
    [] -> do ys <- readTVar write
             case ys of
               [] -> retry
               _  -> do let (z:zs) = reverse ys
                        writeTVar write []
                        writeTVar read zs
                        return z
```

❶ The TBQueue data type is like the TQueue we saw previously but has an extra TVar Int to store the channel's current capacity.

❷ In writeTBQueue, we first read the current capacity.

❸ If the capacity is zero, meaning the channel is full,

❹ we call `retry` to block.

❺ Otherwise, decrease the capacity by 1, because we are about to add another element.

❻ When reading, we always increment the capacity.

In the *chanbench.hs* channel benchmark, the bounded channel performs almost as well as `TQueue` in the first test, although it doesn't do so well in the third test, performing about the same as `TChan`. The second test, which writes a large number of items to the channel, inevitably fails with `TBQueue`.

 The danger with bounded channels is that it is possible to write a program with a lurking deadlock that is only discovered much later when the program is running in production. This is because the vast majority of the time `writeTBQueue` does not block, but once in a while, probably under heavy load, the channel fills up and `writeTBQueue` blocks. If the program depends on `writeTBQueue` not blocking, it may deadlock. How might we get into this situation? It is the dining philosophers problem again:

```
thread 1:
  x <- atomically $ readTBQueue q1
  y <- atomically $ readTBQueue q2

thread 2:
  atomically $ writeTBQueue q2 y
  atomically $ writeTBQueue q1 x
```

This sequence will work perfectly well until q2 becomes full, at which point we get a deadlock. If the communication pattern is obscured by other code, we might not realize there's a problem.

There's no silver bullet. The best advice is to test your code thoroughly with a buffer size of 1, because that will tend to expose any deadlocks of this kind during testing. Note that deadlocks will often be detected by the runtime system and result in an exception rather than a hang; see "Detecting Deadlock" on page 278.

What Can We Not Do with STM?

STM offers a qualitative improvement over `MVar` in various ways: composable atomicity, composable blocking, and simpler error handling. Therefore, it is reasonable to ask whether we need `MVar` at all, and whether there is anything that is harder to accomplish with STM than with `MVar`.

One unsurprising advantage of `MVar` is that it is faster than STM. But even though a straightforward comparison of, say, `takeMVar` against `atomically . takeTMVar` will show that takeMVar is faster, we should not assume that using MVar will always result in faster code. As we saw in the previous section, we can build a channel using STM that outperforms the MVar-based version, and furthermore is composable.

In fact, MVar does have one other important advantage over STM, which we mentioned earlier: *fairness*. When multiple threads block on an MVar, they are guaranteed to be woken up in FIFO order, and no single thread can be blocked in takeMVar indefinitely so long as there is a constant supply of putMVars. In contrast, when multiple threads are blocked in STM transactions that depend on a particular TVar, and the TVar is modified by another thread, it is not enough to just wake up one of the blocked transactions— the runtime must wake them all. To see why, consider the following:

```
do x <- takeTMVar m
   when (x /= 42) retry
```

A transaction can block on an arbitrary condition, so the runtime doesn't know whether any individual transaction will be able to make progress after the TVar is changed; it must run the transaction to find out. Hence, when there are multiple transactions that might be unblocked, we have to run them all; after all, they might *all* be able to continue now. Because the runtime has to run all the blocked transactions, there is no guarantee that threads will be unblocked in FIFO order and no guarantee of fairness.

You might wonder whether we could *implement* fairness using STM. For example, suppose we want to add fairness to our TMVar implementation. We will need to represent explicitly the queue of blocked takeTMVars, perhaps as a list of TVars, each waiting to receive a value. Conversely, the blocked putTMVars could also be a list of TVars, each with a value to put. In fact, we could represent all the blocked threads by a list of TVar (Maybe a).

So this could be the TMVar data type:

```
data TMVar a = TMVar (TVar (Maybe a)) (TVar [TVar (Maybe a)])
```

Now consider how putMVar would work. There are three cases to consider:

The TMVar *is empty, and there are no blocked* takeTMVars
Store the value in the TMVar and return.

The TMVar *is empty, and there are some blocked* takeTMVars
Removes the first blocked takeTMVar from the queue and put the value in its TVar.

The TMVar *is full*
We must create a new TVar containing Just a (the value to be put), add this to the end of the list of blocked putTMVars, and then wait until the TVar contents becomes Nothing.

The last case is the tricky one: we cannot write a transaction that *both* has a visible effect (adds something to the list) *and* calls retry, because calling retry abandons any changes to TVars made by the current transaction.

The only way to implement fairness is to abandon composability. We can implement a TMVar with the structure I suggested, but the operations must be in the IO monad, not the STM monad. The trick is to have the STM transaction return an IO action that is executed after the STM transaction completes. I'll leave the implementation as an exercise for the reader.

In general, the class of operations that STM cannot express are those that involve multi-way communication between threads. The simplest example is a synchronous channel, in which both the reader and the writer must be present simultaneously for the operation to go ahead. We cannot implement this in STM, at least compositionally, for the same reason that we cannot implement TMVar with fairness: the operations need to block *and* have a visible effect—advertise that there is a blocked thread—simultaneously.

Performance

As with most abstractions, STM has a runtime cost. If we understand the cost model, we can avoid writing code that hits the bad cases. So in this section I'll give an informal description of the implementation of STM, with enough detail that the reader can understand the cost model.

An STM transaction works by accumulating a *log* of readTVar and writeTVar operations that have happened so far during the transaction. The log is used in three ways:

- By storing writeTVar operations in the log rather than applying them to main memory immediately, discarding the effects of a transaction is easy; we just throw away the log. Hence, aborting a transaction has a fixed small cost.

- Each readTVar must traverse the log to check whether the TVar was written by an earlier writeTVar. Hence, readTVar is an $O(n)$ operation in the length of the log.

- Because the log contains a record of all the readTVar operations, it can be used to discover the full set of TVars read during the transaction, which we need to know in order to implement retry.

When a transaction reaches the end, the STM implementation compares the log against the contents of memory. If the current contents of memory match the values read by readTVar, the effects of the transaction are *committed* to memory, and if not, the log is discarded and the transaction runs again from the beginning. This process takes place atomically by locking all the TVars involved in the transaction for the duration. The STM implementation in GHC does not use global locks; only the TVars involved in the transaction are locked during commit, so transactions operating on disjoint sets of TVars can proceed without interference.

There are two important rules of thumb:

- Never read an unbounded number of TVars in a single transaction because the $O(n)$ performance of readTVar then gives $O(n^2)$ for the whole transaction.
- Try to avoid expensive evaluation inside a transaction because this will cause the transaction to take a long time, increasing the chance that another transaction will modify one or more of the same TVars, causing the current transaction to be re-executed. In the worst case, a long-running transaction re-executes indefinitely because it is repeatedly aborted by shorter transactions.

It is possible that a future STM implementation may use a different data structure to store the log, reducing the readTVar overhead to $O(\log n)$ or better (on average), but the likelihood that a long transaction will fail to commit would still be an issue. To avoid that problem, intelligent contention-management is required, which is an area of active research.

The retry operation uses the transaction log to find out which TVars were accessed by the transaction, because changes to any of these TVars must trigger a rerun of the current transaction. Hence, each TVar has a *watch list* of threads that should be woken up if the TVar is modified, and retry adds the current thread to the watch list of all the TVars read during the current transaction. Hence, retry is $O(n)$ in the number of TVars read during the transaction. When a transaction is committed, if any of the modified TVars has a watch list, then the threads on the list are all woken up.

One other thing to watch out for is composing too many blocking operations together. If we wanted to wait for a list of TMVars to become full, we might be tempted to do this:

```
atomically $ mapM takeTMVar ts
```

Imagine that the TMVars all started empty and became full one at a time in the same order as the list ts. Each time a new TMVar becomes full, the transaction wakes up and runs again, going to sleep at the next empty TMVar. We'll run the transaction from the start, once for every element of ts, so the whole operation is $O(n^2)$. If instead, we had written this code:

```
mapM (atomically . takeTMVar) ts
```

then it is $O(n)$, although now the semantics are different—it is not a single transaction anymore—but if these semantics are acceptable, then the second form will be much faster.

Summary

To summarize, STM provides several benefits for concurrent programming:

Composable atomicity
> You can construct arbitrarily large atomic operations on shared state, which can simplify the implementation of concurrent data structures with fine-grained locking.

Composable blocking
> You can build operations that choose between multiple blocking operations, which is very difficult with MVars and other low-level concurrency abstractions.

Robustness in the presence of failure and cancellation
> A transaction in progress is aborted if an exception occurs, so STM makes it easy to maintain invariants on state in the presence of exceptions.

CHAPTER 11

Higher-Level Concurrency Abstractions

The preceding sections covered the basic interfaces for writing concurrent code in Haskell. These are enough for simple tasks, but for larger and more complex programs we need to raise the level of abstraction.

The previous chapters developed the `Async` interface for performing operations asynchronously and waiting for the results. In this chapter, we will be revisiting that interface and expanding it with some more sophisticated functionality. In particular, we will provide a way to create an `Async` that is automatically cancelled if its parent dies and then use this to build more compositional functionality.

What we are aiming for is the ability to build *trees of threads*, such that when a thread dies for whatever reason, two things happen: any children it has are automatically terminated, and its parent is informed. Thus the tree is always collapsed from the bottom up, and no threads are ever left running accidentally. Furthermore, all threads are given a chance to clean up when they die, by handling exceptions.

Avoiding Thread Leakage

Let's review the last version of the `Async` API that we encountered from "Async Revisited" on page 182:

```
data Async

async        :: IO a -> IO (Async a)
cancel       :: Async a -> IO ()

waitCatchSTM :: Async a -> STM (Either SomeException a)
waitCatch    :: Async a -> IO (Either SomeException a)

waitSTM      :: Async a -> STM a
wait         :: Async a -> IO a
```

```
waitEither    :: Async a -> Async b -> IO (Either a b)
```

Now we'll define a way to create an Async that is automatically cancelled if the current thread dies. A good motivation for this arises from the example we had in "Error Handling with Async" on page 151, *geturls4.hs*, which contains the following code:

```
main = do
  a1 <- async (getURL "http://www.wikipedia.org/wiki/Shovel")
  a2 <- async (getURL "http://www.wikipedia.org/wiki/Spade")
  r1 <- wait a1
  r2 <- wait a2
  print (B.length r1, B.length r2)
```

Consider what happens when the first Async, a1, fails with an exception. The first wait operation throws the same exception, which gets propagated up to the top of main, resulting in program termination. But this is untidy: we left a2 running, and if this had been deep in a program, we would be not only leaking a thread, but also leaving some I/O running in the background.

What we would like to do is create an Async and install an exception handler that cancels the Async should an exception be raised. This is a typical resource acquire/release pattern, and Haskell has a good abstraction for that: the bracket function. Here is the general pattern:

```
bracket (async io) cancel operation
```

Here, *io* is the IO action to perform asynchronously and *operation* is the code to execute while *io* is running. Typically, *operation* will include a wait to get the result of the Async. For example, we could rewrite *geturls4.hs* in this way:

```
main = do
  bracket (async (getURL "http://www.wikipedia.org/wiki/Shovel"))
          cancel $ \a1 -> do
  bracket (async (getURL "http://www.wikipedia.org/wiki/Shovel"))
          cancel $ \a2 -> do
  r1 <- wait a1
  r2 <- wait a2
  print (B.length r1, B.length r2)
```

But this is a bit of a mouthful. Let's package up the bracket pattern into a function instead:

```
withAsync :: IO a -> (Async a -> IO b) -> IO b
withAsync io operation = bracket (async io) cancel operation
```

Now our main function becomes:

geturls7.hs

```
main =
  withAsync (getURL "http://www.wikipedia.org/wiki/Shovel") $ \a1 ->
```

```
withAsync (getURL "http://www.wikipedia.org/wiki/Spade") $ \a2 -> do
  r1 <- wait a1
  r2 <- wait a2
  print (B.length r1, B.length r2)
```

This is an improvement over *geturls6.hs*. Now the second Async is cleaned up if the first one fails.

Symmetric Concurrency Combinators

Take another look at the example at the end of the previous section. The behavior in the event of failure is lopsided: if a1 fails, then the alarm is raised immediately, but if a2 fails, then the program waits for a result from a1 before it notices the failure of a2. Ideally, we should be able to write this symmetrically so that we notice the failure of either a1 or a2, whichever one happens first. This is somewhat like the waitEither operation that we defined earlier:

```
waitEither :: Async a -> Async b -> IO (Either a b)
```

But here we want to wait for *both* results and terminate early if either Async raises an exception. By analogy with waitEither, let's call it waitBoth:

```
waitBoth :: Async a -> Async b -> IO (a,b)
```

Indeed, we can program waitBoth rather succinctly, thanks to STM's orElse combinator:

```
waitBoth :: Async a -> Async b -> IO (a,b)
waitBoth a1 a2 =
  atomically $ do
    r1 <- waitSTM a1 `orElse` (do waitSTM a2; retry) -- ❶
    r2 <- waitSTM a2
    return (r1,r2)
```

It is worth considering the different cases to convince yourself that line ❶ has the right behavior:

- If a1 threw an exception, then the exception is re-thrown here (remember that if an Async results in an exception, it is re-thrown by waitSTM).
- If a1 returned a result, then we proceed to the next line and wait for a2's result.
- If waitSTM a1 retries, then we enter the right side of orElse:
  - If a2 threw an exception, then the exception is re-thrown here.
  - If a2 returned a result, then we ignore it and call retry, so the whole transaction retries. This case might seem counterintuitive, but the purpose of calling waitSTM a2 here was to check whether a2 had thrown an exception. We aren't interested in its result yet because we know that a1 has still not completed.

— If `waitSTM a2` retries, then the whole transaction retries.

Now, using `withAsync` and `waitBoth`, we can build a nice symmetric function that runs two IO actions concurrently but aborts if either one fails with an exception:

```
concurrently :: IO a -> IO b -> IO (a,b)
concurrently ioa iob =
  withAsync ioa $ \a ->
  withAsync iob $ \b ->
    waitBoth a b
```

Finally, we can rewrite *geturls7.hs* to use `concurrently`:

geturls8.hs

```
main = do
  (r1,r2) <- concurrently
               (getURL "http://www.wikipedia.org/wiki/Shovel")
               (getURL "http://www.wikipedia.org/wiki/Spade")
  print (B.length r1, B.length r2)
```

What if we wanted to download a list of URLs at the same time? The `concurrently` function takes only two arguments, but we can fold it over a list, provided that we use a small wrapper to rebuild the list of results:

geturls9.hs

```
main = do
  xs <- foldr conc (return []) (map getURL sites)
  print (map B.length xs)
 where
  conc ioa ioas = do
    (a,as) <- concurrently ioa ioas
    return (a:as)
```

The `concurrently` function has a companion; if we swap `waitBoth` for `waitEither`, we get a different but equally useful function:

```
race :: IO a -> IO b -> IO (Either a b)
race ioa iob =
  withAsync ioa $ \a ->
  withAsync iob $ \b ->
    waitEither a b
```

The `race` function runs two IO actions concurrently, but as soon as one of them returns a result or throws an exception, the other is immediately cancelled. Hence the name `race`: the two IO actions are racing to produce a result. As we shall see later, `race` is quite useful when we need to fork two threads while letting either one terminate the other by just returning.

These two functions, `race` and `concurrently`, are the essence of constructing trees of threads. Each builds a structure like Figure 11-1.

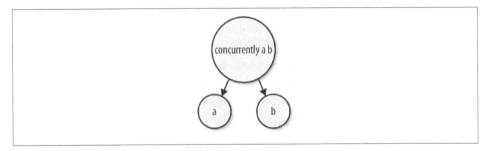

Figure 11-1. Threads created by concurrently

By using multiple race and concurrently calls, we can build up larger trees of threads. If we use these functions consistently, we can be sure that the tree of threads constructed will always be collapsed from the bottom up:

- If a parent throws an exception or receives an asynchronous exception, then the children are automatically cancelled. This happens recursively. If the children have children themselves, then they will also be cancelled, and so on.
- If one child receives an exception, then its sibling is also cancelled.
- The parent chooses whether to wait for a result from both children or just one, by using race or concurrently, respectively.

What is particularly nice about this way of building thread trees is that there is no explicit representation of the tree as a data structure, which would involve a lot of bookkeeping and would likely be prone to errors. The thread tree is completely implicit in the structure of the calls to withAsync and hence concurrently and race.

Timeouts Using race

A simple demonstration of the power of race is an implementation of the timeout function from "Timeouts" on page 164.

timeout2.hs

```haskell
timeout :: Int -> IO a -> IO (Maybe a)
timeout n m
  | n < 0     = fmap Just m
  | n == 0    = return Nothing
  | otherwise = do
      r <- race (threadDelay n) m
      case r of
        Left _  -> return Nothing
        Right a -> return (Just a)
```

Most of the code here is administrative: checking for negative and zero timeout values and converting the `Either ()` a result of `race` into a `Maybe a`. The core of the implementation is simply `race (threadDelay n) m`.

Pedantically speaking, this implementation of `timeout` does have a few differences from the one in "Timeouts" on page 164. First, it doesn't have precisely the same semantics in the case where another thread sends the current thread an exception using `throwTo`. With the original `timeout`, the exception would be delivered to the computation `m`, whereas here the exception is delivered to `race`, which then terminates `m` with `killThread`, and so the exception seen by `m` will be `ThreadKilled`, not the original one that was thrown.

Secondly, the exception thrown to `m` in the case of a timeout is `ThreadKilled`, not a special `Timeout` exception. This might be important if the thread wanted to act on the `Timeout` exception.

Finally, `race` creates an extra thread, which makes this implementation of `timeout` a little less efficient than the one in "Timeouts" on page 164. You won't notice the difference unless `timeout` is in a critical path in your application, though.

Adding a Functor Instance

When an `Async` is created, it has a fixed result type corresponding to the type of the value returned by the `IO` action. But this might be inconvenient: suppose we need to wait for several different `Async`s that have different result types. We would like to emulate the `waitAny` function defined in "Async Revisited" on page 182:

```
waitAny :: [Async a] -> IO a
waitAny asyncs =
  atomically $ foldr orElse retry $ map waitSTM asyncs
```

But if our `Async`s don't all have the same result type, then we can't put them in a list. We could force them all to have the same type when they are created, but that might be difficult, especially if we use an `Async` created by a library function that is not under our control.

A better solution to the problem is to make `Async` an instance of `Functor`:

```
class Functor f where
    fmap :: (a -> b) -> f a -> f b
```

The `fmap` operation lets us map the result of an `Async` into any type we need.

But how can we implement `fmap` for `Async`? The type of the result that the `Async` will place in the `TMVar` is fixed when we create the `Async`; the definition of `Async` is the following:

```
data Async a = Async ThreadId (TMVar (Either SomeException a))
```

Instead of storing the TMVar in the Async, we need to store something more compositional that we can compose with the function argument to fmap to change the result type. One solution is to replace the TMVar with an STM computation that returns the same type:

```
data Async a = Async ThreadId (STM (Either SomeException a))
```

The change is very minor. We only need to move the readTMVar call from waitCatchSTM to async:

```
async :: IO a -> IO (Async a)
async action = do
  var <- newEmptyTMVarIO
  t <- forkFinally action (atomically . putTMVar var)
  return (Async t (readTMVar var))

waitCatchSTM :: Async a -> STM (Either SomeException a)
waitCatchSTM (Async _ stm) = stm
```

And now we can define fmap by building a new STM computation that is composed from the old one by applying the function argument of fmap to the result:

```
instance Functor Async where
  fmap f (Async t stm) = Async t stm'
    where stm' = do
            r <- stm
            case r of
              Left e  -> return (Left e)
              Right a -> return (Right (f a))
```

Summary: The Async API

We visited the Async API several times during the course of the previous few chapters, each time evolving it to add a new feature or to fix some undesirable behavior. The addition of the Functor instance in the previous section represents the last addition I'll be making to Async in this book, so it seems like a good point to take a step back and summarize what has been achieved:

- We started with a simple API to execute an IO action asynchronously (async) and wait for its result (wait).

- We modified the implementation to catch exceptions in the asynchronous code and propagate them to the wait call. This avoids a common error in concurrent programming: forgetting to handle errors in a child thread.

- We reimplemented the Async API using STM, which made it possible to have efficient implementations of combinators that symmetrically wait for multiple Asyncs to complete (waitEither, waitBoth).

- We added `withAsync`, which avoids the accidental leakage of threads when an exception occurs in the parent thread, thus avoiding another common pitfall in concurrent programming.

- Finally, we combined `withAsync` with `waitEither` and `waitBoth` to make the high-level symmetric combinators `race` and `concurrently`. These two operations can be used to build trees of threads that are always collapsed from the bottom up and to propagate errors correctly.

The complete library is available in the `async` package on Hackage.

CHAPTER 12

Concurrent Network Servers

Server-type applications that communicate with many clients simultaneously demand both a high degree of concurrency and high performance from the I/O subsystem. A good web server should be able to handle hundreds of thousands of concurrent connections and service tens of thousands of requests per second.

Ideally, we would like to write these kinds of applications using threads. A thread is the right abstraction. It allows the developer to focus on programming the interaction with a single client and then to lift this interaction to multiple clients by simply forking many instances of the single-client interaction in separate threads. In this chapter, we explore this idea by developing a series of server applications, starting from a trivial server with no interaction between clients, then adding some shared state, and finally building a chat server with state and inter-client interaction.

Along the way, we will need to draw on many of the concepts from previous chapters. We'll discuss the design of the server using both MVar and STM, how to handle failure, and building groups of threads using the abstractions introduced in "Symmetric Concurrency Combinators" on page 199.

A Trivial Server

In this section, we will consider how to build a simple network server with the following behavior:

- The server accepts connections from clients on port 44444.
- If a client sends an integer n, then the service responds with the value of $2n$.
- If a client sends the string "end", then the server closes the connection.

First, we program the interaction with a single client. The function talk defined below takes a Handle for communicating with the client. The Handle will be bound to a network socket so that data sent by the client can be read from the Handle, and data written to the Handle will be sent to the client.

server.hs

```haskell
talk :: Handle -> IO ()
talk h = do
  hSetBuffering h LineBuffering                              -- ❶
  loop                                                       -- ❷
  where
   loop = do
     line <- hGetLine h                                      -- ❸
     if line == "end"                                        -- ❹
       then hPutStrLn h ("Thank you for using the " ++       -- ❺
                         "Haskell doubling service.")
       else do hPutStrLn h (show (2 * (read line :: Integer))) -- ❻
               loop                                          -- ❼
```

❶ First, we set the buffering mode for the Handle to line buffering. If we don't, output sent to the Handle will be buffered up by the I/O layer until there is a full block (which is more efficient for large transfers, but not useful for interactive applications).

❷ We enter a loop to respond to requests from the client.

❸ Each iteration of the loop reads a new line of text.

❹ Then it checks whether the client sent "end".

❺ If so, we emit a polite message and return.

❻ If not, we attempt to interpret the line as an integer and to write the value obtained by doubling it.

❼ Finally, we call loop again to read the next request.

Having dealt with the interaction with a single client, we can now make this into a multiclient server using concurrency. The main function for our server is as follows:

```haskell
main = withSocketsDo $ do
  sock <- listenOn (PortNumber (fromIntegral port))          -- ❶
  printf "Listening on port %d\n" port
  forever $ do                                               -- ❷
    (handle, host, port) <- accept sock                      -- ❸
    printf "Accepted connection from %s: %s\n" host (show port)
    forkFinally (talk handle) (\_ -> hClose handle)          -- ❹

port :: Int
port = 44444
```

❶ First, we create a network socket to listen on port 44444.

❷ Then we enter a loop to accept connections from clients.

❸ This line waits for a new client connection. The `accept` operation blocks until a connection request from a client arrives and then returns a `Handle` for communicating with the client (here bound to `handle`) and some information about the client. Here we bind `host` to the client's hostname and `port` to the local port that accepted the connection but use the variables just to log information to the console.

❹ Next, we call `forkFinally` to create a new thread to handle the request. The interaction with the client is delegated to the function `talk` that we defined above, to which we pass the `handle` returned by the `accept` call. We defined `forkFinally` back in "Catching Asynchronous Exceptions" on page 166.[1] It is used here to ensure that the `Handle` is always closed in the event of an exception in the server thread. If we didn't do this, then GHC's garbage collector would eventually close the `Handle` for us, but it might take a while, and we might run out of `Handle`s in the meantime (there is usually a fixed limit imposed by the operating system on the number of open `Handle`s).

Having forked a thread to handle this client, the main thread then goes back to accepting more connections. All the active client connections and the main thread run concurrently with each other, so the fact that the server is handling multiple clients will be invisible to any individual client.

So making our concurrent server was simple—we did not have to change the single-client code at all, and the code to lift it to a concurrent server was only a handful of lines. We can verify that it works by starting the server in one window:

```
$ ./server
```

In another window, we start a client and try a single request. We send 22 and get 44 in return.[2]

```
$ nc localhost 44444
22
44
```

Next, we leave this client running and start another client:

```
$ ghc -e 'mapM_ print [1..]' | nc localhost 44444
2
4
6
...
```

1. It is provided by `Control.Concurrent` in GHC 7.6.1 and later.
2. *nc* is the *netcat* program, which is useful for simple network interaction. You can also use `telnet` if `nc` is not available.

This client exercises the server a bit more by sending it a continuous stream of numbers to double. For fun, try starting a few of these. Meanwhile we can switch back to our first client and observe that it is still being serviced:

```
$ nc localhost 44444
22
44
33
66
```

Finally, we can end a single client's interaction by typing end:

```
end
Thank you for using the Haskell doubling service.
```

This was just a simple example, but the same ideas underlie several high-performance web server implementations in Haskell. Furthermore, with no additional effort at all, the same server code can make use of multiple cores simply by compiling with -threaded and running with +RTS -N.

There are two technologies that make this structure feasible in Haskell:

- GHC's very lightweight threads mean that having one thread per client is practical.
- GHC's I/O libraries employ an I/O manager thread that multiplexes all the ongoing I/O requests using efficient operating system primitives such as epoll on Linux. Thus applications with lots of lightweight threads, all doing I/O simultaneously, perform very well.

Were it not for lightweight threads and the I/O manager, we would have to resort to collapsing the structure into a single event loop (or worse, multiple event loops to take advantage of multiple cores). The event loop style loses the single-client abstraction. Instead, all clients have to be dealt with simultaneously, which can be complicated if there are different kinds of clients with different behaviors. Furthermore, we have to represent the state of each client somehow, rather than just writing the straight-line code as we did in talk earlier. Imagine extending talk to implement a more elaborate protocol with several states—it would be reasonably straightforward with the single-client abstraction, but if we had to represent each state and the transitions explicitly, things would quickly get complicated.

We ignored many details that would be necessary in a real server application. The reader is encouraged to think about these and try implementing any required changes on top of the provided sample code:

- What happens if the user interrupts the server with Ctrl+C? (Ctrl+C is implemented by sending an asynchronous Interrupted exception to the main thread.)
- What happens in talk if the line does not parse as a number?

- What happens if the client cuts the connection prematurely or the network goes down?
- Should there be a limit on the number of clients we serve simultaneously?
- Can we log the activity of the server to a file?

Extending the Simple Server with State

Next, we'll extend the simple server from the previous section to include some state that is shared amongst the clients and may be changed by client actions.

The new behavior is as follows: instead of multiplying each number by two, the server will multiply each number by the *current factor*. Any connected client can change the current factor by sending the command *N, where N is an integer. When a client changes the factor, the server sends a message to all the other connected clients informing them of the change.

While this seems like a small change in behavior, it introduces some interesting new challenges in designing the server.

- There is a shared state—the current factor—so we must decide how to store it and how it is accessed and modified.
- When one server thread changes the state in response to its client issuing the *N command, we must arrange to send a message to all the connected clients.

Let's explore the design space, taking as a given that we want to serve each client from a separate thread on the server. Over the following sections, I'll outline four possible designs and explain the pros and cons of each one.

Design One: One Giant Lock

This is the simplest approach. The state of the server is stored under a single MVar and looks something like this:

```
data State = State {
  currentFactor :: Int,
  clientHandles :: [Handle]
  }

newtype StateVar = StateVar (MVar State)
```

Note that the state contains all the Handles of the connected clients. This is so that if a server thread receives a factor-change command from its client, it can notify all the other clients of the change by writing a message to their Handle.

However, we have to be careful. If multiple threads write to a Handle simultaneously, the messages might get interleaved in an arbitrary way. To make sure messages don't get interleaved, we can use the MVar as a lock. But this means that every server thread, when it needs to send a message to its client, must hold the MVar while sending the message.

Clearly, the disadvantage of this model is that there will be lots of contention for the shared MVar, since even when clients are not interacting with each other, they still have to take the lock. This design does not have enough concurrency.

Note that we can't reduce contention by using finer-grained locking here because the combination of modifying the state and informing all the clients must be atomic. Otherwise, the notifications created by multiple factor-change commands could interleave with one another and clients may end up being misled about the current factor value.

Design Two: One Chan Per Server Thread

To add more concurrency, we want to design the system so that each server thread can communicate with its client privately without interacting with the other server threads. Therefore, the Handle for communicating with the client must be private to each server thread.

The factor-change command still has to notify all the clients, but since the server thread is the only thread allowed to communicate with a client, we must send a message to all the server threads when a factor-change occurs. Therefore, each server thread must have a Chan on which it receives messages.

The types in this setup would look like this:

```
data State = State {
  clientChans :: [Chan Message]
 }

data Message
  = FactorChange Int
  | ClientInput String

newtype StateVar = StateVar (MVar State)
```

There are two kinds of events that a server thread can act upon: a factor-change event from another server thread or a line of input from the client. Therefore, we make a Message type to combine these two events so that the Chan can carry either. How do the ClientInput events get generated? We need another thread for each server thread whose sole job it is to receive lines of input from the client's Handle and forward them to the Chan in the form of ClientInput events. I'll call this the "receive thread."

This design is an improvement over the first design, although it does still have one drawback. A server thread that receives a factor-change command must iterate over the whole list of Chans sending a message to each one, and this must be done with the lock held, again for atomicity reasons. Furthermore, we have to keep the list of Chans up to date when clients connect and disconnect.

Design Three: Use a Broadcast Chan

To solve the issue that notifying all the clients requires a possibly expensive walk over the list of Chans, we can use a broadcast channel instead, where a broadcast channel is an ordinary Chan that we create a copy of for each server thread using dupChan (see "MVar as a Building Block: Unbounded Channels" on page 135). When an item is written to the broadcast channel, it will appear on all the copies.

So in this design, the only shared state we need is a single broadcast channel, which doesn't even need to be stored in an MVar (because it never changes). The messages sent on the broadcast channel are new factor values. Because all server threads will see messages on this channel in the same order, they all have a consistent view of the state.

```
newtype State = State { broadcastChan :: Chan Int }
```

However, there is one wrinkle with this design. The server thread must listen both for events on the broadcast channel and for input from the client. To merge these two kinds of events, we'll need a Chan as in the previous design, a receive thread to forward the client's input, and another thread to forward messages from the broadcast channel. Hence this design needs a total of three threads per client. The setup is summarized by the diagram in Figure 12-1.

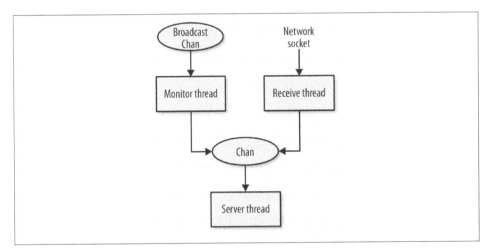

Figure 12-1. Server structure with Chan

Design Four: Use STM

We can improve on the previous design further by using STM. With STM, we can avoid the broadcast channel by storing the current factor in a single shared `TVar`:

```
newtype State = State { currentFactor :: TVar Int }
```

An STM transaction can watch for changes in the `TVar`'s value using the technique that we saw in "Blocking Until Something Changes" on page 179, so we don't need to explicitly send messages when it changes.

Furthermore, as we saw in "Merging with STM" on page 181, we can merge multiple sources of events in STM without using extra threads. We do need a receive thread to forward input from the client because an STM transaction can't wait for IO, but that's all. This design needs two threads per client. The overall structure is depicted in Figure 12-2.

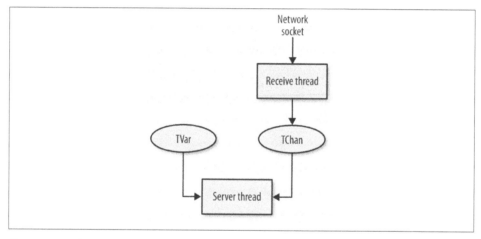

Figure 12-2. Server structure with STM

For concreteness, let's walk through the sequence of events that take place in this setup when a client issues a *N command:

- The receive thread reads the *N command from the `Handle`, and forwards it to the server thread's `TChan`.

- The server thread receives the command on its `TChan` and modifies the shared `TVar` containing the current factor.

- The change of value in the `TVar` is noticed by the other server threads, which all report the new value to their respective clients.

The Implementation

STM results in the simplest architecture, so we'll develop our solution using that. First, the main function, which has a couple of changes compared with the previous version:

server2.hs

```
main = withSocketsDo $ do
  sock <- listenOn (PortNumber (fromIntegral port))
  printf "Listening on port %d\n" port
  factor <- atomically $ newTVar 2                          -- ❶
  forever $ do
    (handle, host, port) <- accept sock
    printf "Accepted connection from %s: %s\n" host (show port)
    forkFinally (talk handle factor) (\_ -> hClose handle)   -- ❷

port :: Int
port = 44444
```

❶ Here, we create the TVar that contains the current factor and initialize its value to 2.

❷ The talk function now takes the factor TVar as an additional argument.

The talk function sets up the threads to handle the new client connection:

```
talk :: Handle -> TVar Integer -> IO ()
talk h factor = do
  hSetBuffering h LineBuffering
  c <- atomically newTChan           -- ❶
  race (server h factor c) (receive h c)  -- ❷
  return ()
```

❶ Creates the new TChan that will carry the messages from the receive thread.

❷ Creates the server and receive threads. (The server and receive functions will be defined shortly.) Note that we are using race from "Symmetric Concurrency Combinators" on page 199. race is particularly useful here because we want to set up a sibling relationship between the two threads. If either thread fails for any reason, then we want to cancel the other thread and raise the exception, which will cause the client connection to be cleanly shut down. Furthermore, race gives us the ability to terminate one thread by simply returning from the other. We don't intend the receive thread to ever voluntarily terminate, but it is useful to be able to shut down cleanly by just returning from the server thread.

The receive function repeatedly reads a line from the Handle and writes it to the TChan:

```
receive :: Handle -> TChan String -> IO ()
receive h c = forever $ do
  line <- hGetLine h
  atomically $ writeTChan c line
```

Next, we have the `server` thread, where most of the application logic resides.

```
server :: Handle -> TVar Integer -> TChan String -> IO ()
server h factor c = do
  f <- atomically $ readTVar factor      -- ❶
  hPrintf h "Current factor: %d\n" f      -- ❷
  loop f                                   -- ❸
 where
  loop f = do
    action <- atomically $ do             -- ❹
      f' <- readTVar factor                -- ❺
      if (f /= f')                         -- ❻
        then return (newfactor f')         -- ❼
        else do
          l <- readTChan c                 -- ❽
          return (command f l)             -- ❾
    action

  newfactor f = do                         -- ❿
    hPrintf h "new factor: %d\n" f
    loop f

  command f s                              -- ⓫
   = case s of
       "end" ->
         hPutStrLn h ("Thank you for using the " ++
                       "Haskell doubling service.")     -- ⓬
       '*':s -> do
         atomically $ writeTVar factor (read s :: Integer) -- ⓭
         loop f
       line  -> do
         hPutStrLn h (show (f * (read line :: Integer)))
         loop f
```

❶ Read the current value of the factor.

❷ Report the current factor value to the client.

❸ Then we enter the loop.

❹ The overall structure is as follows: `loop` waits for the next event, which is either a change in the factor or a command from the client, and calls `newfactor` or `command`, respectively. The `newfactor` and `command` functions take whatever action is necessary and then call back to `loop` to process the next event. The `loop` function itself is implemented as an STM transaction that returns an IO `action`, which is then performed. This is a common pattern in STM. Since we can't invoke IO from inside STM, the transaction instead returns an IO action which is invoked by the caller of `atomically`.[3]

❺ In the transaction, first we read the current factor.

❻ Next, we compare it against the value we previously read, in `f`.

❼ If the two are different, indicating that the factor has been changed, then we call the `newfactor` function.

❽ If the factor has not been changed, we read from the `TChan`. This may `retry` if the channel is empty, but note that in the event of a `retry`, the transaction will be re-executed if either the `factor` TVar *or* the `TChan` changes. You can think of this transaction as a composition of two blocking operations: waiting for the `factor` TVar to change, and reading from the `TChan`. But we can code it without `orElse` thanks to the following equality:

```
(if A then retry else B) `orElse` C  ==>  if A then C else B
```

(Convince yourself that the two versions do the same thing, and also consider why it isn't possible to *always* transform away an `orElse`). Sometimes it isn't necessary to use `orElse` to compose blocking operations in STM.

❾ Having read a line of input from the `TChan`, we call `command` to act upon it.

❿ The `newfactor` function reports the change in factor to the client and continues with `loop`.

⓫ The `command` function executes a command received from the client.

⓬ If the client said `end`, then we terminate the connection by simply returning, instead of recursively calling `loop`. As mentioned earlier, this will cause `race` to terminate the `receive` thread.

⓭ If the client requests a change in factor, then we update the global factor value and call `loop`, *passing the old factor value*. Thus the transaction will immediately notice the change in factor and report it, giving the client confirmation that the factor was changed.

---

3. In fact, this pattern is more succinctly expressed using `Control.Monad.join`, but here it is written without `join` for clarity.

Try this server yourself by compiling and running the `server2.hs` program. Start up a few clients with the `nc` program (or another suitable telnet-style application) and check that it is working as expected. Test the error handling: what happens when you close the client connection without sending the end command, or if you send a non-number? You might want to add some additional debugging output to various parts of the program in order to track more clearly what is happening.

A Chat Server

Continuing on from the simple server examples in the previous sections, we now consider a more realistic example: a network chat server. A chat server enables multiple clients to connect and type messages to one another interactively. Real chat servers (e.g., IRC) have multiple channels and allow clients to choose which channels to participate in. For simplicity, we will be building a chat server that has a single channel, whereby every message is seen by every client.

The informal specification for the server is as follows:

- When a client connects, the server requests the name that the client will be using. The client must choose a name that is not currently in use; otherwise, the server will request that the user choose a different name.

- Each line received from the client is interpreted as a command, which is one of the following:

  /tell *name message*
  : Sends *message* to the user *name*.

  /kick *name*
  : Disconnects user *name*.[4]

  /quit
  : Disconnects the current client.

  message
  : Any other string (not beginning with /) is broadcast as a message to all the connected clients.

- Whenever a client connects or disconnects, all other connected clients are notified.

- We will be handling errors correctly and aiming for consistent behavior. For example, when two clients connect at the same time, one of them is always deemed to have connected first and gets notified about the other client connecting.

---

4. In real chat servers, this command would typically be available only to privileged users, but for simplicity here we will allow any user to kick any other user.

- If two clients simultaneously try to kick each other, only one of them will succeed. This may seem obvious, but as we shall see it is easy to get this wrong.

Architecture

As in the factor example of the previous section, the requirements dictate that a server thread must act on events from multiple sources: input from the client over the network, /tell messages and broadcasts from other clients, being kicked by another client, and clients connecting or disconnecting,

The basic architecture will be similar. We need a receive thread to forward the network input into a TChan and a server thread to wait for the different kinds of events and act upon them. Compared to the previous example, though, we have a lot more shared state. A client needs to be able to send messages to any other client, so the set of clients and their corresponding TChans must be shared.

We should consider how to handle /kick because we want to guarantee that two clients cannot simultaneously kick each other. This implies some synchronized, shared state for each client to indicate whether it has been kicked. A server thread can then check that it has not already been kicked itself before kicking another client. To inform the victim that it has been kicked, we could send a message to its TChan, but because we are using STM, we might as well just watch the global state for changes as we did in the factor example in the previous section.

Next, we need to consider how the various events (apart from /kick) arrive at the server thread. There is input from the client over the network and also messages from other clients to be sent back to this client. We could use separate TChans for the different kinds of events, but it is slightly better to use just one; the ordering on events is retained, which makes things more predictable for the client. So the design we have so far is a TVar to indicate whether the client has been kicked and a TChan to carry both network input and events from other clients.

Client Data

Now that we have established the main architectural design, we can fill in the details. In the previous examples, we passed around the various pieces of state explicitly, but now that things are more complicated, it will help to separate the state into the global server state and the per-client state. The per-client state is defined as follows:

chat.hs

```
type ClientName = String

data Client = Client
  { clientName   :: ClientName
  , clientHandle :: Handle
```

```
  , clientKicked    :: TVar (Maybe String)
  , clientSendChan :: TChan Message
  }
```

We have one TVar indicating whether this client has been kicked (clientKicked). Normally, this TVar contains Nothing, but after the client is kicked, the TVar contains Just s, where s is a string describing the reason for the client being kicked.

The TChan clientSendChan carries all the other messages that may be sent to a client. These have type Message:

```
data Message = Notice String
             | Tell ClientName String
             | Broadcast ClientName String
             | Command String
```

Where, respectively: Notice is a message from the server, Tell is a private message from another client, Broadcast is a public message from another client, and Command is a line of text received from the user (via the receive thread).

We need a way to construct a new instance of Client, which is Straightforward:

```
newClient :: ClientName -> Handle -> STM Client
newClient name handle = do
  c <- newTChan
  k <- newTVar Nothing
  return Client { clientName     = name
                , clientHandle   = handle
                , clientSendChan = c
                , clientKicked   = k
                }
```

Next, we define a useful function for sending a Message to a given Client:

```
sendMessage :: Client -> Message -> STM ()
sendMessage Client{..} msg =
  writeTChan clientSendChan msg
```

The syntax Client{..} is a *record wildcard* pattern, which brings into scope all the fields of the Client record with their declared names. In this case, we are using only clientSendChan, but when there are lots of fields it is a convenient shorthand, so we will be using it quite often from here on. (Remember to enable the RecordWildCards extension to use this syntax.)

Note that this function is in the STM monad, not IO. We will be using it inside some STM transactions later.

Server Data

The data structure that stores the server state is just a TVar containing a mapping from ClientName to Client.

```
data Server = Server
  { clients :: TVar (Map ClientName Client)
  }

newServer :: IO Server
newServer = do
  c <- newTVarIO Map.empty
  return Server { clients = c }
```

This state must be accessible from all the clients, because each client needs to be able to broadcast to all the others. Furthermore, new clients need to ensure that they are choosing a username that is not already in use and hence the set of active usernames is shared knowledge.

Here is how we broadcast a Message to all the clients:

```
broadcast :: Server -> Message -> STM ()
broadcast Server{..} msg = do
  clientmap <- readTVar clients
  mapM_ (\client -> sendMessage client msg) (Map.elems clientmap)
```

The Server

Now we will work top-down and write the code of the server. The main function is almost identical to the one in the previous section:

```
main :: IO ()
main = withSocketsDo $ do
  server <- newServer
  sock <- listenOn (PortNumber (fromIntegral port))
  printf "Listening on port %d\n" port
  forever $ do
      (handle, host, port) <- accept sock
      printf "Accepted connection from %s: %s\n" host (show port)
      forkFinally (talk handle server) (\_ -> hClose handle)

port :: Int
port = 44444
```

The only difference is that we create a new empty server state up front by calling newServer and pass this to each new client as an argument to talk.

Setting Up a New Client

When a new client connects, we need to do the following tasks:

- Ask the client for a username.
- If the username already exists, ask the client to choose another name.

- Otherwise, create a new `Client` and insert it into the `Server` state, ensuring that the `Client` will be removed when it disconnects or any failure occurs.
- Notify all existing clients that the new client has connected.
- Set up the threads to handle the client connection and start processing messages.

Let's start by defining an auxiliary function `checkAddClient`, which takes a username and attempts to add a new client with that name to the state, returning `Nothing` if a client with that name already exists, or `Just client` if the addition was successful. It also broadcasts the event to all the other connected clients:

```
checkAddClient :: Server -> ClientName -> Handle -> IO (Maybe Client)
checkAddClient server@Server{..} name handle = atomically $ do
  clientmap <- readTVar clients
  if Map.member name clientmap
    then return Nothing
    else do client <- newClient name handle
            writeTVar clients $ Map.insert name client clientmap
            broadcast server  $ Notice (name ++ " has connected")
            return (Just client)
```

And we will need a corresponding `removeClient` that removes the client again:

```
removeClient :: Server -> ClientName -> IO ()
removeClient server@Server{..} name = atomically $ do
  modifyTVar' clients $ Map.delete name
  broadcast server $ Notice (name ++ " has disconnected")
```

Now we can put the pieces together. Unfortunately we can't reach for the usual tool for these situations, namely `bracket`, because our "resource acquisition" (`checkAddClient`) is conditional. So we need to write the code out explicitly:

```
talk :: Handle -> Server -> IO ()
talk handle server@Server{..} = do
  hSetNewlineMode handle universalNewlineMode
      -- Swallow carriage returns sent by telnet clients
  hSetBuffering handle LineBuffering
  readName
 where
  readName = do
    hPutStrLn handle "What is your name?"
    name <- hGetLine handle
    if null name
      then readName
      else do
             ok <- checkAddClient server name handle  -- ❶
             case ok of
               Nothing -> do                           -- ❷
                 hPrintf handle
                     "The name %s is in use, please choose another\n" name
                 readName
```

```
Just client ->                                    -- ❸
    runClient server client
        `finally` removeClient server name
```

❶ After reading the requested username from the client, we attempt to add it to the server state with checkAddClient.

❷ If we were unsuccessful, then print a message to the client, and recursively call readName to read another name.

❸ If we were successful, then call a function named runClient (to be defined shortly) to handle the client interaction and use finally to arrange that whatever happens, we eventually call removeClient to remove this client from the state.

This is *almost* right, but strictly speaking we should mask asynchronous exceptions to eliminate the possibility that an exception is received just after checkAddClient but before runClient, which would leave a stale client in the state. This is what bracket would have done for us, but because we're rolling our own logic here, we have to handle the exception safety, too (for reference, the definition of bracket is given in "Asynchronous Exception Safety for Channels" on page 162).

The correct version of readName is as follows:

```
readName = do
  hPutStrLn handle "What is your name?"
  name <- hGetLine handle
  if null name
    then readName
    else mask $ \restore -> do        -- ❶
            ok <- checkAddClient server name handle
            case ok of
              Nothing -> restore $ do  -- ❷
                hPrintf handle
                    "The name %s is in use, please choose another\n" name
                readName
              Just client ->
                restore (runClient server client) -- ❸
                    `finally` removeClient server name
```

❶ We mask asynchronous exceptions.

❷ We restore them again before trying again if the name was already in use.

❸ If the name is accepted, then we unmask asynchronous exceptions when calling runClient but being careful to do it inside the argument to finally so there's no danger that a stale Client will be left in the state.

Running the Client

Having initialized the client, created the Client data structure, and added it to the Server state, we now need to create the client threads themselves and start processing events. The main functionality of the client will be implemented in a function called runClient:

```
runClient :: Server -> Client -> IO ()
```

runClient returns or throws an exception only when the client is to be disconnected. Recall that we need two threads per client: a *receive* thread to read from the network socket and a *server* thread to listen for messages from other clients and to send messages back over the network. As before, we can use race to create the two threads with a sibling relationship so that if either thread returns or fails, the other will be cancelled.

```
runClient :: Server -> Client -> IO ()
runClient serv@Server{..} client@Client{..} = do
  race server receive
  return ()
 where
  receive = forever $ do
    msg <- hGetLine clientHandle
    atomically $ sendMessage client (Command msg)

  server = join $ atomically $ do
    k <- readTVar clientKicked
    case k of
      Just reason -> return $
        hPutStrLn clientHandle $ "You have been kicked: " ++ reason
      Nothing -> do
        msg <- readTChan clientSendChan
        return $ do
            continue <- handleMessage serv client msg
            when continue $ server
```

So runClient is just race applied to the server and receive threads. In the receive thread, we read one line at a time from the client's Handle and forward it to the server thread as a Command message.

In the server thread, we have a transaction that tests two pieces of state: first, the clientKicked TVar, to see whether this client has been kicked. If it has not, then we take the next message from clientSendChan and act upon it. Note that this time, we have expressed server using join applied to the STM transaction: the join function is from Control.Monad and has the following type:

```
join :: Monad m => m (m a) -> m a
```

Here, m is instantiated to IO. The STM transaction returns an IO action, which is run by join, and in most cases this IO action returned will recursively invoke server.

The `handleMessage` function acts on a message and is entirely straightforward:

```
handleMessage :: Server -> Client -> Message -> IO Bool
handleMessage server client@Client{..} message =
  case message of
     Notice msg          -> output $ "*** " ++ msg
     Tell name msg       -> output $ "*" ++ name ++ "*: " ++ msg
     Broadcast name msg -> output $ "<" ++ name ++ ">: " ++ msg
     Command msg ->
       case words msg of
          ["/kick", who] -> do
              atomically $ kick server who clientName
              return True
          "/tell" : who : what -> do
              tell server client who (unwords what)
              return True
          ["/quit"] ->
              return False
          ('/':_):_ -> do
              hPutStrLn clientHandle $ "Unrecognized command: " ++ msg
              return True
          _ -> do
              atomically $ broadcast server $ Broadcast clientName msg
              return True
  where
    output s = do hPutStrLn clientHandle s; return True
```

Note that the function returns a `Bool` to indicate whether the caller should continue to handle more messages (`True`) or exit (`False`).

Recap

We have now given most of the code for the chat server. The full code is less than 250 lines total, which is not at all bad considering that we have implemented a complete and usable chat server. Moreover, without changes the server will scale to many thousands of connections and can make use of multiple CPUs if they are available.

There were two tools that helped a lot here:

race
  Helped to create threads that propagate errors to their parents and are automatically cancelled when their siblings terminate.

STM
  Helped to build consistency properties, such as the requirement that two clients may not kick each other simultaneously, and helps when we need to handle multiple sources of events.

Care should be taken with STM with respect to performance, though. Take a look at the definition of broadcast in "Server Data" on page 218. It is an STM transaction that operates on an unbounded number of TChans and thus builds an unbounded transaction. We noted earlier in "Performance" on page 193 that long transactions should be avoided because they cost $O(n^2)$. Hence, broadcast should be reimplemented to avoid this. As an exercise, why not try to fix this yourself: one way to do it would be to use a broadcast channel.

CHAPTER 13

Parallel Programming Using Threads

We have been discussing concurrency as a means to modularize programs with multiple interactions. For instance, concurrency allows a network server to interact with a multitude of clients simultaneously while letting you separately write and maintain code that deals with only a single client at a time. Sometimes these interactions are batch-like operations that we want to overlap, such as when downloading multiple URLs simultaneously. There the goal was to speed up the program by overlapping the I/O, but it is not true parallelism because we don't need multiple processors to achieve a speedup; the speedup was obtained by overlapping the time spent waiting for multiple web servers to respond.

But concurrency can also be used to achieve true parallelism. In this book, we have tried to emphasize the use of the parallel programming models—Eval, Strategies, the Par monad, and so on—for parallelism where possible, but there are some problems for which these pure parallel programming models cannot be used. These are the two main classes of problem:

- Problems where the work involves doing some I/O
- Algorithms that rely on some nondeterminism internally

Having side effects does not necessarily rule out the use of parallel programming models because Haskell has the ST monad for encapsulating side-effecting computations. However, it is typically difficult to use parallelism *within* the ST monad, and in that case probably the only solution is to drop down to concurrency unless your problem fits into the Repa model (Chapter 5).

How to Achieve Parallelism with Concurrency

In many cases, you can achieve parallelism by forking a few threads to do the work. The Async API can help by propagating errors appropriately and cleaning up threads. As with the parallel programs we saw in Part I, you need to do two things to run a program on multiple cores:

- Compile the program with -threaded.

- Run the program with +RTS -N*cores* where *cores* is the number of cores to use, e.g., +RTS -N2 to use two cores. Alternatively, use +RTS -N to use all the cores in your machine.

When multiple cores are available, the GHC runtime system automatically migrates threads between cores so that no cores are left idle. Its load-balancing algorithm isn't very sophisticated, though, so don't expect the scheduling policy to be fair, although it does try to ensure that threads do not get starved.

Many of the issues that we saw in Part I also arise when using concurrency to program parallelism; for example, static versus dynamic partitioning, and granularity. Forking a fixed number of threads will gain only a fixed amount of parallelism, so instead you probably want to fork plenty of threads to ensure that the program scales beyond a small number of cores. On the other hand, forking too many threads creates overhead that we want to avoid. The next section tackles these issues in the context of a concrete example.

Example: Searching for Files

We start by considering how to parallelize a simple program that searches the filesystem for files with a particular name. The program takes a filename to search for and the root directory for the search as arguments, and prints either Just p if the file was found with pathname p or Nothing if it was not found.

This problem may be either I/O-bound or compute-bound, depending on whether the filesystem metadata is already cached in memory or not, but luckily the same solution will allow us to parallelize the work in both cases.

Sequential Version

The search is implemented in a recursive function find, which takes the string to search for and the directory to start searching from, respectively, and returns a Maybe FilePath indicating whether the file was found (and its path) or not. The algorithm is a recursive walk over the filesystem, using the functions getDirectoryContents and doesDirectoryExist from System.Directory:

findseq.hs

```
find :: String -> FilePath -> IO (Maybe FilePath)
find s d = do
  fs <- getDirectoryContents d                    -- ❶
```

```
      let fs' = sort $ filter (`notElem` [".",".."]) fs    -- ❷
      if any (== s) fs'                                      -- ❸
         then return (Just (d </> s))
         else loop fs'                                       -- ❹
  where
   loop [] = return Nothing                                 -- ❺
   loop (f:fs) = do
     let d' = d </> f                                        -- ❻
     isdir <- doesDirectoryExist d'                          -- ❼
     if isdir
        then do r <- find s d'                               -- ❽
                case r of
                   Just _  -> return r                       -- ❾
                   Nothing -> loop fs                         -- ❿
         else loop fs                                        -- ⓫
```

❶   Read the list of filenames in the directory d.

❷   Filter out "." and ".." (the two special entries corresponding to the current and the parent directory, respectively). We also sort the list so that the search is deterministic.

❸   If the filename we are looking for is in the current directory, then return the result: d </> s is the filename constructed by appending the filename s to the directory d.

❹   If the filename was not found, then loop over the filenames in the directory d, recursively searching each one that is a subdirectory.

❺   In the loop, if we reach the end of the list, then we did not find the file. Return Nothing.

❻   For a filename f, construct the full path d </> f.

❼   Ask whether this pathname corresponds to a directory.

❽   If it does, then make a recursive call to find to search the subdirectory.

❾   If the file was found in this subdirectory, then return the name.

❿   Otherwise, loop to search the rest of the subdirectories.

⓫   If the name was not a directory, then loop again to search the rest.

The main function that wraps find into a program expects two command-line arguments and passes them as the arguments to find:

```
main :: IO ()
main = do
  [s,d] <- getArgs
  r <- find s d
  print r
```

To search a tree consisting of about 7 GB of source code on my computer, this program takes 1.14s when all the metadata is in the cache.[1] The program isn't as efficient as it could be. The system find program is about four times faster, mainly because the Haskell program is using the notoriously inefficient String type and doing Unicode conversion. If you were optimizing this program for real, it would obviously be important to fix these inefficiencies before trying to parallelize it, but we gloss over that here.

Parallel Version

Parallelizing this program is not entirely straightforward because doing it naively could waste a lot of work; if we search multiple subdirectories concurrently and we find the file in one subdirectory, then we would like to stop searching the others as soon as possible. Moreover, if an error is encountered at any point, then we need to propagate the exception correctly. We must be careful to keep the deterministic behavior of the sequential version, too. If we encounter an error while searching a subtree, then the error should not prevent the return of a correct result if the sequential program would have done so.

To implement this, we're going to use the Async API with its withAsync facility for creating threads and automatically cancelling them later. This is just what we need for spawning threads to search subtrees: the search threads should be automatically cancelled as soon as we have a result for a subtree.

Recall the type of withAsync:

```
withAsync :: IO a -> (Async a -> IO b) -> IO b
```

It takes the inner computation as its second argument. So to set off several searches in parallel, we have to nest multiple calls of withAsync. This implies a fold of some kind, and furthermore we need to collect up the Async values so we can wait for the results. The function we are going to fold is this:

```
subfind :: String -> FilePath
        -> ([Async (Maybe FilePath)] -> IO (Maybe FilePath))
        ->  [Async (Maybe FilePath)] -> IO (Maybe FilePath)

subfind s p inner asyncs = do
  isdir <- doesDirectoryExist p
  if not isdir
     then inner asyncs
     else withAsync (find s p) $ \a -> inner (a:asyncs)
```

The subfind function takes the string to search for, s, the path to search, p, the inner IO computation, inner, and the list of Asyncs, asyncs. If the path corresponds to a

---

1. The performance characteristics of this program depend to some extent on the structure of the filesystem used as a benchmark, so don't be too surprised if the results are a bit different on your system.

---

directory, we create a new Async to search it using withAsync, and inside withAsync we call inner, passing the original list of Asyncs with the new one prepended. If the pathname is not a directory, then we simply invoke the inner computation without creating a new Async.

Using this piece, we can now update the find function to create a new Async for each subdirectory:

findpar.hs

```
find :: String -> FilePath -> IO (Maybe FilePath)
find s d = do
  fs <- getDirectoryContents d
  let fs' = sort $ filter (`notElem` [".",".."]) fs
  if any (== s) fs'
     then return (Just (d </> s))
     else do
       let ps = map (d </>) fs'        -- ❶
       foldr (subfind s) dowait ps []  -- ❷
 where
   dowait as = loop (reverse as)       -- ❸

   loop [] = return Nothing
   loop (a:as) = do                    -- ❹
     r <- wait a
     case r of
       Nothing -> loop as
       Just a  -> return (Just a)
```

The differences from the previous find are as follows:

❶ Create the list of pathnames by prepending d to each filename.

❷ Fold subfind over the list of pathnames, creating the nested sequence of withAsync calls to create the child threads. The inner computation is the function dowait, defined next.

❸ dowait enters a loop to wait for each Async to finish, but first we must reverse the list. The fold generated the list in reverse order, and to make sure we retain the same behavior as the sequential version, we must check the results in the same order.

❹ The loop function loops over the list of Asyncs and calls wait for each one. If any of the Asyncs returns a Just result, then loop immediately returns it. Returning from here will cause all the Asyncs to be cancelled, as we return up through the nest of withAsync calls. Similarly, if an error occurs inside any of the Async computations, then the exception will propagate from the wait and cancel all the other Asyncs.

Performance and Scaling

You might wonder whether creating a thread for every subdirectory is expensive, both in terms of time and space. Let's compare `findseq` and `findpar` on the same 7 GB tree of source code, searching for a file that does not exist so that the search is forced to traverse the whole tree:

```
$ ./findseq nonexistent ~/code +RTS -s
Nothing
  2,392,886,680 bytes allocated in the heap
     76,466,184 bytes copied during GC
      1,179,224 bytes maximum residency (26 sample(s))
         37,744 bytes maximum slop
              4 MB total memory in use (0 MB lost due to fragmentation)

  MUT     time    1.05s  (  1.06s elapsed)
  GC      time    0.07s  (  0.07s elapsed)
  Total   time    1.13s  (  1.13s elapsed)

$ ./findpar nonexistent ~/code +RTS -s
Nothing
  2,523,910,384 bytes allocated in the heap
    601,596,552 bytes copied during GC
     34,332,168 bytes maximum residency (21 sample(s))
      1,667,048 bytes maximum slop
             80 MB total memory in use (0 MB lost due to fragmentation)

  MUT     time    1.28s  (  1.29s elapsed)
  GC      time    1.16s  (  1.16s elapsed)
  Total   time    2.44s  (  2.45s elapsed)
```

The parallel version does indeed take about twice as long, and it needs a lot more memory (80 MB compared to 4 MB). But let's see how well it scales, first with two processors:

```
$ ./findpar nonexistent ~/code +RTS -s -N2
Nothing
  2,524,242,200 bytes allocated in the heap
    458,186,848 bytes copied during GC
     26,937,968 bytes maximum residency (21 sample(s))
      1,242,184 bytes maximum slop
             62 MB total memory in use (0 MB lost due to fragmentation)

  MUT     time    1.28s  (  0.65s elapsed)
  GC      time    0.86s  (  0.43s elapsed)
  Total   time    2.15s  (  1.08s elapsed)
```

We were lucky. This program scales super-linearly (better than double performance with two cores), and just about beats the sequential version when using -N2. The reason for super-linear performance may be because running in parallel allowed some of the data structures to be garbage-collected earlier than they were when running sequentially.

Note the lower GC time compared with findseq and the lower memory use compared with the single-processor findpar. Running with -N4 shows the good scaling continue:

```
$ ./findpar nonexistent ~/code +RTS -s -N4
Nothing
   2,524,666,176 bytes allocated in the heap
     373,621,096 bytes copied during GC
      23,306,264 bytes maximum residency (23 sample(s))
       1,084,456 bytes maximum slop
              55 MB total memory in use (0 MB lost due to fragmentation)

  MUT     time    1.42s  (  0.36s elapsed)
  GC      time    0.83s  (  0.21s elapsed)
  Total   time    2.25s  (  0.57s elapsed)
```

Relative to the sequential program, this is a speedup of two on four cores. Not bad, but we ought to be able to do better.

Limiting the Number of Threads with a Semaphore

The findpar program is scaling quite nicely, which indicates that there is plenty of parallelism available. Indeed, a quick glance at a ThreadScope profile confirms this (Figure 13-1).

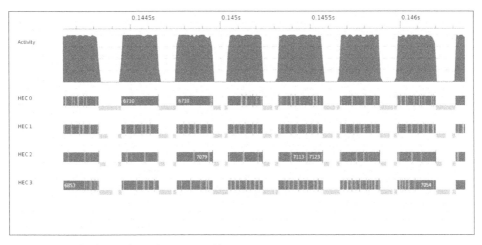

Figure 13-1. findpar ThreadScope profile

So the reason for the lack of speedup relative to the sequential version is the extra overhead in the parallel program. To improve performance, therefore, we need to focus on reducing the overhead.

The obvious target is the creation of an Async, and therefore a thread, for every single subdirectory. This is a classic granularity problem—the granularity is too fine.

One solution to granularity is chunking, where we increase the grain size by making larger chunks of work (we used this technique with the K-Means example in "Parallelizing K-Means" on page 40). However, here the computation is tree-shaped, so we can't easily chunk. A depth threshold is more appropriate for divide-and-conquer algorithms, as we saw in "Example: A Conference Timetable" on page 70, but here the problem is that the tree shape is dependent on the filesystem structure and is therefore not naturally balanced. The tree could be *very* unbalanced—most of the work might be concentrated in one deep subdirectory. (The reader is invited to try adding a depth threshold to the program and experiment to see how well it works.)

So here we will try a different approach. Remember that what we are trying to do is limit the number of threads created so we have just the right amount to keep all the cores busy. So let's program that behavior explicitly: keep a shared counter representing the number of threads we are allowed to create, and if the counter reaches zero we stop creating new ones and switch to the sequential algorithm. When a thread finishes, it increases the counter so that another thread can be created.

A counter used in this way is often called a *semaphore*. A semaphore contains a number of units of a resource and has two operations: acquire a unit of the resource or release one. Typically, acquiring a unit of the resource would *block* if there are no units available, but in our case we want something simpler. If there are no units available, then the program will do something different (fall back to the sequential algorithm). There are of course semaphore implementations for Concurrent Haskell available on Hackage, but since we only need a nonblocking semaphore, the implementation is quite straightforward, so we will write our own. Furthermore, we will need to tinker with the semaphore implementation later.

The nonblocking semaphore is called NBSem:

findpar2.hs

```
newtype NBSem = NBSem (MVar Int)

newNBSem :: Int -> IO NBSem
newNBSem i = do
  m <- newMVar i
  return (NBSem m)

tryAcquireNBSem :: NBSem -> IO Bool
tryAcquireNBSem (NBSem m) =
  modifyMVar m $ \i ->
    if i == 0
       then return (i, False)
       else let !z = i-1 in return (z, True)

releaseNBSem :: NBSem -> IO ()
releaseNBSem (NBSem m) =
  modifyMVar m $ \i ->
    let !z = i+1 in return (z, ())
```

We used an MVar to implement the NBSem, with straightforward tryAcquireNBSem and releaseNBSem operations to acquire a unit and release a unit of the resource, respectively. The implementation uses things we have seen before, e.g., modifyMVar for operating on the MVar.

We will use the semaphore in subfind, which is where we implement the new decision about whether to create a new Async or not:

```
subfind :: NBSem -> String -> FilePath
        -> ([Async (Maybe FilePath)] -> IO (Maybe FilePath))
        -> [Async (Maybe FilePath)] -> IO (Maybe FilePath)

subfind sem s p inner asyncs = do
  isdir <- doesDirectoryExist p
  if not isdir
    then inner asyncs
    else do
      q <- tryAcquireNBSem sem          -- ❶
      if q
        then do
          let dofind = find sem s p `finally` releaseNBSem sem -- ❷
          withAsync dofind $ \a -> inner (a:asyncs)
        else do
          r <- find sem s p             -- ❸
          case r of
            Nothing -> inner asyncs
            Just _  -> return r
```

❶ When we encounter a subdirectory, first try to acquire a unit of the semaphore.

❷ If we successfully grabbed a unit, then create an Async as before, but now the computation in the Async has an additional finally call to releaseNBSem, which releases the unit of the semaphore when this Async has completed.

❸ If we didn't get a unit of the semaphore, then we do a synchronous call to find instead of an asynchronous one. If this find returns an answer, then we can return it; otherwise, we continue to perform the inner action.

The changes to the find function are straightforward, just pass around the NBSem. In main, we need to create the NBSem, and the main question is how many units to give it to start with. For now, we defer that question and make the number of units into a command-line parameter:

findpar2.hs

```
main = do
  [n,s,d] <- getArgs
  sem <- newNBSem (read n)
  find sem s d >>= print
```

Let's see how well this performs. First, set n to zero so we never create any Asyncs, and this will tell us whether the NBSem has any impact on performance compared to the plain sequential version:

```
$ ./findpar2 0 nonexistent ~/code +RTS -N1 -s
Nothing
   2,421,849,416 bytes allocated in the heap
      84,264,920 bytes copied during GC
       1,192,352 bytes maximum residency (34 sample(s))
          33,536 bytes maximum slop
               4 MB total memory in use (0 MB lost due to fragmentation)

  MUT     time    1.09s  (  1.10s elapsed)
  GC      time    0.08s  (  0.08s elapsed)
  Total   time    1.18s  (  1.18s elapsed)
```

This ran in 1.18s, which is close to the 1.14s that the sequential program took, so the NBSem impacts performance by around 4% (these numbers are quite stable over several runs).

Now to see how well it scales. Remember that the value we choose for n is the number of *additional* threads that the program will use, aside from the main thread. So choosing n == 1 gives us 2 threads, for example. With n == 1 and +RTS -N2:

```
$ ./findpar2 1 nonexistent ~/code +RTS -N2 -s
Nothing
   2,426,329,800 bytes allocated in the heap
      90,600,280 bytes copied during GC
       2,399,960 bytes maximum residency (40 sample(s))
          80,088 bytes maximum slop
               6 MB total memory in use (0 MB lost due to fragmentation)

  MUT     time    1.23s  (  0.65s elapsed)
  GC      time    0.16s  (  0.08s elapsed)
  Total   time    1.38s  (  0.73s elapsed)
```

If you experiment a little, you might find that setting n == 2 is slightly better. We seem to be doing better than findpar, which ran in 1.08s with -N2.

I then increased the number of cores to -N4, with n == 8, and this is a typical run on my computer:

```
$ ./findpar2 8 nonexistent ~/code +RTS -N4 -s
Nothing
   2,464,097,424 bytes allocated in the heap
     121,144,952 bytes copied during GC
       3,770,936 bytes maximum residency (47 sample(s))
          94,608 bytes maximum slop
              10 MB total memory in use (0 MB lost due to fragmentation)
```

```
MUT     time    1.55s  (  0.47s elapsed)
GC      time    0.37s  (  0.09s elapsed)
Total   time    1.92s  (  0.56s elapsed)
```

The results vary a lot but hover around this value. The original findpar ran in about 0.57s with -N4; so the advantage of findpar2 at -N2 has evaporated at -N4. Furthermore, experimenting with values of n doesn't seem to help much.

Where is the bottleneck? We can take a look at the ThreadScope profile; for example, Figure 13-2 is a typical section:

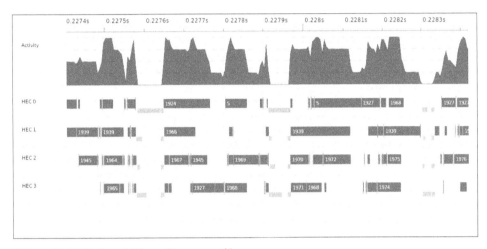

Figure 13-2. findpar2 ThreadScope profile

Things look quite erratic, with threads often blocked. Looking at the raw events in ThreadScope shows that threads are getting blocked on MVars, and that is the clue: there is high contention for the MVar in the NBSem.

So how can we improve the NBSem implementation to behave better when there is contention? One solution would be to use STM because STM transactions do not block, they just re-execute repeatedly. In fact STM does work here, but instead we will introduce a different way to solve the problem, one that has less overhead than STM. The idea is to use an ordinary IORef to store the semaphore value and operate on it using atomicModifyIORef:

```
atomicModifyIORef :: IORef a -> (a -> (a, b)) -> IO b
```

The atomicModifyIORef function modifies the contents of an IORef by applying a function to it. The function returns a pair of the new value to be stored in the IORef and a value to be returned by atomicModifyIORef. You should think of atomicModifyIORef as a very limited version of STM; it performs a transaction on a single mutable cell. Because it is much more limited, it has less overhead than STM.

Using `atomicModifyIORef`, the NBSem implementation looks like this:

findpar3.hs

```
newtype NBSem = NBSem (IORef Int)

newNBSem :: Int -> IO NBSem
newNBSem i = do
  m <- newIORef i
  return (NBSem m)

tryWaitNBSem :: NBSem -> IO Bool
tryWaitNBSem (NBSem m) = do
  atomicModifyIORef m $ \i ->
    if i == 0
       then (i, False)
       else let !z = i-1 in (z, True)

signalNBSem :: NBSem -> IO ()
signalNBSem (NBSem m) =
  atomicModifyIORef m $ \i ->
    let !z = i+1 in (z, ())
```

Note that we are careful to evaluate the new value of i inside `atomicModifyIORef`, using a bang-pattern. This is a standard trick to avoid building up a large expression inside the IORef: 1 + 1 + 1 + ...

The rest of the implementation is the same as *findpar2.hs*, except that we added some logic in `main` to initialize the number of units in the NBSem automatically:

findpar3.hs

```
main = do
  [s,d] <- getArgs
  n <- getNumCapabilities
  sem <- newNBSem (if n == 1 then 0 else n * 4)
  find sem s d >>= print
```

The function `getNumCapabilities` comes from `GHC.Conc` and returns the value passed to +RTS -N, which is the number of cores that the program is using. This value can actually be changed while the program is running, by calling `setNumCapabilities` from the same module.

If the program is running on multiple cores, then we initialize the semaphore to n * 4, which experimentation suggests to be a reasonable value.

The results with -N4 look like this:

```
$ ./findpar3 nonexistent ~/code +RTS -s -N4
Nothing
```

```
  2,495,362,472 bytes allocated in the heap
    138,071,544 bytes copied during GC
      4,556,704 bytes maximum residency (50 sample(s))
        141,160 bytes maximum slop
             12 MB total memory in use (0 MB lost due to fragmentation)

  MUT     time    1.38s  (  0.36s elapsed)
  GC      time    0.35s  (  0.09s elapsed)
  Total   time    1.73s  (  0.44s elapsed)
```

This represents a speedup of about 2.6—our best yet, but in the next section we will improve on this a bit more.

The ParIO monad

In Chapter 4, we encountered the Par monad, a simple API for programming deterministic parallelism as a dataflow graph. There is another version of the Par monad called ParIO, provided by the module Control.Monad.Par.IO with two important differences from Par:[2]

- IO operations are allowed inside ParIO. To inject an IO operation into a ParIO computation, use liftIO from the MonadIO class.

- For this reason, the pure runPar is not available for ParIO. Instead, a parallel computation is performed by the following:

    ```
    runParIO :: ParIO a -> IO a
    ```

Of course, unlike Par, ParIO computations are not guaranteed to be deterministic. Nevertheless, the full power of the Par framework is available: very lightweight tasks, multicore scheduling, and the same dataflow API based on IVars. ParIO is ideal for parallel programming in the IO monad, albeit with one caveat that we will discuss shortly.

Let's look at the filesystem-searching program using ParIO. The structure will be identical to the Async version; we just need to change a few lines. First, subfind:

findpar4.hs

```
subfind :: String -> FilePath
        -> ([IVar (Maybe FilePath)] -> ParIO (Maybe FilePath))
        -> [IVar (Maybe FilePath)] -> ParIO (Maybe FilePath)

subfind s p inner ivars = do
  isdir <- liftIO $ doesDirectoryExist p
  if not isdir
     then inner ivars
```

2. In monad-par-0.3.3 and later.

```
else do v <- new              -- ❶
        fork (find s p >>= put v)  -- ❷
        inner (v : ivars)          -- ❸
```

Note that instead of a list of Asyncs, we now collect a list of IVars that will hold the results of searching each subdirectory.

❶ Create a new IVar for this subdirectory.

❷ fork the computation to search the subdirectory, putting the result into the IVar.

❸ Perform the inner computation, adding the IVar we just created to the list.

I've omitted the definition of find, which has only one difference compared with the Async version: we call the Par monad's get function to get the result of an IVar, instead of Async's wait.

In main, we need to call runParIO to start the parallel computation:

findpar4.hs

```
main = do
  [s,d] <- getArgs
  runParIO (find s d) >>= print
```

That's it. Let's see how well it performs, at -N4:

```
$ ./findpar4 nonexistent ~/code +RTS -s -N4
Nothing
   2,460,545,952 bytes allocated in the heap
     102,831,928 bytes copied during GC
       1,721,200 bytes maximum residency (44 sample(s))
          78,456 bytes maximum slop
               7 MB total memory in use (0 MB lost due to fragmentation)

  MUT     time    1.26s  (  0.32s elapsed)
  GC      time    0.27s  (  0.07s elapsed)
  Total   time    1.53s  (  0.39s elapsed)
```

In fact, this version beats our carefully coded NBSem implementation, achieving a speed-up of 2.92 on 4 cores. Why is that? Well, one reason is that we didn't have to consult some shared state and choose whether to fork or continue our operation in the current thread, because fork is very cheap in Par and ParIO (note the low-memory overhead in the results above). Another reason is that the Par monad has a carefully tuned work-stealing scheduler implementation that is designed to achieve good parallel speedup.[3]

---

3. In fact, the Par monad implementation is built using nothing more than the concurrency APIs that we have seen so far in this book.

However, we cheated slightly here. ParIO has no error handling: exceptions raised by an IO computation might (or might not) be silently dropped, depending on which thread the Par monad scheduler happens to be using to run the computation. It *is* possible to fix this; if you enjoy a programming puzzle, why not have a go at finding a good way yourself—preferably one that requires few changes to the application code? My attempt can be found in *findpar5.hs*.

CHAPTER 14

Distributed Programming

Up until now, we have been considering programs that run on a single machine, while possibly making use of multiple processors to exploit parallelism. But there is a far more plentiful source of parallelism: running a program on multiple *machines* simultaneously. We call this *distributed* programming, and Haskell supports it through a framework called `distributed-process`.[1]

Aside from the obvious advantages of multimachine parallelism, there are other reasons to write distributed programs. For example:

- A distributed server can make more efficient use of network resources by moving the servers closer to the clients. We will see an example of this in "A Distributed Chat Server" on page 262.

- A distributed program can exploit a heterogeneous environment, where certain resources are available only to certain machines. An example of this might be a cluster of machines with local disks, where a large data structure is spread across the disks and we wish to run our computation on the machine that has the appropriate part of the data structure on its local disk.

So what should distributed programming look like from the programmer's perspective? Should it look like Concurrent Haskell, with `forkIO`, `MVar`, and `STM`? In fact, there are some good reasons to treat distributed computation very differently from computation on a shared-memory multicore:

- There is a realistic possibility of partial hardware failure: that is, some of the machines involved in a computation may go down while others continue to run. Indeed, given a large enough cluster of machines, having nodes go down becomes the

---

1. Also known as "Cloud Haskell."

norm. It would be unacceptable to simply abort the entire program in this case. Recovery is likely to be application-specific, so it makes sense to make failure visible to the programmer and let him handle it in an appropriate way for his application.

- Communication time becomes significant. In the shared-memory setting, it is convenient and practical to allow unrestricted sharing. This is because, for example, passing a pointer to a large data structure from one thread to another has no cost (beyond the costs imposed by the hardware and the runtime memory manager, but again it is convenient and practical to ignore these). In a distributed setting, however, communication can be costly, and sharing a data structure between threads is something the programmer will want to think about and explicitly control.

- In a distributed setting, it becomes far more difficult to provide any global consistency guarantees of the kind that, for example, STM provides in the shared-memory setting. Achieving a consistent view of the state of the system becomes a very hard problem indeed. There are algorithms for achieving agreement between nodes in a distributed system, but the exact nature of the consistency requirements depend on the application, so we don't want to build a particular algorithm into the system.

For these reasons, the Haskell developers decided that the model for distributed programming should be based on explicit *message passing*, and not the MVar and STM models that we provide for shared-memory concurrency.[2] Think of it as having TChan be the basic primitive available for communication. It is possible to build higher-level abstractions on top of the explicit message-passing layer, just as we built higher-level abstractions on top of STM and MVar in earlier chapters.

The Distributed-Process Family of Packages

There is no built-in support for distributed programming in Haskell. It is all implemented as libraries using the concurrency facilities we have covered in earlier chapters.

The package providing the core APIs for distributed programming is called distributed-process. It must be used together with a separate *transport layer* package that provides infrastructure for sending and receiving messages between nodes in the distributed network. The distributed-process package is deliberately independent of the transport layer so we can plug in different transport layer implementations. The most common transport layer is likely to be TCP/IP, as provided by the network-transport-tcp package, but we could imagine a transport layer that used shared memory to communicate among multiple nodes on the same multicore machine, or transport layers supporting some of the faster networks designed for clusters, such as InfiniBand.

---

2. This is also known as the *actor model*.

Each transport layer needs a different mechanism for creating and shutting down nodes on the network and discovering which nodes are available (*peer discovery*). We will be using the package `distributed-process-simplelocalnet` that provides a simple implementation on top of the `network-transport-tcp` transport layer.

At the time of writing, the `distributed-process` framework is somewhat new and a little rough around the edges, but it is already quite fully featured and we expect it to mature in due course.[3]

It is reasonable to wonder whether we even need a framework to do distributed message-passing. After all, can't we just use the `network` package directly and program our own message passing? Certainly you could do this, but the packages described in this chapter provide a lot of functionality that makes it much easier to build a distributed application. They let you think about your application as *single program that happens to run on multiple machines*, rather than a collection of programs running on different machines that talk to one another.

For example, with the `distributed-process` framework, we can call a function `spawn` that spawns a process (like a thread) on a different machine, and we can exchange messages with the remote process directly in the form of Haskell data types. Even though we are writing a single program to execute on multiple machines, there is no need for all the machines to be identical; indeed, programmers often want to exploit some non-uniformity. For example, we might want to run a caching service on a machine with lots of memory while sending compute-intensive tasks to machines with lots of fast cores. There may also be nonuniformity in the network topology. We might want to perform a database query on a machine close to the database server, for example, or put services that communicate with each other frequently close to one another in the network.

The `distributed-process` framework provides a whole infrastructure suite that supports the distributed application domain. These are some of the important facilities it provides:

- Remote spawning of processes
- Serialization of Haskell data for message passing
- Process linking (receiving notification when another process dies)
- Receiving messages on multiple channels
- A dedicated per-process channel for receiving dynamically typed messages
- Automatic peer discovery

---

3. The `distributed-process` package is in fact the second implementation of these ideas, the first prototype being the `remote` package.

Distributed Concurrency or Parallelism?

We have included distribution in the concurrency part of this book for the simple reason that the explicit message-passing API we'll describe is concurrent and nondeterministic. And yet, the main reason to want to use distribution is to exploit the parallelism of running on multiple machines simultaneously. So this setting is similar to parallel programming using threads described in Chapter 13, except that here we have only message passing and no shared state for coordination.

It is a little unfortunate that we have to resort to a nondeterministic programming model to achieve parallelism just because we want to exploit multiple machines. There are efforts under way to build deterministic programming models atop the distributed-process framework, although at the time of writing these projects are too experimental to include in this book.[4]

A First Example: Pings

To get acquainted with the basics of distributed programming, we will start with a simple example: a ping/pong message exchange. To start with, there will be a single master process that creates a child process. The master process will send a "ping" message to the child, which will respond with a "pong" message and the program will then exit.

The ping example will illustrate the basic pattern for setting up a program to use the distributed-process framework and introduce the APIs for creating processes and simple message passing. The first version of the program will run on a single *node* (machine) so we can get familiar with the basics of the interface before moving on to working with multiple nodes.

For reference, the subset of the Control.Distributed.Process API that we will be using is shown here:

```
data Process    -- instance Monad, MonadIO

data NodeId    -- instance Eq, Ord, Show, Typeable, Binary
data ProcessId -- instance Eq, Ord, Show, Typeable, Binary

getSelfPid  :: Process ProcessId
getSelfNode :: Process NodeId

spawn  :: NodeId -> Closure (Process ()) -> Process ProcessId

send   :: Serializable a => ProcessId -> a -> Process ()
expect :: Serializable a => Process a
```

---

4. For example, meta-par and HdpH.

```
terminate :: Process a

say :: String -> Process ()
```

Processes and the Process Monad

First, a bit of terminology. A distributed program consists of a set of *processes* that may communicate with one another by sending and receiving messages. A process is like a thread. Processes run concurrently with one another, and every process has a unique `ProcessId`. There are a couple of important differences between threads and processes, however:

- Threads are always created on the current node, whereas a process can be created on a remote node (we won't be using this facility until the next section, though).

- Processes run in the `Process` monad, rather than the `IO` monad. `Process` is an instance of `MonadIO`, so you can perform `IO` operations in `Process` by wrapping them in `liftIO`. All message-passing operations are in `Process`, so only processes, not threads, can engage in message passing.

Defining a Message Type

We start by defining the type of messages that our processes will send and receive:

distrib-ping/ping.hs

```
data Message = Ping ProcessId
             | Pong ProcessId
   deriving (Typeable, Generic)          -- ❶

   instance Binary Message               -- ❷
```

The `Ping` message contains the `ProcessId` of the process that sent it so that the target of the message knows where to send the response. The `Pong` response also includes the `ProcessId` of the responder so that the master process can tell which process a particular response comes from.

Messages in a distributed program can be sent over the network, which Involves *serializing* the Haskell data into a stream of bytes before it is sent and *deserializing* the bytes back into Haskell data at the other end. The `distributed-process` framework uses the `Binary` class from the `binary` package to implement serialization and deserialization, and hence every message type must be an instance of `Binary`.

The serialization format is under your control. If you want, you can define your own `Binary` instance that uses a specialized serialization format. Normally, however, you'll just want an automatically derived `Binary` instance. Fortunately, the `binary` package[5] lets you derive `Binary` instances using GHC's `DeriveGeneric` extension.[6] To do this, we first derive the `Generic` class (❶) and then declare an instance of `Binary` for `Message` (❷); GHC fills in the method definitions of this instance for us.

Message types must also be an instance of `Typeable`, because they can be sent to dynamically typed channels (more about this later). For `Typeable`, we can derive the instance directly (❶).

`Typeable` and `Binary` are normally packaged up together and referred to as `Serializable` using the following class provided by `Control.Distributed.Process.Serializable`:

```
class (Binary a, Typeable a) => Serializable a
instance (Binary a, Typeable a) => Serializable a
```

There's nothing magic about `Serializable`. Just think of `Serializable a` as shorthand for `(Binary a, Typeable a)`. You'll see `Serializable` used a lot in the `Control.Distributed.Process` APIs.

The Ping Server Process

Next, we'll write the code for a "ping server" process. The ping server must wait for a `Ping` message and then respond with a `Pong` message.

```
pingServer :: Process ()
pingServer = do
  Ping from <- expect                           -- ❶
  say $ printf "ping received from %s" (show from) -- ❷
  mypid <- getSelfPid                           -- ❸
  send from (Pong mypid)                        -- ❹
```

First of all, notice that we are in the `Process` monad. As we mentioned earlier, virtually all of the `Control.Distributed.Process` API is in this monad, and only code running in the `Process` monad can communicate with other processes and spawn new processes. There has to be a way to get into `Process` in the first place; we'll see how that happens shortly, but for now let's assume we're already in `Process` and we need to program the ping server.

At ❶ we receive the next message using `expect`:

```
expect :: Serializable a => Process a
```

---

5. As of `binary` version 0.6.3.0.

6. As of GHC version 7.2.1.

The expect function receives a message sent directly to this process. Each process has a channel associated with it, and the channel can receive messages of any type. The expect call receives a message of a particular type, where the type is determined by the context. If the type cannot be determined, the compiler will complain that the type is ambiguous, and the usual fix is to add a type signature. In the example just shown, the type of messages to receive is determined by the pattern match on the result, which matches directly on the Ping constructor and thus forces expect to receive messages of the type Message.

The expect function is a little like Haskell's read function, in that it returns a value whose type depends on the context. But whereas read fails if its argument cannot be parsed as the desired type, expect skips over messages in the queue that do not match and returns the first one that matches. Messages that don't match the expected type are left in the channel for the time being.

If there are no messages of the right type, expect will block until one arrives. Therefore, it should be used with care: the other messages in the queue are ignored while expect is waiting for the right kind of message to arrive, which could lead to a deadlock. We'll see later how to wait for several different types of message at the same time.

The say function, called at ❷, causes a message to be logged, which is a useful way to debug your program. Usually, the message will be logged to stderr, but it might be sent somewhere else if the transport layer overrides the default logging process.

At ❸ we call getSelfPid to obtain the ProcessId of the current process. The ProcessId of the current process is needed because the Pong message will contain it:

```
getSelfPid  :: Process ProcessId
```

And at ❹ we send a response back to the originator of the Ping. The function send is used to send a message to a process, and it has the following type:

```
send :: (Serializable a) => ProcessId -> a -> Process ()
```

We know which ProcessId to send the Pong to because it was contained in the original Ping message.

Now we need to be able to create processes running pingServer. Although in this example we will be creating the process on the local node, in general we might be creating the process on another node. Functions that will be executed remotely in this way need to be declared explicitly.[7] The following declaration invokes a bit of Template Haskell

---

7. We expect that in the future, GHC will provide syntactic sugar to make remote code execution easier.

magic that creates the necessary infrastructure to allow `pingServer` to be executed remotely:[8]

```
remotable ['pingServer]
```

The Master Process

Next, we will write the code for the master process. As you might expect, this is an operation of type `Process ()`:

```
master :: Process ()
master = do
  node <- getSelfNode                                -- ❶

  say $ printf "spawning on %s" (show node)
  pid <- spawn node $(mkStaticClosure 'pingServer)   -- ❷

  mypid <- getSelfPid                                -- ❸
  say $ printf "sending ping to %s" (show pid)
  send pid (Ping mypid)                              -- ❹

  Pong _ <- expect                                   -- ❺
  say "pong."

  terminate                                          -- ❻
```

❶ Call `getSelfNode`, which returns the `NodeId` of the current node. A `NodeId` is needed when creating a new process.

---

8. Template Haskell is a feature provided by GHC that allows Haskell code to be manipulated and generated at compile time. For more details, see the GHC User's Guide.

❷ Call `spawn` to create the child process. Here is the function's signature:

```
spawn :: NodeId -> Closure (Process ()) -> Process ProcessId
```

The `spawn` function creates a new process on the given `NodeId` (which here is the current node). The new process runs the computation supplied as the second argument to `spawn`, which is a value of type `Closure (Process ())`. Ultimately, we want to spawn a computation of type `Process ()`, but such values cannot be serialized because in practice a value of type `Process ()` could refer to an arbitrary amount of local data, including things that cannot be sent to other nodes (such as a `TVar`). Hence the type `Closure` is used to represent serializable computations.

How do we get one of these? First, the function to call must be declared `remotable`, as we did above. Then, if there are no arguments to pass, the Template Haskell function `mkStaticClosure` generates the appropriate code for the closure. (If there are arguments, then we need to use a different function, which we will see later.)

The `spawn` operation returns the `ProcessId` of the new process, which we bind to `pid`.

❸ Call `getSelfPid` to return the `ProcessId` of the current process. We need this to send in the `Ping` message.

❹ Send the `Ping` message to the child process.

❺ Call `expect` to receive the `Pong` message from the child process.

❻ Finally, terminate the process by calling `terminate`. In this case, simply returning from `master` would terminate the process, but sometimes we need to end the process in a context where it is not practical to arrange the top-level function to return, and in those cases `terminate` is useful. Moreover, it is good practice to indicate the end of the process explicitly.

The main Function

All that remains to complete the program is to define our `main` function, and here it is:

```
main :: IO ()
main = distribMain (\_ -> master) Main.__remoteTable
```

The `main` function calls `distribMain` from `DistribUtils`, which is a small module of utilities provided with the sample code to make these examples a bit less cluttered. The `distribMain` function is a wrapper around the lower-level startup facilities from the `distributed-process-simplelocalnet` package. It starts up the distributed-process framework with the distributed-process-simplelocalnet backend on a single node.

The first argument to distribMain is the Process computation to run as the master process on the node. It has type [NodeId] -> Process (), where the list of NodeIds are the other nodes in our distributed network. Because this example is running on a single node, we ignore the [NodeId] and just invoke the master function as our master process.

The second argument to distribMain is the metadata used to execute remote calls; in this case we pass Main.__remoteTable, which is generated by the Template Haskell call to remotable we showed earlier.

When you run the program, you should see output like this:[9]

```
$ ./ping
pid://localhost:44444:0:3: spawning on nid://localhost:44444:0
pid://localhost:44444:0:3: sending ping to pid://localhost:44444:0:4
pid://localhost:44444:0:4: ping received from pid://localhost:44444:0:3
pid://localhost:44444:0:3: pong.
```

Each of these messages corresponds to one of the calls to say in the example program, and they are tagged with the date, time, and ProcessId of the process that called say.

Summing Up the Ping Example

In this section, we built the simplest distributed program possible: it spawns a single child process and performs a simple ping/pong message exchange. Here are the key things to take away:

- To create a process, we call spawn, passing a NodeId and a Closure (Process ()). The former we got from getSelfNode (there are other ways, which we will encounter shortly), and the latter was generated by a call to the Template Haskell function mkStaticClosure.

- Processes run in the Process monad, which is a layer over the IO monad.

- Messages can be sent to a process using send and received by calling expect. Messages are ordinary Haskell data; the only requirement is that the type of the message is an instance of the Binary and Typeable classes.

There is a certain amount of boilerplate associated with distributed programming: deriving Binary instances, declaring remotable functions with remotable, starting up the framework with distribMain, and so on. Remember that the distributed-process

---

9. The log messages produced by say are normally prefixed by a timestamp, but I have omitted the timestamps here for clarity.

framework is currently implemented as a library entirely in Haskell. There is no support for distributed programming built into the language or GHC itself, and this accounts for some of the boilerplate. As the framework matures, distributed programming will likely become a smoother experience.

Multi-Node Ping

The previous example showed how to create a process and exchange some simple messages. Now we will extend the program to be truly distributed. Instead of spawning a process on the local node, we will run the program on several nodes, create a process on each one, and perform the ping/pong protocol with all nodes simultaneously.

The Message type and pingServer remain exactly as before. The only changes will be to the master and main functions. The new master function is shown below, along with a waitForPongs helper function:

distrib-ping/ping-multi.hs

```
master :: [NodeId] -> Process ()                 -- ❶
master peers = do

  ps <- forM peers $ \nid -> do                  -- ❷
          say $ printf "spawning on %s" (show nid)
          spawn nid $(mkStaticClosure 'pingServer)

  mypid <- getSelfPid

  forM_ ps $ \pid -> do                          -- ❸
    say $ printf "pinging %s" (show pid)
    send pid (Ping mypid)

  waitForPongs ps                                -- ❹

  say "All pongs successfully received"
  terminate

waitForPongs :: [ProcessId] -> Process ()        -- ❺
waitForPongs [] = return ()
waitForPongs ps = do
  m <- expect
  case m of
    Pong p -> waitForPongs (filter (/= p) ps)
    _      -> say "MASTER received ping" >> terminate
```

❶ This time, the master process takes an argument of type [NodeId], containing a NodeId for each node in the distributed network. This list is supplied by the framework when it starts up, after it has discovered the set of peers in the network. We'll see shortly how to start up the program on multiple nodes.

❷   Spawn a new process on each of the peer nodes, and bind the resulting list of `ProcessIds` to `ps`.

❸   Call `waitForPongs` (defined below) to receive all the pong messages. When `waitForPongs` returns, the program emits a diagnostic and terminates.

❹   `waitForPongs` is a simple algorithm that removes each `ProcessId` from the list as its pong message is received and returns when the list is empty.

The `main` function is almost the same as before:

```
main :: IO ()
main = distribMain master Main.__remoteTable
```

The only difference is that the [`Node`] argument gets passed along to `master` instead of being discarded here.

Running with Multiple Nodes on One Machine

First, I'll illustrate starting multiple nodes on the same machine and then progress on to multiple machines.

A distributed program consists of a single master node and one or more *slave* nodes. The master is the node that begins with a process running; the slave nodes just wait until processes are spawned on them.

Let's start by creating two slave nodes:

```
$ ./ping-multi slave 44445 &
[3] 58837
$ ./ping-multi slave 44446 &
[4] 58847
```

The `ping-multi` program takes two command-line arguments; these are interpreted by the `distrbMain` function and tell it how to initialize the framework. The first argument is either `master` or `slave` and indicates which kind of node to create. The second argument is the TCP port number that this node should use to communicate on, with the default being 44444.[10] Always use different port numbers when creating multiple nodes on the same machine.

I used & to create these as background processes in the shell. If you're on Windows, just open a few Command Prompt windows and run the program in each one.

Having started the slaves, we now start the master node:

```
$ ./ping-multi
pid://localhost:44444:0:3: spawning on nid://localhost:44445:0
```

---

10. The default port is chosen by our `distribMain` wrapper, not the `distributed-process` framework.

```
pid://localhost:44444:0:3: spawning on nid://localhost:44446:0
pid://localhost:44444:0:3: pinging pid://localhost:44445:0:4
pid://localhost:44444:0:3: pinging pid://localhost:44446:0:4
pid://localhost:44446:0:4: ping received from pid://localhost:44444:0:3
pid://localhost:44445:0:4: ping received from pid://localhost:44444:0:3
pid://localhost:44444:0:3: All pongs successfully received
```

The first thing to note is that the master node automatically found the two slave nodes. The `distributed-process-simplelocalnet` package includes a *peer discovery* mechanism that is designed to automatically locate and connect to other instances running on the same machine or other machines on the local network.

It is also possible to restart the master without restarting the slaves—try invoking `ping-multi` again, and you should see the same result. The new `master` node discovers and reconnects to the existing slaves.

Running on Multiple Machines

If we have multiple machines connected on the same network, we can run a distributed Haskell program on them. The first step is to distribute the binary to all the machines; every machine must be running the same binary. A mismatch in the binary on different machines can cause strange failures, such as errors when decoding messages.

Next, we start the slaves as before, but this time we start slaves on the remote machines and pass an extra argument:

```
$ ./ping-multi slave 192.168.1.100 44444
$ ./ping-multi slave 192.168.1.101 44444
```

(The above commands are executed on the appropriate machines.) The second argument is new and gives the IP address that identifies the slave. This is the address that the other nodes will use to contact it, so it must be an address that resolves to the correct machine. It doesn't have to be an IP address, but using IP addresses is simpler and eliminates a potential source of failure (the DNS).

When the slaves are running, we can start the master:

```
$ ./ping-multi master 44444
pid://localhost:44444:0:3: spawning on nid://192.168.1.100:44444:0
pid://localhost:44444:0:3: spawning on nid://192.168.1.101:44444:0
pid://localhost:44444:0:3: pinging pid://192.168.1.100:44444:0:5
pid://localhost:44444:0:3: pinging pid://192.168.1.101:44444:0:5
pid://192.168.1.100:44444:0:5: ping received from pid://localhost:44444:0:3
pid://192.168.1.101:44444:0:5: ping received from pid://localhost:44444:0:3
pid://localhost:44444:0:3: All pongs successfully received
```

The program successfully identified the remote nodes, spawned a processes on each one, and exchanged ping-pong messages with the process on each node.

Typed Channels

In the examples so far, we saw messages being delivered to a process and the process receiving the messages by using expect. This scheme is quite convenient: we need to know only a process's ProcessId to send it messages, and we can send it messages of any type. However, all the messages for a process go into the same queue, which has a couple of disadvantages:

- Each time we call expect, the implementation has to search the queue for a message of the right type, which could be slow.

- If we are receiving messages of the same type from multiple senders, then we need to explicitly include some information in the message that lets us tell them apart (e.g., the ProcessId of the sender).

The distributed-process framework provides an alternative means of message passing based on *typed channels*, which addresses these two problems. The interface is as follows:

```
data SendPort a      -- instance of Typeable, Binary
data ReceivePort a

newChan :: Serializable a => Process (SendPort a, ReceivePort a)

sendChan :: Serializable a => SendPort a -> a -> Process ()

receiveChan :: Serializable a => ReceivePort a -> Process a
```

A typed channel consists of two ports, a SendPort and a ReceivePort. Messages are sent to the SendPort by sendChannel and received from the ReceivePort using receiveChannel. As the name suggests, a typed channel can carry messages only of a particular type.

Typed channels imply a different pattern of interaction. For example, suppose we were making a request to another process and expecting a response. Using typed channels, we could program this as follows:

- The client creates a new channel for an interaction.
- The client sends the request, along with the SendPort.
- The server responds on the SendPort it was sent.

In general, the server might make its own channel and send that to the client, and the subsequent interaction would happen over these two channels.

The advantage of creating a channel to carry the response is that the client knows that a message arriving on this channel can only be a response to the original request, and it is not possible to mix up this response with other responses. The channel serves as a link between the original request and the response; we know that it is a response to *this* particular request, because it arrived on the right channel.

In the absence of typed channels, ensuring that the response can be uniquely identified would involve creating a new identifier to send along with the original message.[11]

Let's look at how to modify the ping example to use typed channels:

distrib-ping/ping-tc.hs

```
data Message = Ping (SendPort ProcessId)
  deriving (Typeable, Generic)

instance Binary Message
```

Note that we don't need a Pong message anymore. Instead, the Ping message will contain a SendPort on which to send the reply, and the reply is just the ProcessId of the sender. In fact, in this example we don't really need to send any content back at all—just sending () would be enough—but for the purposes of illustration we will send back the ProcessId.

```
pingServer :: Process ()
pingServer = do
  Ping chan <- expect
  say $ printf "ping received from %s" (show chan)
  mypid <- getSelfPid
  sendChan chan mypid

master :: [NodeId] -> Process ()
master peers = do

  ps <- forM peers $ \nid -> do
          say $ printf "spawning on %s" (show nid)
          spawn nid $(mkStaticClosure 'pingServer)

  mapM_ monitor ps

  ports <- forM ps $ \pid -> do

    say $ printf "pinging %s" (show pid)
    (sendport,recvport) <- newChan       --❶
    send pid (Ping sendport)             --❷
    return recvport

  forM_ ports $ \port -> do              --❸
    _ <- receiveChan port
    return ()
```

---

11. Indeed, some of Erlang's libraries use exactly this technique.

```
say "All pongs successfully received"
terminate
```

❶ Create a new channel to carry the response.

❷ Send the ping message, including the SendPort of the channel.

❸ Where previously we needed a function waitForPongs to collect all the responses and match them up with the peers, this time we can just wait for a response on each of the channels we created.

This code is simpler than the previous version in "Multi-Node Ping" on page 251. However, note that we still sent the Ping messages directly to the process, rather than using a typed channel. If we wanted to use a typed channel here too, things get more complicated. We want to do something like this (considering just a single worker for simplicity):

```
do
  (s1,r1) <- newChan
  spawn nid ($(mkClosure `pingServer) r1)

  (s2,r2) <- newChan
  sendChan s1 (Ping s2)

  receiveChan r2
```

This seems quite natural: we create a channel with send port s1 and receive port r1 on which to send the Ping message. Then we give the receive port of the channel to the pingServer process when we spawn it. The code shows how to use spawn to apply a function (here pingServer) to an argument (here r1): use mkClosure instead of mkStaticClosure, and then pass the argument to it (we'll come back to this later; the details aren't important right now).

But there's a big problem here. ReceivePorts are not Serializable, which prevents us passing the ReceivePort r1 to the spawned process. GHC will reject the program with a type error.

Why are ReceivePorts not Serializable? If you think about it a bit, this makes a lot of sense. If a process were allowed to send a ReceivePort somewhere else, the implementation would have to deal with two things: routing messages to the correct destination when a ReceivePort has been forwarded (possibly multiple times), and routing messages to *multiple* destinations, because sending a ReceivePort would create a new copy. This would introduce a vast amount of complexity to the implementation, and it is not at all clear that it is a good feature to allow. So the remote framework explicitly disallows it, which fortunately can be done using Haskell's type system.

This means that we have to jump through an extra hoop to fix the previous code, though. Instead of passing the ReceivePort to the spawned process, the spawned process must create the channel and send us back the `SendPort`. This means we need *another* channel so that the spawned process can send us back its `SendPort`.

```
do
  (s,r) <- newChan  -- throw-away channel
  spawn nid ($(mkClosure 'pingServer) s)
  ping <- receiveChan r

  (sendpong,recvpong) <- newChan
  sendChan ping (Ping sendpong)

  receiveChan recvpong
```

Since this extra handshake is a bit of a hassle, you might well prefer to send messages directly to the spawned process using `send` rather than using typed channels, which is exactly what the example code at the beginning of this section did.

Merging Channels

In the previous section, we waited for a response from each child process in turn, whereas the old `waitForPongs` version processed the messages in the order they arrived. In this case it isn't a problem, but suppose some of these messages required a response. Then we might have introduced some extra latency: if a process toward the end of the list replies early, it won't get a response until the master process has dealt with the messages from the other processes earlier in the list, some of which might take a while to reply.

So we need a way to wait for messages from multiple channels simultaneously. The `distributed-process` framework has an elegant way to do this. Channels can be merged together to make a single channel that receives messages from any of the original channels. There are two ways to do this:

```
mergePortsBiased :: Serializable a => [ReceivePort a] -> Process (ReceivePort a)
mergePortsRR     :: Serializable a => [ReceivePort a] -> Process (ReceivePort a)
```

The difference is in the order in which messages arrive on the merged channel. In `mergePortsBiased`, each receive searches the ports in left-to-right order for a message, returning the first message it finds. The alternative is `mergePortsRR` (the RR stands for "round robin") which also searches left to right, but rotates the list by one element after each receive, with the leftmost port moving to the end of the list.

One important thing to note is that merging channels does not affect the original channel; we can still receive messages from either source, and indeed there is no problem with merging multiple overlapping sets of channels.[12]

---

12. The current implementation of channels uses STM, and channels are merged using `orElse`.

Here is the ping example with channels, where instead of waiting for the responses one by one, we merge the channels together and wait for all the responses simultaneously.

distrib-ping/ping-tc-merge.hs

```
master :: [NodeId] -> Process ()
master peers = do

  ps <- forM peers $ \nid -> do
          say $ printf "spawning on %s" (show nid)
          spawn nid $(mkStaticClosure 'pingServer)

  ports <- forM ps $ \pid -> do
    say $ printf "pinging %s" (show pid)
    (sendport,recvport) <- newChan
    send pid (Ping sendport)
    return recvport

  oneport <- mergePortsBiased ports     -- ❶
  waitForPongs oneport ps               -- ❷

  say "All pongs successfully received"
  terminate

waitForPongs :: ReceivePort ProcessId -> [ProcessId] -> Process ()
waitForPongs _ [] = return ()
waitForPongs port ps = do
  pid <- receiveChan port
  waitForPongs port (filter (/= pid) ps)
```

❶ Merge the ReceivePorts together into a single ReceivePort.

❷ Now we need a loop to wait for the responses, which is written as a separate function waitForPongs. Each message received from the channel removes the corresponding ProcessId from the list until all the spawned processes have responded.

Handling Failure

One of the important benefits provided by the distributed-process framework is handling and recovering from failure. Failure is a fact of life in distributed computing, and we should be prepared for the possibility that any of our processes might fail at any time, whether due to network outage, a hardware crash, or software faults.

Here is a basic example showing how the failure of one process can be caught and acted upon by another process. In the original ping example from "Defining a Message Type" on page 245, recall that the Message type has two constructors:

```
data Message = Ping ProcessId
             | Pong ProcessId
```

and the code for pingServer matches explicitly on the Ping constructor:

distrib-ping/ping-fail.hs

```
pingServer :: Process ()
pingServer = do
  Ping from <- expect
  say $ printf "ping received from %s" (show from)
  mypid <- getSelfPid
  send from (Pong mypid)
```

What will happen if the message is a Pong, rather than a Ping? Both messages have the type Message, so expect cannot distinguish them; if the context requires a message of type Message, expect can return either a Ping or a Pong. Clearly, if expect returns a Pong here, then the pattern match against Ping will fail, and as usual in Haskell this throws an exception. Since there are no exception handlers, the exception will result in the termination of the pingServer process.

There are ways to prevent the error, of course, but for now let's see how we can catch this failure from another process. We'll use withMonitor, which has the following signature:

```
withMonitor :: ProcessId -> Process a -> Process a
```

withMonitor takes a ProcessId to monitor and an action to perform. During the action, if the specified process fails in any way, a special message of type ProcessMonitorNotification is sent to the current process.

To wait for either the ProcessMonitorNotification message or a Pong, we need to know how to wait for different types of message at the same time. The basic pattern for this is as follows:

```
receiveWait
  [ match $ \p -> do ...
  , match $ \q -> do ...
  ]
```

where p and q are patterns that match different types of message. The types of these functions are shown here:

```
receiveWait    ::        [Match b] -> Process b
receiveTimeout :: Int -> [Match b] -> Process (Maybe b)

match   :: Serializable a =>                  (a -> Process b) -> Match b
matchIf :: Serializable a => (a -> Bool) -> (a -> Process b) -> Match b
```

The function receiveWait waits until any of the match functions applies to a message in the queue, and then executes the associated action. The receiveTimeout operation is similar, but instead of waiting indefinitely for a matching message, it takes a time in milliseconds and returns Nothing if a matching message did not arrive before the time.

Here is how we monitor the `pingServer` process and then wait for either a `Pong` message or a `ProcessMonitorNotification`:

distrib-ping/ping-fail.hs

```
withMonitor pid $ do
  send pid (Pong mypid)              -- ❶
  receiveWait
    [ match $ \(Pong _) -> do
        say "pong."
        terminate
    , match $ \(ProcessMonitorNotification _ref deadpid reason) -> do
        say (printf "process %s died: %s" (show deadpid) (show reason))
        terminate
    ]
```

Note that we deliberately send the child a `Pong` message (❶) to cause it to fail. Running the program results in this:

```
pid://localhost:44444:0:3: spawning on nid://localhost:44444:0
pid://localhost:44444:0:3: sending ping to pid://localhost:44444:0:4
pid://localhost:44444:0:3: process pid://localhost:44444:0:4 died:
  DiedException "user error (Pattern match failure in do expression at
    distrib-ping/ping-fail.hs:24:3-11)"
```

The third log message indicates that the master received the notification of the failed process, and gives the details of the failure: a pattern-match error, as we expected.

It is worth asking whether having a single `Message` data type for our messages was a good idea in the first place. Perhaps we should have made separate types, as in:

```
newtype Pong = Pong ProcessId
newtype Ping = Ping ProcessId
```

The choice comes down to whether we are using typed channels or not. With typed channels, we could use only a single message type, whereas using the per-process dynamically typed channel with `send` and `expect` or `receiveWait`, we could use multiple message types. Having one type for each message would avoid the possibility of a pattern-match failure when matching on a message, but unless we also have a catch-all case to match unrecognized messages, the other messages could be left in the queue forever, which could amount to an undetected error or deadlock. So there might well be cases where we *want* to match both messages because one is definitely an error, and so using a single message type would help ensure that we always match on all the possible messages.

The more appropriate choice depends on the particular circumstances in your application.

A summary of the API for process monitoring follows:

```
monitor     :: ProcessId -> Process MonitorRef
unmonitor   :: MonitorRef -> Process ()
```

```
withMonitor :: ProcessId -> Process a -> Process a

data ProcessMonitorNotification
  = ProcessMonitorNotification MonitorRef ProcessId DiedReason

data MonitorRef -- abstract

data DiedReason
  = DiedNormal            -- Normal termination
  | DiedException !String -- The process exited with an exception
  | DiedDisconnect        -- We got disconnected from the process node
  | DiedNodeDown          -- The process node died
  | DiedUnknownId         -- Invalid (process/node/channel) identifier
```

In addition to the withMonitor function mentioned earlier, a process can also be monitored by calling the monitor function. This function returns a token of type MonitorRef, which can be passed to unmonitor to stop monitoring the process again. In general, it is better to use withMonitor than the monitor and unmonitor pair if possible, because withMonitor will automatically stop monitoring the remote process in the event of an exception. However, sometimes withMonitor doesn't fit the control flow, which is when monitor and unmonitor are useful.

The Philosophy of Distributed Failure

In a distributed system, parts of the running program may fail at any time due to circumstances beyond our control. Such a failure typically results in one or more of the processes in our network becoming disconnected without warning; there is no exception and no opportunity to clean up whatever it was doing. Perhaps the hardware it was running on failed, or the network on which we were communicating with it stopped working.

A far-reaching approach for such failures can be seen in Erlang, a programming language with distributed programming at its heart. The only mechanism for communication is message passing, so every concurrent Erlang program is fundamentally distributable. The Erlang designers promote a particular philosophy for dealing with failure, often known by its catchphrase: "Let it crash." The basic principle is that since in a distributed system we must already be prepared for a process to simply disappear, we might as well deal with *all* kinds of failure in this way because doing so makes failure handling much simpler. And since failure handling is difficult to test, making it simpler is highly desirable.

Concretely, instead of trying to enumerate local failure conditions and handle them in some way, we can just let them propagate to the top of the process and let the process die. The distributed program must be prepared for this eventuality already (since this is a distributed system), so the system will recover in some way: perhaps by restarting the failed process in some known-good state and logging the failure somewhere.

Thus the granularity at which we have to consider failure is the process, and we can design our applications such that individual processes can fail without catastrophic consequences. A process will probably have some *internal* state that is lost when it dies, but the parent should know how to construct the initial state to restart the process or to propagate the failure to a higher layer that can.

A Distributed Chat Server

In "A Chat Server" on page 216, we built a multithreaded chat server using Concurrent Haskell and STM. In this section, we will extend the chat server to be distributed. The server will be running across multiple machines, clients may connect to any of the machines, and any client will be able to chat with any other client connected via any of the servers. Essentially, the distributed chat server will behave just like the single-threaded server (minus some subtle differences that we will discuss shortly), except that clients have a choice of machines to connect to.

A distributed chat network saves bandwidth. For example, suppose we set up a chat network with two servers A and B on each side of the Atlantic Ocean. Each server has a large number of clients connected, with each client connecting to its closest server. When a client on server A broadcasts a message, it needs to be sent across the trans-Atlantic link to server B only once, and server B then forwards it to each of its connected clients. The broadcast message crosses the Atlantic only once, instead of once for each of the clients on the other side.

We have already written all the code for the multithreaded server, so it seems a shame to throw it away and rewrite it all to use distributed-process instead. Fortunately, we don't have to do that. We can simply add some extra code to handle distribution, using the original server code nearly intact. Each client will still be managed by ordinary IO threads synchronized using STM, but additionally we will have some code communicating with the other servers using distributed-process. In Haskell, distributed programming is not all or nothing. We can freely mix distributed and concurrent programming in the same program. This means we can take advantage of the simplicity and performance of ordinary concurrent programming on each node, while using the heavier-weight distributed interfaces for the parts of the program that need to work across multiple nodes.

In this first version, we will use a master/slave configuration in which the master will start up server instances on all the slaves once at the beginning. Later, we will consider how to modify the program so that all nodes are equal, and nodes may come and go at arbitrary times.

Data Types

We will need a few changes to the data structures compared with the multithreaded server. When one client sends a message to another client connected to a different server, we need to know where to send the message. So each server will need to keep a list of all the clients connected to any server in the network, along with the server to which the client is connected. The information about a client now has two possibilities: either it is a *local client* (connected to this server), or a *remote client* (connected to a different server).

distrib-chat/chat.hs

```
type ClientName = String

data Client
  = ClientLocal    LocalClient
  | ClientRemote   RemoteClient

data RemoteClient = RemoteClient
      { remoteName :: ClientName
      , clientHome :: ProcessId
      }

data LocalClient = LocalClient
      { localName      :: ClientName
      , clientHandle   :: Handle
      , clientKicked   :: TVar (Maybe String)
      , clientSendChan :: TChan Message
      }

clientName :: Client -> ClientName
clientName (ClientLocal  c) = localName c
clientName (ClientRemote c) = remoteName c

newLocalClient :: ClientName -> Handle -> STM LocalClient
newLocalClient name handle = do
  c <- newTChan
  k <- newTVar Nothing
  return LocalClient { localName      = name
                     , clientHandle   = handle
                     , clientSendChan = c
                     , clientKicked   = k
                     }
```

LocalClient is what we previously called Client, and RemoteClient is a client connected to another server. The Client type is now a disjunction of these two, with constructors ClientLocal and ClientRemote.

The Message type is as before, except that we need to derive Typeable and Binary, because Messages will be sent over the network:

```
data Message = Notice String
             | Tell ClientName String
             | Broadcast ClientName String
             | Command String
  deriving (Typeable, Generic)

instance Binary Message
```

Servers need to communicate with one another, and the kinds of messages they need
to send are richer than Message. For example, servers need to tell one another when a
new client connects, or one client kicks another. So we have a new type for messages
sent between servers, which we call PMessage:

```
data PMessage
  = MsgServers           [ProcessId]
  | MsgSend              ClientName Message
  | MsgBroadcast         Message
  | MsgKick              ClientName ClientName
  | MsgNewClient         ClientName ProcessId
  | MsgClientDisconnected ClientName ProcessId
  deriving (Typeable, Generic)

instance Binary PMessage
```

Most of these are self-explanatory, except for one: MsgServers is a special message sent
to each server node when it starts up, telling it the ProcessIds of all the server nodes in
the network.

The Server type previously contained only the mapping from ClientName to Client,
but now it needs some more information:

```
data Server = Server
  { clients   :: TVar (Map ClientName Client)
  , proxychan :: TChan (Process ())
  , servers   :: TVar [ProcessId]
  , spid      :: ProcessId
  }

newServer :: [ProcessId] -> Process Server
newServer pids = do
  pid <- getSelfPid
  liftIO $ do
    s <- newTVarIO pids
    c <- newTVarIO Map.empty
    o <- newTChanIO
    return Server { clients = c, servers = s, proxychan = o, spid = pid }
```

clients is the client mapping, as before; servers is the list of other server
ProcessIds, and spid is the ProcessId of this server (for convenience).

The proxychan field pertains to an added bit of complexity in our distributed architecture. Remember that we are leaving as much of the existing server infrastructure intact

as possible; that means the existing server threads are ordinary forkIO threads. A forkIO thread cannot perform operations in the Process monad, yet we certainly need to be able to do that somehow because certain actions by a client must trigger communication with other servers in the network. So the trick we use is a *proxy*, which is a process that reads actions from a TChan and performs them in the Process monad. To have a Process action performed from an IO thread, we simply queue it on the proxy TChan. Each server has a single proxy channel, created when the server starts up and stored in the proxychan field of Server.

Sending Messages

Next, we need a few small utilities. First, a way to send a Message to a LocalClient:

```
sendLocal :: LocalClient -> Message -> STM ()
sendLocal LocalClient{..} msg = writeTChan clientSendChan msg
```

The following function, sendRemote, sends a PMessage to a remote server. To do this, it needs to use the proxychan (which it gets from the Server) and it needs the pid of the destination process:

```
sendRemote :: Server -> ProcessId -> PMessage -> STM ()
sendRemote Server{..} pid pmsg = writeTChan proxychan (send pid pmsg)
```

Now that we can send both local and remote messages, we can define sendMessage, which sends a Message to any client:

```
sendMessage :: Server -> Client -> Message -> STM ()
sendMessage server (ClientLocal client) msg =
    sendLocal client msg
sendMessage server (ClientRemote client) msg =
    sendRemote server (clientHome client) (MsgSend (remoteName client) msg)
```

A variant sends a message to a named client or returns False if the client is not connected:

```
sendToName :: Server -> ClientName -> Message -> STM Bool
sendToName server@Server{..} name msg = do
    clientmap <- readTVar clients
    case Map.lookup name clientmap of
        Nothing     -> return False
        Just client -> sendMessage server client msg >> return True
```

Broadcasting

Next, we consider broadcasting messages. First, we need a way to send a PMessage to all the connected servers:

```
sendRemoteAll :: Server -> PMessage -> STM ()
sendRemoteAll server@Server{..} pmsg = do
```

```
        pids <- readTVar servers
        mapM_ (\pid -> sendRemote server pid pmsg) pids
```

We also need a `broadcastLocal` function that sends a message to the local clients only:

```
broadcastLocal :: Server -> Message -> STM ()
broadcastLocal server@Server{..} msg = do
    clientmap <- readTVar clients
    mapM_ sendIfLocal (Map.elems clientmap)
  where
    sendIfLocal (ClientLocal c)  = sendLocal c msg
    sendIfLocal (ClientRemote _) = return ()
```

This function works by calling an auxiliary function `sendIfLocal` on each of the clients, which calls `sendLocal` if the client is local and does nothing if the client is remote.

Putting `sendRemoteAll` and `broadcastLocal` together, we can broadcast a `Message` to everyone:

```
broadcast :: Server -> Message -> STM ()
broadcast server@Server{..} msg = do
    sendRemoteAll server (MsgBroadcast msg)
    broadcastLocal server msg
```

Distribution

The rest of the local server code is almost identical to that in "A Chat Server" on page 216, so we don't reproduce it here. The only important differences are that we need to inform other servers whenever a client connects or disconnects by calling `sendRemoteAll` with a `MsgNewClient` or `MsgClientDisconnected` respectively.

The interesting part is how we handle distribution. Previously, the `main` function was responsible for setting up the network socket and accepting new connections. This is now delegated to a function `socketListener`, which is otherwise identical to the previous `main`:

```
socketListener :: Server -> Int -> IO ()
socketListener server port = withSocketsDo $ do
  sock <- listenOn (PortNumber (fromIntegral port))
  printf "Listening on port %d\n" port
  forever $ do
      (handle, host, port) <- accept sock
      printf "Accepted connection from %s: %s\n" host (show port)
      forkFinally (talk server handle)
                  (\_ -> hClose handle)
```

We need a function to implement the proxy, described above in "Sending Messages" on page 265. All it does is repeatedly read `Process ()` values from the `proxychan` and execute them:

```
proxy :: Server -> Process ()
proxy Server{..} = forever $ join $ liftIO $ atomically $ readTChan proxychan
```

Now, the chatServer function is the main Process () action that implements a chat
server:

```
chatServer :: Int -> Process ()
chatServer port = do
  server <- newServer []
  liftIO $ forkIO (socketListener server port)        -- ❶
  spawnLocal (proxy server)                            -- ❷
  forever $ do m <- expect; handleRemoteMessage server m -- ❸
```

❶   Starts up the socketListener thread.

❷   Creates the proxy. Note here that we use spawnLocal, which is like spawn except
     that the new process is always created on the current node. This means that the
     computation to be spawned doesn't need to be serialized, so spawnLocal takes
     an ordinary Process value rather than a Closure, which makes it easier to use.

❸   Repeatedly grabs the next message and calls handleRemoteMessage (defined
     next) to act on it.

```
handleRemoteMessage :: Server -> PMessage -> Process ()
handleRemoteMessage server@Server{..} m = liftIO $ atomically $
  case m of
    MsgServers pids  -> writeTVar servers (filter (/= spid) pids) -- ❶
    MsgSend name msg -> void $ sendToName server name msg         -- ❷
    MsgBroadcast msg -> broadcastLocal server msg                 -- ❸
    MsgKick who by   -> kick server who by                        -- ❹

    MsgNewClient name pid -> do                                   -- ❺
        ok <- checkAddClient server (ClientRemote (RemoteClient name pid))
        when (not ok) $
          sendRemote server pid (MsgKick name "SYSTEM")

    MsgClientDisconnected name pid -> do                          -- ❻
        clientmap <- readTVar clients
        case Map.lookup name clientmap of
          Nothing -> return ()
          Just (ClientRemote (RemoteClient _ pid')) | pid == pid' ->
            deleteClient server name
          Just _ ->
            return ()
```

❶   The special MsgServers message is sent once at startup to tell each server the
     ProcessIds of all the servers in the network. This is used to set the servers field
     of Server.

❷ ❸   MsgSend, MsgBroadcast, and MsgKick are straightforward. They cause the
❹   appropriate action to take place just as if a local client had initiated it.

❺   MsgNewClient indicates that a client has connected to a remote server. We
     attempt to add the remote client to the local state, but it may be that this server
     already has a client with the same name. Unlike in the single server case where
     we relied on STM to ensure that inconsistencies like this could never arise, in a
     distributed system there is no global consistency. So we have to handle the case
     where two clients connect at the same time on different servers. The method we
     choose here is simple but brutal: reply with a MsgKick to kick the other client.
     It is likely that the remote server will simultaneously do the same, so both clients
     will end up being kicked, but at least the inconsistency is resolved, and this case
     will be rare in practice.

❻   MsgClientDisconnected is not difficult, but we do have to be careful to check
     that the client being disconnected is in fact the correct client, just in case an
     inconsistency has arisen (in particular, this might be the response to the MsgKick
     initiated by the MsgNewClient case just shown).

Now that the server code is in place, we just need to write the code to start up the whole
distributed network. The main function invokes master on the master node:

```
port :: Int
port = 44444

master :: [NodeId] -> Process ()
master peers = do

  let run nid port = do
          say $ printf "spawning on %s" (show nid)
          spawn nid ($(mkClosure 'chatServer) port)

  pids <- zipWithM run peers [port+1..]
  mypid <- getSelfPid
  let all_pids = mypid : pids
  mapM_ (\pid <- send pid (MsgServers)) all_pids

  chatServer port

main = distribMain master Main.__remoteTable
```

The master function is fairly straightforward. It spawns chatServer on each of the
slaves, using increasing port numbers, and then sends a MsgServers message to each
server process containing a list of all the server ProcessIds.[13]

---

13. This is mainly so that we can test the server on a single machine; in practice, you would want to choose the
    port number via a command-line option or some other method.

Testing the Server

We can start up a few nodes on a single machine like so:

```
$ ./chat slave 55551 & ./chat slave 55552 & ./chat master 55553
pid://localhost:55553:0:3: spawning on nid://localhost:55552:0
pid://localhost:55553:0:3: spawning on nid://localhost:55551:0
Listening on port 44444
Listening on port 44445
Listening on port 44446
```

(Remember the port numbers given on the command line are the ports used by the `distributed-process` framework; the ports that the chat server listens to are hardcoded to 44444, 44445, …)

Then connect to one of the nodes:

```
$ nc localhost 44445
What is your name?
Fred
*** Fred has connected
```

And connect to a different node:

```
$ nc localhost 44446
What is your name?
Bob
*** Bob has connected
hi
<Bob>: hi
```

We should now see the new activity on the first connection:

```
*** Bob has connected
<Bob>: hi
```

Failure and Adding/Removing Nodes

Our distributed server works only with a fixed set of nodes, which makes it quite limited. In practice, we want to be able to add and remove nodes from the network at will. Nodes will disconnect due to network and hardware outages, and we would like to be able to add new nodes without restarting the entire network.

My sketch implementation can be found in *distrib-chat/chat-noslave.hs*, but you might want to try implementing this for yourself. Some hints on how to go about it follow.

We need to abandon the master/slave architecture; every node will be equal. Instead of using our `DistribUtils` module, we can use the following sequence to initialize the `simplelocalnet` backend and start up a node:

```
main = do
  [port, chat_port] <- getArgs
  backend <- initializeBackend "localhost" port
                    (Main.__remoteTable initRemoteTable)
  node <- newLocalNode backend
  Node.runProcess node (master backend chat_port)
```

Now the function `master` has type `Backend -> String -> Process ()` and runs on every node. The outline of the rest of the implementation is as follows:

1. When a node starts up, it calls `findPeers` to get the other nodes in the network.

   ```
   findPeers :: Backend -> Int {- timeout -} -> IO [NodeId]
   ```

2. It registers the current process as `"chatServer"` on the local node using the `register` function:

   ```
   register :: String -> ProcessId ->
   Process ()
   ```

3. Next we call `whereisRemoteAsync` for each of the other nodes, asking for the `ProcessId` of `"chatServer"`.

   ```
   whereisRemoteAsync :: NodeId -> String -> Process ()
   ```

   The remote node will respond with a `WhereIsReply`:

   ```
   data WhereIsReply = WhereIsReply String (Maybe ProcessId)
   ```

   We won't wait for the reply immediately; it will be received along with other messages in the main message loop.

4. Then we start up the `chatServer` as before, but now we need to also handle `WhereIsReply` messages. When one of these messages is received, if it indicates that we found a `"chatServer"` process on another node, then we move on to the next step.

5. Send that `ProcessId` a message to tell it that we have joined the network. This is a new `PMessage` that we call `MsgServerInfo`. It contains the current `ProcessId` and the list of local clients we have (because clients may have already connected by now).

6. On receipt of a `MsgServerInfo`, add that `ProcessId` to the `servers` list if it isn't already there.

7. Add the information about the remote clients to the state. There may need to be some conflict resolution at this point if the remote server has clients with the same names as clients that we already know about.

8. If the new server is not already known to us, then we should respond with a `MsgServerInfo` of our own to tell the other server which local clients are on *this* server.

---

9. Start monitoring the remote process. Then we can be informed when the remote process dies and remove its clients from our local state.

Exercise: A Distributed Key-Value Store

A key-value store is a simple database that supports only operations to store and retrieve values associated with keys. Key-value stores have become popular over recent years because they offer scalability advantages over traditional relational databases in exchange for supporting fewer operations (in particular, they lack database joins).

This exercise is to use the `distributed-process` framework to implement a *distributed fault-tolerant key-value store* (albeit a very simplistic one).

The interface exposed to clients is the following:

```
type Database
type Key   = String
type Value = String

createDB :: Process Database
set      :: Database -> Key -> Value -> Process ()
get      :: Database -> Key -> Process (Maybe Value)
```

Here, `createDB` creates a database, and `set` and `get` perform operations on it. The `set` operation sets the given key to the given value, and `get` returns the current value associated with the given key or `Nothing` if the key has no entry.

Part 1. In *distrib-db/db.hs*, I supplied a sample `main` function that acts as a client for the database, and you can use this to test your database. The skeleton for the database code itself is in *Database.hs* in the same directory. The first exercise is to implement a single-node database by modifying *Database.hs*. That is:

- `createDB` should spawn a process to act as the database. It can spawn on the current node.

- `get` and `set` should talk to the database process via messages; you need to define the message type and the operations.

When you run *db.hs*, it will call `createDB` to create a database and then populate it using the *Database.hs* source file itself. Every word in the file is a key that maps to the word after it. The client will then look up a couple of keys and then go into an interactive mode where you can type in keys that are looked up in the database. Try it out with your database implementation and satisfy yourself that it is working.

Part 2. The second stage is to make the database *distributed*. In practice, the reason for doing this is to store a database much larger than we can store on a single machine and still have fast access to all of it.

The basic plan is that we are going to divide up the key space uniformly and store each portion of the key space on a separate node. The exact method used for splitting up the key space is important in practice because if you get it wrong, then the load might not be well-balanced between the nodes. For the purposes of this exercise, though, a simple scheme will do: take the first character of the key modulo the number of workers.

There will still be a single process handling requests from clients, so we still have `type Database = ProcessId`. However, this process needs to delegate requests to the correct worker process according to the key:

- Arrange to start worker processes on each of the nodes. The list of nodes in the network is passed to `createDB`.
- Write the code for the worker process. You probably need to put it in a different module (e.g., called `Worker`) due to restrictions imposed by Template Haskell. The worker process needs to maintain its own `Map` and handle `get` and `set` requests.
- Make the main database process delegate operations to the correct worker. You should be able to make the worker reply directly to the original client rather than having to forward the response from the worker back to the client.

Compile *db.hs* against your distributed database to make sure it still works.

Part 3. Make the main database process monitor all the worker processes. Detect failure of a worker and emit a message using `say`. You will need to use `receiveWait` to wait for multiple types of messages; see the *ping-fail.hs* example for hints.

Note that we can't yet do anything sensible if a worker dies. That is the next part of the exercise.

Part 4. Implement *fault tolerance* by replicating the database across multiple nodes.

- Instead of dividing the key space evenly across workers, put the workers in pairs and give each pair a slice of the key space. Both workers in the pair will have exactly the same data.
- Forward requests to both workers in the pair (it doesn't matter that there will be two responses in the case of a `get`).
- If a worker dies, you will need to remove the worker from your internal list of workers so that you don't try to send it messages in the future.[14]

---

14. A real fault-tolerant database would restart the worker on a new node and copy the database slice from its partner. The solution provided in this book doesn't do this, but by all means have a go at doing it.

This *should* result in a distributed key-value store that is robust to individual nodes going down, as long as we don't kill too many nodes too close together. Try it out—kill a node while the database is running and check that you can still look up keys.

A sample solution can be found in *distrib-db/DatabaseSample.hs* and *distrib-db/WorkerSample.hs*.

CHAPTER 15

Debugging, Tuning, and Interfacing with Foreign Code

Debugging Concurrent Programs

In this section, I've collected a few tricks and techniques that you might find useful when debugging Concurrent Haskell programs.

Inspecting the Status of a Thread

The `threadStatus` function (from `GHC.Conc`) returns the current state of a thread:

```
threadStatus :: ThreadId -> IO ThreadStatus
```

Here, `ThreadStatus` is defined as follows:

```
data ThreadStatus
  = ThreadRunning          -- ❶
  | ThreadFinished         -- ❷
  | ThreadBlocked  BlockReason  -- ❸
  | ThreadDied             -- ❹
  deriving (Eq, Ord, Show)
```

❶ The thread is currently running (or runnable).

❷ The thread has finished.

❸ The thread is blocked (the `BlockReason` type is explained shortly).

❹ The thread died because an exception was raised but not caught. This should never happen under normal circumstances because `forkIO` includes a default exception handler that catches and prints exceptions.

The `BlockReason` type gives more information about why a thread is blocked and is self-explanatory:

```
data BlockReason
  = BlockedOnMVar
  | BlockedOnBlackHole
  | BlockedOnException
  | BlockedOnSTM
  | BlockedOnForeignCall
  | BlockedOnOther
  deriving (Eq, Ord, Show)
```

Here's an example in GHCi:

```
> t <- forkIO (threadDelay 3000000)
> GHC.Conc.threadStatus t
ThreadBlocked BlockedOnMVar
> -- wait a few seconds
> GHC.Conc.threadStatus t
ThreadFinished
>
```

While threadStatus can be very useful for debugging, don't use it for normal control flow in your program. One reason is that it breaks abstractions. For instance, in the previous example, it showed us that threadDelay is implemented using MVar (at least in this version of GHC). Another reason is that the result of threadStatus is out of date as soon as threadStatus returns, because the thread may now be in a different state.

Event Logging and ThreadScope

While we should never underestimate the usefulness of adding putStrLn calls to our programs to debug them, sometimes this isn't quite lightweight enough. putStrLn can introduce some extra contention for the stdout Handle, which might perturb the concurrency in the program you're trying to debug. So in this section, we'll look at another way to investigate the behavior of a concurrent program at runtime.

We've used ThreadScope a lot to diagnose performance problems in this book. ThreadScope generates its graphs from the information in the .eventlog file that is produced when we run a program with the +RTS -l option. This file is a mine of information about what was happening behind the scenes when the program ran, and we can use it for debugging our programs, too.

You may have noticed that ThreadScope identifies threads by their number. For debugging, it helps a lot to know which thread in the program corresponds to which thread number; this connection can be made using labelThread:

```
labelThread :: ThreadId -> String -> IO ()
  -- defined in GHC.Conc
```

The labelThread function has no effect on the running of the program but causes the program to emit a special event into the event log.

There are also a couple of ways to put your own information in the eventlog file:

```
traceEvent   :: String -> a -> a
traceEventIO :: String -> IO ()
  -- defined in Debug.Trace
```

Here's a simple program to demonstrate labelThread and traceEventIO in action:

mvar4.hs

```
main = do
  t <- myThreadId
  labelThread t "main"
  m <- newEmptyMVar
  t <- forkIO $ putMVar m 'a'
  labelThread t "a"
  t <- forkIO $ putMVar m 'b'
  labelThread t "b"
  traceEventIO "before takeMVar"
  takeMVar m
  takeMVar m
```

This program forks two threads. Each of the threads puts a value into an MVar, and then the main thread calls takeMVar on the MVar twice.

Compile the program with -eventlog and run it with +RTS -l:

```
$ ghc mvar4.hs -threaded -eventlog
$ ./mvar4 +RTS -l
```

This generates the file *mvar4.eventlog*, which is a space-efficient binary representation of the sequence of events that occurred in the runtime system when the program ran. You need a program to display the contents of a .eventlog file; ThreadScope of course is one such tool, but you can also just display the raw event stream using the ghc-events program:[1]

```
$ ghc-events show mvar4.eventlog
```

As you might expect, there is a lot of implementation detail in the event stream, but with the help of labelThread and traceEventIO, you can sort through it to find the interesting bits. Note that if you try this program yourself, you might not see exactly the same event log; such is the nature of implementation details.

We labeled the main thread "main", so searching for main in the log finds this section:

```
912458: cap 0: running thread 3
950678: cap 0: thread 3 has label "main"          -- ❶
953569: cap 0: creating thread 4                  -- ❷
956227: cap 0: thread 4 has label "a"             -- ❸
```

---

1. The ghc-events program is installed along with the ghc-events package, which is a dependency of Thread-Scope, so you should have it if you have ThreadScope. If not, cabal install ghc-events should get it.

```
 957001: cap 0: creating thread 5                              -- ❹
 958450: cap 0: thread 5 has label "b"
 960835: cap 0: stopping thread 3 (thread yielding)            -- ❺
 997067: cap 0: running thread 4                               -- ❻
1007167: cap 0: stopping thread 4 (thread finished)
1008066: cap 0: running thread 5                               -- ❼
1010022: cap 0: stopping thread 5 (blocked on an MVar)
1045297: cap 0: running thread 3                               -- ❽
1064248: cap 0: before takeMVar                                -- ❾
1066973: cap 0: waking up thread 5 on cap 0                    -- ❿
1067747: cap 0: stopping thread 3 (thread finished)            -- ⓫
```

❶　This event was generated by labelThread. GHC needs some threads for its own purposes, so it turns out that in this case the main thread is thread 3.

❷　This is the first forkIO executed by the main thread, creating thread 4.

❸　The main thread labels thread 4 as a.

❹　The second forkIO creates thread 5, which is then labeled as b.

❺　Next, the main thread "yields." This means it stops running to give another thread a chance to run. This happens at regular intervals during execution due to pre-emption.

❻　The next thread to run is thread 4, which is a. This thread will put a value into the MVar and then finish.

❼　Next, thread 5 (b) runs. It also puts in the MVar but gets blocked because the MVar is already full.

❽　The main thread runs again.

❾　This is the effect of the call to traceEventIO in the main thread; it helps us to know where in the code we're currently executing. Be careful with traceEventIO and traceEvent, though. They have to convert String values into raw bytes to put in the event log and can be expensive, so use them only to annotate things that don't happen too often.

❿　When the main thread calls takeMVar, this has the effect of waking up thread 5 (b), which was blocked in putMVar.

⓫　The main thread has finished, so the program exits.

So from this event log we can see the sequence of actions that happened at runtime, including which threads got blocked when, and some information about why they got blocked. These clues can often be enough to point you to the cause of a problem.

Detecting Deadlock

As I mentioned briefly in "Communication: MVars" on page 128, the GHC runtime system can detect when a thread has become deadlocked and send it the

`BlockedIndefinitelyOnMVar` exception. How exactly does this work? Well, in GHC both threads and `MVar`s are objects on the heap, just like other data values. An `MVar` that has blocked threads is represented by a heap object that points to a list of the blocked threads. Heap objects are managed by the garbage collector, which traverses the heap starting from the *roots* to discover all the live objects. The set of roots consists of the running threads and the stack associated with each of these threads. Any thread that is not *reachable* from the roots is definitely deadlocked. The runtime system cannot ever find these threads by following pointers, so they can never become runnable again.

For example, if a thread is blocked in `takeMVar` on an `MVar` that is not referenced by any other thread, then both the `MVar` that it is blocked on and the thread itself will be unreachable. When a thread is found to be unreachable, it is sent the `BlockedIndefinitelyOnMVar` exception (there is also a `BlockedIndefinitelyOnSTM` exception for when a thread is blocked in an STM transaction). The exception gives the thread a chance to clean up any resources it may have been holding and also allows the program to quit with an error message rather than hanging in the event of a deadlock.

The concept extends to mutual deadlock between a group of threads. Suppose we create two threads that deadlock on each other like this:

```
a <- newEmptyMVar
b <- newEmptyMVar
forkIO (do takeMVar a; putMVar b ())
forkIO (do takeMVar b; putMVar a ())
...
```

Then both threads are blocked, each on an `MVar` that is reachable from the other. As far as the garbage collector is concerned, both threads and the `MVar`s a and b are unreachable (assuming the rest of the program does not refer to a or b). When there are multiple unreachable threads, they are all sent the `BlockedIndefinitelyOnMVar` exception at the same time.

This all seems quite reasonable, but you should be aware of some consequences that might not be immediately obvious. Here's an example:[2]

deadlock1.hs

```
main = do
  lock <- newEmptyMVar
  complete <- newEmptyMVar
  forkIO $ takeMVar lock `finally` putMVar complete ()
  takeMVar complete
```

Study the program for a moment and think about what you expect to happen.

---

2. Courtesy of Edward Yang.

The child thread is clearly deadlocked, and so it should receive the BlockedIndefinitelyOnMVar exception. This will cause the finally action to run, which performs putMVar complete (), which will in turn unblock the main thread. However, this is not what happens. At the point where the child thread is deadlocked, *the main thread is also deadlocked.* The runtime system has no idea that sending the exception to the child thread will cause the main thread to become unblocked, so the behavior when there is a group of deadlocked threads is to send them all the exception at the same time. Hence the main thread also receives the BlockedIndefinitelyOnMVar exception, and the program prints an error message.

The second consequence is that the runtime can't always prove that a thread is deadlocked even if it seems obvious to you. Here's another example:

deadlock2.hs

```
main = do
  lock <- newEmptyMVar
  forkIO $ do r <- try (takeMVar lock); print (r :: Either SomeException ())
  threadDelay 1000000
  print (lock == lock)
```

We might expect the child thread to be detected as deadlocked here because it is clear that nothing is ever going to put into the lock MVar. But the child thread never receives an exception, and the program completes printing True. The reason the deadlock is not detected here is that the main thread is holding a reference to the MVar lock because it is used in the (slightly contrived) expression (lock == lock) on the last line. Deadlock detection works using garbage collection, which is necessarily a conservative approximation to the true future behavior of the program.

Suppose that instead of the last line, we had written this:

```
  if isPrime 43 then return () else putMVar lock ()
```

Provided that the compiler optimizes away isPrime 43, we would get a deadlock exception. You can't in general know how clever the compiler is going to be, so *you should not rely on deadlock detection for the correct working of your program.* Deadlock detection is a debugging feature; in the event of a deadlock, you get an exception rather than a silent hang, but you should aim to never have any deadlocks in your program.

Tuning Concurrent (and Parallel) Programs

In this section, I'll cover a few tips and techniques for improving the performance of concurrent programs. The standard principles apply here, just as much as in ordinary sequential programming:

- Avoid premature optimization. Don't overoptimize code until you know there's a problem. That said, "avoiding premature optimization" is not an excuse for writing awful code. For example, don't use wildly inappropriate data structures if using the right one is just a matter of importing a library. I like to "write code with efficiency in mind": know the complexity of your algorithms, and if you find yourself using something worse than $O(n\log n)$, think about whether it might present a problem down the road. The more of this you do, the better your code will cope with larger and larger problems.

- Don't waste time optimizing code that doesn't contribute much to overall runtime. Profile your program so that you can focus your efforts on the important parts. GHC has a reasonable space and time profiler that should point out at least where the inner loops of your code are. In concurrent programs, the problem can often be I/O or contention, in which case using ThreadScope together with labelThread and traceEvent can help track down the culprits (see "Event Logging and Thread-Scope" on page 276).

Thread Creation and MVar Operations

GHC strives to provide an extremely efficient implementation of threads. This section explores the performance of a couple of very simple concurrent programs to give you a feel for the efficiency of the basic concurrency operations and how to inspect the performance of your programs.

The first program creates 1,000,000 threads, has each of them put a token into the same MVar, and then reads the 1,000,000 tokens from the MVar:

threadperf1.hs

```
numThreads = 1000000

main = do
  m <- newEmptyMVar
  replicateM_ numThreads $ forkIO (putMVar m ())
  replicateM_ numThreads $ takeMVar m
```

This program should give us an indication of the memory overhead for threads because all the threads will be resident in memory at once. To find out the memory cost, we can run the program with +RTS -s (the output is abbreviated slightly here):

```
$ ./threadperf1 +RTS -s
  1,048,049,144 bytes allocated in the heap
  3,656,054,520 bytes copied during GC
    799,504,400 bytes maximum residency (10 sample(s))
    146,287,144 bytes maximum slop
          1,768 MB total memory in use (0 MB lost due to fragmentation)

  INIT    time    0.00s  (  0.00s elapsed)
  MUT     time    0.75s  (  0.76s elapsed)
  GC      time    2.21s  (  2.22s elapsed)
```

```
   EXIT    time     0.18s  (   0.18s elapsed)
   Total   time     3.14s  (   3.16s elapsed)
```

So about 1 GB was allocated, although the total memory required by the program was 1.7 GB. The amount of allocated memory tells us that threads require approximately 1 KB each, and the extra memory used by the program is due to copying GC overheads. In fact, it is possible to tune the amount of memory given to a thread when it is allocated, using the +RTS -k<size> option; here is the same program using 400-byte threads:

```
$ ./threadperf1 +RTS -s -k400
     424,081,144 bytes allocated in the heap
   1,587,567,240 bytes copied during GC
     387,551,912 bytes maximum residency (9 sample(s))
      87,195,664 bytes maximum slop
             902 MB total memory in use (0 MB lost due to fragmentation)

   INIT    time     0.00s  (   0.00s elapsed)
   MUT     time     0.59s  (   0.59s elapsed)
   GC      time     1.60s  (   1.61s elapsed)
   EXIT    time     0.13s  (   0.13s elapsed)
   Total   time     2.32s  (   2.33s elapsed)
```

A thread will allocate more memory for its stack on demand, so whether it is actually a good idea to use +RTS -k400 will depend on your program. In this case, the threads were doing very little before exiting, so it did help the overall performance.

The second example also creates 1,000,000 threads, but this time we create a separate MVar for each thread to put a token into and then take all the MVars in the main thread before exiting:

threadperf2.hs

```
numThreads = 1000000

main = do
  ms <- replicateM numThreads $ do
          m <- newEmptyMVar
          forkIO (putMVar m ())
          return m
  mapM_ takeMVar ms
```

This program has quite different performance characteristics:

```
$ ./threadperf2 +RTS -s
   1,153,017,744 bytes allocated in the heap
     267,061,032 bytes copied during GC
      62,962,152 bytes maximum residency (8 sample(s))
       4,662,808 bytes maximum slop
             121 MB total memory in use (0 MB lost due to fragmentation)

   INIT    time     0.00s  (   0.00s elapsed)
   MUT     time     0.70s  (   0.72s elapsed)
   GC      time     0.50s  (   0.50s elapsed)
```

```
EXIT    time    0.02s  (  0.02s elapsed)
Total   time    1.22s  (  1.24s elapsed)
```

Although it allocated a similar amount of memory, the total memory in use by the program at any one time was only 121 MB. This is because each thread can run to completion independently, unlike the previous example where all the threads were present and blocked on the same MVar. So while the main thread is busy creating more threads, the threads it has already created can run, complete, and be garbage-collected, leaving behind only the MVar for the main thread to take later.

Note that the GC overheads of this program are much lower than the first example. The total time gives us a rough indication of the time it takes to create an MVar and a thread, and for the thread to run, put into the MVar, complete, and be garbage-collected. We did this 1,000,000 times in about 1.2s, so the time per thread is about 1.2 microseconds.

The conclusion is that threads are cheap in GHC, in both creation time and memory overhead. Context-switch performance is also efficient, as it does not require a kernel round-trip, although we haven't measured that here. The memory used by threads is automatically recovered when the thread completes, and because thread stacks are movable in GHC, you don't have to worry about memory fragmentation or running out of address space, as you do with OS threads. The number of threads we can have is limited only by the amount of memory.

We covered one trick here: the +RTS -k<size> option, which tunes the initial stack size of a thread. If you have a lot of very tiny threads, it might be worth tweaking this option from its default 1k to see if it makes any difference.

Shared Concurrent Data Structures

We've encountered shared data structures a few times so far: the phonebook example in "MVar as a Container for Shared State" on page 133, the window-manager in Chapter 10, and the semaphore in "Limiting the Number of Threads with a Semaphore" on page 231, not to mention various versions of channels. Those examples covered most of the important techniques to use with shared data structures, but we haven't compared the various choices directly. In this section, I'll briefly summarize the options for shared state, with a focus on the performance implications of the different choices.

Typically, the best approach when you want some shared state is to take an existing pure data structure, such as a list or a Map, and store it in a mutable container. Not only is this straightforward to accomplish, but there are a wide range of well-tuned pure data structures to choose from, and using a pure data structure means that reads and writes are automatically concurrent.

There are a couple of subtle performance issues to be aware of, though. The first is the effect of lazy evaluation when writing a new value into the container, which we covered in "MVar as a Container for Shared State" on page 133. The second is the choice of mutable container itself, which exposes some subtle performance trade-offs. There are three choices:

MVar

We found in "Limiting the Number of Threads with a Semaphore" on page 231 that using an MVar to keep a shared counter did not perform well under high contention. This is a consequence of the fairness guarantee that MVar offers: if a thread relinquishes an MVar and there is another thread waiting, it *must* then hand over to the waiting thread; it cannot continue running and take the MVar again.

TVar

Using a TVar sometimes performs better than MVar under contention and has the advantage of being composable with other STM operations. However, be aware of the other performance pitfalls with STM described in "Performance" on page 193.

IORef

Using an IORef together with atomicModifyIORef is often a good choice for performance, as we saw in "Limiting the Number of Threads with a Semaphore" on page 231. The main pitfall here is lazy evaluation; getting enough strictness when using atomicModifyIORef is quite tricky. This is a good pattern to follow:

```
b <- atomicModifyIORef ref
        (\x -> let (a, b) = f x
               in (a, a `seq` b))
b `seq` return b
```

The seq call on the last line forces the second component of the pair, which itself is a seq call that forces a, which in turn forces the call to f. All of this ensures that both the value stored inside the IORef and the return value are evaluated strictly, and no chains of thunks are built up.

RTS Options to Tweak

GHC has plenty of options to tune the behavior of the runtime system (RTS). For full details, see the GHC User's Guide (*http://www.haskell.org/ghc/docs/latest/html/users_guide/*). Here, I'll highlight a few of the options that are good targets for tuning concurrent and parallel programs.

RTS options should be placed between +RTS and -RTS, but the -RTS can be omitted if it would be at the end of the command line.

-N[*cores*]

(Default: 1) We encountered -N many times throughout Part I. But what value should you pass? GHC can automatically determine the number of processors in your machine if you use -N without an argument, but that might not always be the best choice. The GHC runtime system scales well when it has exclusive access to the number of processors specified with -N, but performance can degrade quite rapidly if there is contention for some of those cores with other processes on the machine.

Should you include hyperthreaded cores in the count? Anecdotal evidence suggests that using hyperthreaded cores often gives a small performance boost, but obviously not as much as a full core. On the other hand, it might be wise to leave the hyperthreaded cores alone in order to provide some insulation against any contention arising from other processes. Be aware that using -N alone normally includes hyperthreaded cores.

-qa

(Default: off) Enables the use of *processor affinity*, which locks the Haskell program to specific cores. Normally the operating system is free to migrate the threads that run the Haskell program around the cores in the machine in response to other activity, but using -qa prevents it from doing so. This can improve performance or degrade it, depending on the scheduling behavior of your operating system and the demands of the program.

-A*size*

(Default: 512k) This option controls the size of the memory allocation area for each core. A good rule of thumb is to keep this around the size of the L2 cache *per core* on your machine. Cache sizes vary a lot and are often shared between cores, and sometimes there is even an L3 cache, too. So setting the -A value is not an exact science.

There are two opposing factors at play here: using more memory means we run the garbage collector less, but using less memory means we use the caches more. The sweet spot depends on the characteristics of the program and the hardware, so the only consistent advice is to try various values and see what helps.

-I*seconds*

(Default: 0.3) This option affects deadlock detection ("Detecting Deadlock" on page 278). The runtime needs to perform a full garbage collection in order to detect deadlocked threads. When the program is idle, the runtime doesn't know whether a thread will wake up again, or the program is deadlocked and the garbage collector should be run to detect the deadlock. The compromise is to wait until the program has been idle for a short period of time before running the garbage collector, which by default is 0.3 seconds. This might be a bad idea if a full GC takes a long time (because your program has lots of data) and it regularly goes idle for short periods of time, in which case you might want to tune this value higher.

-C[*seconds*]

(Default 0.02) This option sets the context-switch interval, which determines how often the scheduler interrupts the current thread to run the next thread on the run queue. The scheduler switches between runnable threads in a round-robin fashion. As a rule of thumb, this option should not be set too low because frequent context switches harm performance, and should not be set too high because that can cause jerkiness and stuttering in interactive threads.

Concurrency and the Foreign Function Interface

Haskell has a *foreign function interface* (FFI) that allows Haskell code to call, and be called by, foreign language code (primarily C). Foreign languages also have their own threading models—in C, there are POSIX and Win32 threads, for example—so we need to specify how Concurrent Haskell interacts with the threading models of foreign code.

All of the following assumes the use of GHC's `-threaded` option. Without `-threaded`, the Haskell process uses a single OS thread only, and multithreaded foreign calls are not supported.

Threads and Foreign Out-Calls

An *out-call* is a call made from Haskell to a foreign language. At the present time, the FFI supports only calls to C, so that's all we describe here. In the following, we refer to threads in C (i.e., POSIX or Win32 threads) as "OS threads" to distinguish them from the Haskell threads created with `forkIO`.

As an example, consider making the POSIX C function `read()` callable from Haskell:

```
foreign import ccall "read"
  c_read :: CInt        -- file descriptor
         -> Ptr Word8   -- buffer for data
         -> CSize       -- size of buffer
         -> CSSize      -- bytes read, or -1 on error
```

This declares a Haskell function `c_read` that can be used to call the C function `read()`. Full details on the syntax of `foreign` declarations and the relationship between C and Haskell types can be found in the Haskell 2010 Language Report (*http:// www.haskell.org/onlinereport/haskell2010/*).

Just as Haskell threads run concurrently with one another, when a Haskell thread makes a foreign call, that foreign call runs concurrently with the other Haskell threads, and indeed with any other active foreign calls. The only way that two C calls can be running concurrently is if they are running in two separate OS threads, so that is exactly what happens; if several Haskell threads call `c_read` and they all block waiting for data to be read, there will be one OS thread per call blocked in `read()`.

This has to work even though Haskell threads are not normally mapped one to one with OS threads; in GHC, Haskell threads are lightweight and managed in user space by the runtime system. So to handle concurrent foreign calls, the runtime system has to create more OS threads, and in fact it does this on demand. When a Haskell thread makes a foreign call, another OS thread is created (if necessary), and the responsibility for running the remaining Haskell threads is handed over to the new OS thread, while the current OS thread makes the foreign call.

The implication of this design is that a foreign call may be executed in *any* OS thread, and subsequent calls may even be executed in different OS threads. In most cases, this isn't a problem, but sometimes it is; some foreign code must be called by a *particular* OS thread. There are two situations where this happens:

- Libraries that allow only one OS thread to use their API. GUI libraries often fall into this category. Not only must the library be called by only one OS thread, but it must often be one particular thread (e.g., the main thread). The Win32 GUI APIs are an example of this.

- APIs that use internal thread-local state. The best known example of this is OpenGL, which supports multithreaded use but stores state between API calls in thread-local storage. Hence, subsequent calls must be made in the same OS thread; otherwise, the later call will see the wrong state.

To handle these requirements, Haskell has a concept of *bound threads*. A bound thread is a Haskell thread/OS thread pair that guarantees that foreign calls made by the Haskell thread always take place in the associated OS thread. A bound thread is created by forkOS:

```
forkOS :: IO () -> IO ThreadId
```

Care should be taken when calling forkOS; it creates a complete new OS thread, so it can be quite expensive. Furthermore, bound threads are much more expensive than unbound threads. When context-switching to or from a bound thread, the runtime system has to switch OS threads, which involves a trip through the operating system and tends to be very slow. Use bound threads sparingly.

For more details on bound threads, see the documentation for the Control. Concurrent module.

There is a common misconception about forkOS, which is partly a consequence of its poorly chosen name. Upon seeing a function called forkOS, one might jump to the conclusion that you need to use forkOS to call a foreign function like read() and have it run concurrently with the other Haskell threads. This isn't the case. As I mentioned earlier, the GHC runtime system creates more OS threads on demand for running foreign calls. Moreover, using forkOS instead of forkIO will make your code a lot slower.

The *only* reason to call forkOS is to create a bound thread, and the only reason for wanting bound threads is to work with foreign libraries that have particular requirements about the OS thread in which a call is made.

The thread that runs main in a Haskell program is a bound thread. This can give rise to a serious performance problem if you use the main thread heavily; communication between the main thread and other Haskell threads will be extremely slow. If you notice that your program runs several times slower when -threaded is added, this is the most likely cause.

The best way around this problem is just to create a new thread from main and work in that instead.

Asynchronous Exceptions and Foreign Calls

When a Haskell thread is making a foreign call, it cannot receive asynchronous exceptions. There is no way in general to interrupt a foreign call, so the runtime system waits until the call returns before raising the exception. This means that a thread blocked in a foreign call may be unresponsive to timeouts and interrupts, and moreover that calling throwTo will block if the target thread is in a foreign call.

The trick for working around this limitation is to perform the foreign call in a separate thread. For example:

```
do
  a <- async $ c_read fd buf size
  r <- wait a
  ...
```

Now the current thread is blocked in wait and can be interrupted by an exception as usual. Note that if an exception is raised it won't cancel the read() call, which will continue in the background. Don't be tempted to use withAsync here because withAsync will attempt to kill the thread calling read() and will block in doing so.

Operations in the standard System.IO library already work this way behind the scenes because they delegate blocking operations to a special IO manager thread. So there's no need to worry about forking extra threads when calling standard IO operations.

Threads and Foreign In-Calls

In-calls are calls to Haskell functions that have been exposed to foreign code with a foreign export declaration. For example, if we have a function f of type Int -> IO Int, we could expose it like this:

```
foreign export ccall "f" f :: Int -> IO Int
```

This would create a C function with the following signature:

```
HsInt f(HsInt);
```

Here, HsInt is the C type corresponding to Haskell's Int type.

In a multithreaded program, it is entirely possible for f to be called by multiple OS threads concurrently. The GHC runtime system supports this (provided you use -threaded) with the following behavior: each call becomes a new *bound thread*. That is, a new Haskell thread is created for each call, and the Haskell thread is bound to the OS thread that made the call. Hence, any further out-calls made by the Haskell thread will take place in the same OS thread that made the original in-call. This turns out to be important for dealing with GUI callbacks. The GUI wants to run in the main OS thread only, so when it makes a callback into Haskell, we need to ensure that GUI calls made by the callback happen in the same OS thread that invoked the callback.

Index

Symbols

! operator
  in Accelerate, 106
  in Repa, 87
  indexing arrays with, 108
$ operator (infix operator), 135
$! operator, 135
-02 optimization option, 93
-A (RTS option), 285
-C (RTS option), 285
-ddump-cc option, 116
-dverbose option, 116
-fllvm optimization option, 93
-I (RTS option), 285
-k (RTS option), 283
-N(RTS option), 284
-qa (RTS option), 285
-s (RTS option), 21
-threaded option, 94
/quit::, 216
:. constructor, 86, 105
>-> operator, 114

A

Accelerate, 103–111
  Arrays class, 108
  arrays in, 105–106
  conditionals, working with, 116–122
  constant function, 111
  creating arrays, 109–110
  debugging, 116
  Elt class, 108
  GPUs, programming with, 103–104
  implementing Floyd-Warshall algorithm, 112–116
  indices in, 105–106
  Mandelbrot set generator in, 116–122
  programs, executing, 106–107
  Shape class, 108
  type classes in, 108
accept operation, for multiclient servers, 207
addition, in Accelerate, 118
addToPointSum function, 37
adjacency matrix
  algorithms run over, 62
  defined, 91
  foldS function with, 96
Amdahls law, 28
Applicative type class, 64
arrays
  delayed, 88–90
  large-scale, 85
  manifest, 90
  nested, 106
  unboxed, 89
Arrays class (Accelerate), 108

We'd like to hear your suggestions for improving our indexes. Send email to index@oreilly.com.

typed channels, 254–258
  merging, 257–258
  untyped channels vs., 260

U

unbounded channels
  bounded channels vs., 189
  constructing, 135–139
Unbox type class, 86
unboxed arrays, computeS function and, 89
unevaluated computations, 10
unGetChan operation, 139, 185
Unicode conversion, 228
uninterruptibleMask, 160
unit operation, in Accelerate, 108
Unlift class, 110
unlift function, 110, 119
Unmasked constructor, 160
unresponsive threads, deadlocks and, 155
update function, 63
use function, in Accelerate, 107
user interface, multiple threads with, 155
user interrupt, asynchronous exceptions and, 170
using function, 32
  and garbage-collected sparks, 50

W

wait function
  error handling with, 151–152
  for asynchronous actions, 144
waitAny function, 154, 183, 202
waitBoth operation
  and orElse combinator, 199
  and withAsync function, 200
waitCatch function
  error handling with, 152
  implementing, 157
waitCatchSTM function, 182

waitEither function, 153, 200
  and symmetric concurrency combinators, 199
  in STM, 182, 183
waitSTM function, 182
wall-clock time, elapsed and, 21
watch list, in TVars, 194
weak head normal form (WHNF), 9–15
web browsers, interrupting several activiites with, 155
web pages, concurrent downloading of, 143
weight function, Floyd-Warshall algorithm and, 62
WHNF (weak head normal form), 9–15
window manager example, 173–177
withAsync function
  and waitBoth operation, 200
  foreign calls with, 288–289
  installing exception handlers with, 198
  nesting calls of, 228
withMonitor function, 259
withStrategy, parallelizing lazy streams with, 52
work items, number of, 47–48
work pools, 59
work stealing, 25, 238
write pointer (channel), 136
writeChan operations
  concurrent, 137
  definition of, 163
writeImage operation, 97
writeTBQueue, deadlock caused by, 191

Y

yields (term), 278

Z

Z constructor, 86
zeroPoint operation, 37
zipWith function (Accelerate), 111

About the Author

Simon Marlow has been a prominent figure in the Haskell community for many years. He is the author of large parts of the Glasgow Haskell Compiler, including in particular its highly regarded multicore runtime system, along with many of the libraries and tools that Haskell programmers take for granted. Simon also contributes to the functional programming research community and has a string of papers on subjects ranging from garbage collection to language design. In recent years, Simon's focus has been on making Haskell an ideal programming language for parallel and concurrent applications, both by developing new programming models and building a high quality implementation. Simon spent 14 years at Microsoft's Research laboratory in Cambridge before taking a break in the spring of 2013 to work on this book. He currently works at Facebook UK.

Colophon

The animal on the cover of *Parallel and Concurrent Programming in Haskell* is a scrawled butterflyfish (*Chaetodon meyeri*). This fish can grow up to 8 inches in length and is characterized by its white or blue-white body and yellow-edged black bar running through its eyes.

This species of butterflyfish can be found in the Pacific and Indian Oceans, at depths of 2 to 25 meters. Because they generally prefer coral-rich areas, these fish are susceptible to habitat loss. Though there have been no population declines documented to date, this species' food source is live coral and is sensitive to climate-induced coral depletion.

The cover image is of unknown origin. The cover font is Adobe ITC Garamond. The text font is Adobe Minion Pro; the heading font is Adobe Myriad Condensed; and the code font is Dalton Maag's Ubuntu Mono.

Have it your way.

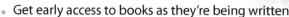

Get even more for your money.

Join the O'Reilly Community, and register the O'Reilly books you own. It's free, and you'll get:

- $4.99 ebook upgrade offer
- 40% upgrade offer on O'Reilly print books
- Membership discounts on books and events
- Free lifetime updates to ebooks and videos
- Multiple ebook formats, DRM FREE
- Participation in the O'Reilly community
- Newsletters
- Account management
- 100% Satisfaction Guarantee

Signing up is easy:

1. **Go to: oreilly.com/go/register**
2. **Create an O'Reilly login.**
3. **Provide your address.**
4. **Register your books.**

Note: English-language books only

To order books online:
oreilly.com/store

For questions about products or an order:
orders@oreilly.com

To sign up to get topic-specific email announcements and/or news about upcoming books, conferences, special offers, and new technologies:
elists@oreilly.com

For technical questions about book content:
booktech@oreilly.com

To submit new book proposals to our editors:
proposals@oreilly.com

O'Reilly books are available in multiple DRM-free ebook formats. For more information:
oreilly.com/ebooks

Spreading the knowledge of innovators   oreilly.com